Solmaz Yadollahi
Urban Heritage Planning in Tehran and Beyond

Cultural Heritage Studies | Volume 9

Solmaz Yadollahi (Dr.), a conservation architect, earned her doctorate in heritage studies. Her academic journey includes positions as a research fellow at the Chair of Urban Management and an affiliated post-doctoral fellow at the DFG Research Training Group 1913, both at Brandenburgische Technische Universität Cottbus-Senftenberg. Namely, she assumed the role of Principal Investigator for the DFG-funded research project entitled "Assembling Iran's Urban Heritage Conservation Policy and Practice: Problematized in Tehran".

Solmaz Yadollahi

Urban Heritage Planning in Tehran and Beyond

Sequences of Disrupted Spatial-Discursive Assemblages

[transcript]

This work received support from the German Research Foundation (DFG), the Publication Fund for Open Access Monographs of the Federal State of Brandenburg, Germany, and a publication grant from the Equal Opportunities Office at the Brandenburg University of Technology (BTU).

Bibliographic information published by the Deutsche Nationalbibliothek
The Deutsche Nationalbibliothek lists this publication in the Deutsche Nationalbibliografie; detailed bibliographic data are available in the Internet at http://dnb.d-nb.de

This work is licensed under the Creative Commons Attribution 4.0 (BY) license, which means that the text may be remixed, transformed and built upon and be copied and redistributed in any medium or format even commercially, provided credit is given to the author.
https://creativecommons.org/licenses/by/4.0/
Creative Commons license terms for re-use do not apply to any content (such as graphs, figures, photos, excerpts, etc.) not original to the Open Access publication and further permission may be required from the rights holder. The obligation to research and clear permission lies solely with the party re-using the material.

First published in 2023 by transcript Verlag, Bielefeld
© Solmaz Yadollahi

Cover layout: Jan Gerbach, Bielefeld
Copy-editing: Lara Bastajian, Limassol, Cyprus
Printed by: Majuskel Medienproduktion GmbH, Wetzlar
https://doi.org/10.14361/9783839471623
Print-ISBN: 978-3-8376-7162-9
PDF-ISBN: 978-3-8394-7162-3
ISSN of series: 2752-1516
eISSN of series: 2752-1524

Printed on permanent acid-free text paper.

Contents

A note on dates, translations, and transliterations..........................7

Glossary 9

List of Abbreviations 11

List of Figures 13

Acknowledgements 19

Introduction...21
The academic scope of the book 22
Underlying concepts 26
Methods of data collection and analysis: Unravelling the book's structure 32

Part One

Urban heritage planning in Iran: Repeated cycles of struggle for territorialization 39
The first cycle: Assembling the conservation fundaments between two revolutions 40
The second cycle: Re-assembling conservation and heritage planning 65
The third cycle: A renewed endeavour to reform urban heritage assemblage .. 115

Part Two

Assembling urban heritage in Tehran: Collecting heritage fragments here and there 147
An introduction to Tehran's historic centre and its spatial-economic setting .. 147
Short stories around renewal, beautification, and place-making in Tehran's historic centre 154
Tehran's socio-spatial urban heritage assemblage 207

Conclusion 215
Urban heritage assemblage in Iran: A sequence of ephemeral territorialization endeavours foiled by de-territorializing forces 215

References 227

Index 265

A note on dates, translations, and transliterations

The presentation of dates, translations, and transliterations in this book is influenced by several considerations. To begin with, the Iranian solar calendar's initiation on the 21st of March, which distinguishes it from the Gregorian calendar, could potentially perplex non-Iranian readers. As a solution, I have used Iranian dates sparingly and instead opted to incorporate corresponding Gregorian dates obtained through a calendar calculation platform. I utilized time.ir, a platform that generates the calendar based on computations provided by the Calendar Centre at the Geophysics Institute of the University of Tehran.

To enhance comprehensibility for a wider audience, I deliberately minimized intricate transliterations and diacritical marks. Rather, I focused on presenting words in their familiar Persian pronunciation. This approach is consistently applied to technical terms commonly utilized within the realm of conservation in Iran. For example, I substituted the widely recognized Persian pronunciation 'miras' for the term 'heritage' in Farsi, eschewing the Arabic pronunciation 'mirath'. Similarly, the term 'maremmat', prevalent among conservation professionals and academics in Iran, is employed for the concept of 'conservation'. Likewise, 'hefazat' is used interchangeably with 'preservation'.

When it came to formal titles, I stayed true to the official version of their translation and transliteration. This means that names of publications and organizations subject to transliteration by relevant authorities or editors maintain their original transliteration and translation. For instance, the journal *Athar* retains its established transliteration, rather than adopting the Farsi-pronounced *Asar*. Also, the term 'Awqaf', which employs the officially recognized Arabic pronunciation instead of the common Persian pronunciation 'Owqaf', exemplifies this approach.

I must also highlight that throughout the text, when introducing a non-English term for the first time, I enclose it in brackets alongside its English equivalent. Subsequently, I rely on the English translation to ensure clarity and to avoid overwhelming readers, particularly those unacquainted with Farsi. When citing non-English publications, I transliterate the original title, followed by enclosing the English translation within brackets. This approach reduces the necessity for an extensive glossary within this section. Nevertheless, I furnish a concise compilation of frequently employed non-English terms in the book.

Glossary

Anjoman	Council
Arg	Citadel
Awqaf	Assets obtained from donations, inheritance, or acquisition and placed in a trust for charitable and social aims, all under the supervision of religious authorities. In Persian technical and administrative texts, the term 'Awqaf' is often employed to refer to both the organization and the assets under its management.
Azadi	Freedom
Baladiyeh	The municipality, also related to the municipality building.
Baz zendeh sazi	Revitalization
Bazafarini-ye shahri	Urban regeneration
Bonyad	Foundation
Enghelab	Revolution
Farhang	Culture
Golha	A radio programme that aired on Iranian National Radio spanning from 1956 to 1979. The term means 'flowers'.
Hosseineh	A religious institution or building in Iran primarily used for Shia Islamic rituals and gatherings.
Imam Jum'a	A high-profile religious figure, normally appointed by the Supreme Leader, who leads the politically symbolic Friday prayers in Iranian cities.

Iranshahr	Traced back to the pre-Islamic Sassanid Dynasty (3rd century AD), the term refers to their expansive political domain, spanning from the Oxus to the Euphrates. Certain academics and political figures drew upon the historical governance traditions of Iranshahr to propose a model for contemporary governance in Iran.
Khaneh	House
Konkur	The annual university admission competition in Iran.
Maremmat	Conservation
Maremmat-e shahri	Urban conservation
Meidan	Square
Miras	Heritage
Musalla	An Arabic term referring to a large area typically used for congregational prayer, especially at outdoor gatherings or religious events.
Nafayes	Irreplaceable treasures
Nosazi	Renovation
Sazman	Organization
Setad	Headquarters
Taghut	A Quranic word referring to the disbeliever and oppressive rulers.
Takiyeh	A place where Shia Muslims gather during the month of Muharram to commemorate the death of Husayn ibn Ali, their third Imam.
Zibasazi	Beautification

List of Abbreviations

BOT	Build-operate-transfer
CBO	Community-based organization
HCAUP	High Council of Architecture and Urban Planning
HDCC	Housing Development and Construction Company
HEC	Higher Education Centre (part of the Iranian Cultural Heritage Organization)
HUL	Historic Urban Landscape
ICHHTO	Iranian Cultural Heritage, Handicrafts and Tourism Organization
ICHO	Iranian Cultural Heritage Organization
IRGC	Islamic Revolutionary Guard Corps
MCHHT	Ministry of Cultural Heritage, Handicrafts and Tourism
MHUD	Ministry of Housing and Urban Development
MHUP	Ministry of Housing and Urban Planning
MRUD	Ministry of Roads and Urban Development
NCM	National Council for Monuments
NDO	Neighbourhood Development Office
NOPHM	National Organization for the Preservation of Historical Monuments
PBO	Planning and Budget Organization
TCHO	Tehran Cultural Heritage Organization
URC	Urban Regeneration Company

List of Figures

Figure 1:	The overlapping spheres of influence in urban heritage planning.	30
Figure 2:	Persepolis, Gate of All Nations, photographed during the 1939 excavation season.	42
Figure 3:	Arg-e Alishah in the Tabriz Master Plan of 1970	48
Figure 4:	Public exhibitions in Fars (left) and Qazvin (right) on the occasion of the NOPHM's founding anniversary	49
Figure 5:	Monument Relevé programme for undergraduates, University of Tehran	50
Figure 6:	Image captured by Walter Mittelholzer in 1925, showing Naqsh-e Jahan Square in Isfahan	52
Figure 7:	An announcement regarding the admission of students to the conservation programme under an agreement between Farabi University and NOPHM. The third individual from the left is Bagher Ayatollah Zadeh Shirazi, who led the NOPHM's Technical Office in Isfahan during that period. Following the 1979 Revolution, he assumed the directorship of NOPHM until its integration into the Iranian Cultural Heritage Organization.	53
Figure 8:	The Second Symposium of Iranian Architecture in Tehran (1973)	54
Figure 9:	An aerial picture of Tabriz Bazaar and its surrounding neighbourhoods	59

Figure 10:	Dariush Borbor, Architect and Urban Planner, presenting the Urban Renewal of Mashhad City Centre to the Shah, Alam (Ministry of the Royal Court), Eghbal (Chairman of the National Iranian Oil Company), and Valiyan (Governor of Khorasan and Vice-Regent of the Shrine) in Mashhad (1973) 60
Figure 11:	In 1978, Tamasha Magazine published an interview with architect and designer Keyvan Khosravani about protecting Tehran's old neighbourhoods. 61
Figure 12:	A public exhibition of original sketches by architect, Keyvan Khosravani in the Oudlajan neighbourhood of Tehran in the late 1970s, calling on the government to save the neighbourhood 62
Figure 13:	Iraqi war prisoners forming a choral group at Tehran's Evin Prison, performing on a stage that features the monarchy's downfall and the collapse of the pillars of the pre-Islamic historical site, Persepolis 71
Figure 14:	The initial plan proposed for the musalla was inspired by the Islamic Republic's emblem and covered the historical Arg under its gigantic dome. 73
Figure 15:	The 'Hello Commander' [Salam Farmandeh] chant at the gathering ceremony near the Imam Khomeini Musalla and in front of the Arg, Tabriz August 2022 74
Figure 16:	President Hassan Rouhani visiting the House of the Constitution in Tabriz 86
Figure 17:	Mostafa Chamran's museum-house in Tehran 90
Figure 18:	General Qasem Soleimani visiting the Alavi Shrine project in Najaf in 2018 93
Figure 19:	Development plan connecting the holy shrines in Karbala 93
Figure 20:	The Shahecheragh Development project in Shiraz 95
Figure 21:	Imam Reza Shrine in Mashhad 95
Figure 22:	The 2004 International Workshop on the Recovery of Bam's Cultural Heritage 97
Figure 23:	Yazd, an aerial view 99
Figure 24:	The preserved roofscape of Tabriz Bazaar, the 1990s 100

Figure 25: Ahmadinejad at the World Heritage listing ceremony for Tabriz Bazaar 109
Figure 26: The courtyard of the Urban Dialogue House of Tehran, also known as Vartan House, decorated with a mural depicting an epic story from the Shahnameh about the legendary Iranian prince, Siavash remembering his homeland, Iranshahr 122
Figure 27: Seyyed Hassan Modarres's Museum-house, Tehran 124
Figure 28: A cartoon of Zarghami, the Minister of Cultural Heritage submitting his approval to General Ghalibaf, the Chairman of the Parliament, for the demolition of historic neighbourhoods, starting with Shiraz and moving on to other cities 132
Figure 29: The Shahecheragh project in Shiraz 134
Figure 30: ICOMOS-Iran public meeting on tourism 139
Figure 31: Public meeting organized by Ivan Cultural Group in Isfahan 139
Figure 32: A frequently shared photograph of Reza Shah, which gained significant traction on social media after the Trans-Iranian Railway was added to the World Heritage List. The image captures Reza Shah and his son, the Crown Prince, framed within a train window in 1932. 141
Figure 33: The location of the Safavid (red) and Qajar (blue) boundaries in the 1967 development plan of Tehran (yellow) 148
Figure 34: The spatial-economic setting of the historic centre of Tehran ... 152
Figure 35: The fading remains of a once stately entrance to a historic house in Oudlajan, now under the pressure of the bustling bazaar 153
Figure 36: Aerial photos of Oudlajan in 1956, 2000, and 2007................ 157
Figure 37: The Borazjan area in Oudlajan and Mirza Hamid's murals on its ruins 158
Figure 38: A skyline view of Sangeladge looking west from the rooftop of the Hajrajabali Mosque 161
Figure 39: Examples of beautification works in Marvi, the bazaar neighbourhood, and Khayam Street 167
Figure 40: Oudlajan Cluster Bazaar 169
Figure 41: The beautified back alley of the Oudlajan Cluster Bazaar......... 170
Figure 42: Examples of beautified facades in Enghelab Street 175

Figure 43: Top, Vida Movahed in front of France Pastry and bottom, the bakery 176
Figure 44: Tiles with lyrics from Shajarian's popular songs 177
Figure 45: Two visitors sitting in front of the bakery's picture of the 1960s .. 177
Figure 46: Pastry boxes of France Pastry, left: Fifth Shiraz Art Festival and right: Reconstruction of the censored box based on the original posters of the festival 178
Figure 47: The city centre's pedestrian network as outlined in the 2006 Detailed Plan of District 12 186
Figure 48: Food street in Bab-e Homayoun 187
Figure 49: Instances of social media content within the sphere of boundary action, aiming to bridge the gap between collective memories and the established political narrative of Tehran's past 190
Figure 50: Posts of the official Instagram pages of the municipality and city council on reconstruction of demolished Qajar monuments 192
Figure 51: Poster of a 'Bukhara Evenings' event about Toopkhaneh Square with the picture of the demolished Telegraph Building (Telegrafkhaneh) 196
Figure 52: The Municipality of Tehran (Baladiyeh) in 1930s 197
Figure 53: The ongoing reconstruction project of the Baladiyeh 197
Figure 54: Ghazali Cinema Town, today a Tehran tourist attraction 201
Figure 55: A scene featuring Lalehzar from the 'Hezar-dastan' series filmed in the Ghazali Cinema Town 201
Figure 56: A scene from the 'Shahrzad' series featuring the 1953 events in Lalehzar 202
Figure 57: Lalehzar Street in the 1960s.....................................203
Figure 58: Cinema Iran 206
Figure 59: An example of the beautified areas in Lalehzar 207
Figure 60: 'The tank in the city', an illustration of Khabaronline News Agency showing Zakani with the logo of the municipality and a tank. 212
Figure 61: A cognitive map of Vali-e Asr Street created by a participant (Fatemeh Mahmoudi Panah) in the Minaee House workshops, exemplifying the discussed attempts to blend Tehran's official and popular heritage.. 213

Figure 62: Disrupted efforts to territorialize urban heritage planning in Iran from the Constitutional Revolution of 1905 to the unified rule of conservative factions in August 2021 218

Acknowledgements

Writing this book has been a transformative journey, and I owe my heartfelt gratitude to all those who have played a significant role in making it possible. Without their support and encouragement, this endeavour would not have been as fulfilling and successful.

First and foremost, I express my deepest appreciation to the German Research Foundation (DFG) for granting me the invaluable opportunity to immerse myself fully in this investigation. Their support allowed me to dedicate time and focus to this work without the burden of academic career uncertainties, far from my homeland. I express my sincere gratitude to the anonymous reviewers of my DFG grant proposal for their constructive feedback, which proved invaluable in guiding me through my research journey.

I extend my gratitude to Professor Christiane Hipp, Vice President of Research (at the time of writing the grant proposal for this research), and Dr. Katrin Weise, DFG Research Funding Advisor, for their unwavering support, which allowed me to present and write a proposal for this research. Their belief in the significance of this work motivated me to strive for excellence throughout this process. In this vein, I extend my sincere appreciation to the Open Access Brandenburg initiative and the Equal Opportunities Office at the BTU for their instrumental co-funding of the publication costs of this book.

I am deeply grateful to Professor Silke Weidner, Chair of Urban Management at BTU, for creating a nurturing environment for my research to thrive and for her constant support. I extend my sincere thanks to Professor Klaus Rheidth, former Chair of Architectural History and

Spokesman of the DFG Research Training Group 1913, for his generous advice and guidance right from the early stages of formulating the grant proposal. His insights and encouragement laid the foundation for this book, and I am truly grateful for his mentorship. I am immensely grateful to the DFG Research Training Group 1913 for providing a nurturing space where I could exchange ideas and thoughts with international colleagues from diverse research fields, including architectural history, archaeology, and philosophy. Their support fostered an enriching environment that greatly contributed to the development of this work.

During challenging times when travel restrictions hindered my progress, Mr. Hossein Bayat provided indispensable help with archive research. His dedication and assistance were instrumental in overcoming the obstacles caused by the COVID-19 pandemic and advancing this project. I extend my wholehearted thanks to all 29 interviewees, both anonymous and named, for their invaluable contributions to this work. Their time, openness, and patience in answering my questions enriched this study and added a human dimension to the research. Additionally, I wish to extend my appreciation to Lara Bastajian for not only her dedication in editing the final draft but also for providing valuable and constructive feedback.

Lastly, I extend my heartfelt gratitude to my family in Tehran. Their encouragement and presence have been a constant source of strength throughout this journey, and I cherish the bond we share, even when miles apart.

Concluding this journey, I express my profound gratitude to everyone who has provided direct or indirect assistance along the way. While their perspectives may not have always corresponded with the standpoints laid out in this book, their invaluable contributions have significantly influenced its creation. Thank you all for being a part of this adventure.

Introduction

During the initial phase of my research, I engaged in an interview with Mohammad Mansour Falamaki, an eminent figure among the early generation of Iranian urban and architectural conservationists whose impact on the field dates back to the early 1970s. When I inquired about the evolution of the field of conservation in Iran, Falamaki characterized it as an overwhelming story, one that would shock any reasonable person. Through my comprehensive examination of the legal, administrative, and social trajectories of the field in Iranian cities, I have discerned a recurring tendency whereby accumulated resources and structures are deliberately dumped, only to be rebuilt in subsequent cycles. Speaking of shocking, Falamaki was, in a way, alluding to this tendency.

I started my investigation without any preconceived assumptions about heritage planning in Iran and relied solely on empirical observations to interpret my findings. Nevertheless, the deeper I delved into my investigation, the stronger my conviction became that the evolution of urban heritage planning in Iran exemplifies the thesis put forth by the historian Homa Katouzian about Iranian society. In the broader domain of Iranian socio-political history, Katouzian has identified a similar pattern: Iran is a "short-term society" resembling a "pick-axe", in other words, a near-crumbling building subjected to constant teardowns and reconstructions based on the transient desires of its rulers.[1] Katouzian

---

1   Homa Katouzian, 'The Short-Term Society: A Study in the Problems of Long-Term Political and Economic Development in Iran', *Middle Eastern Studies* 40, no. 1 (2004): 2.

asserts that the arbitrariness of the states and societies in Iran has created a history consisting of "a series of short runs", interrupted by successive waves of groups in political and economic power. In other words, it is a pick-axe society undergoing a recurring cycle of revolutionary detachment from established structures, re-establishment of new structures, and detachment once again. Every governing authority endeavours to dismantle the prevailing system and institute a fresh one, yet paradoxically, this very process perpetuates the cycle.

The historical trajectory of conservation and urban heritage planning in Iran throughout the past six decades is characterized by a series of fragmented aspirations, transient accomplishments, and iterative fresh beginnings. This pattern endures, whether instigated by revolutionary upheavals, transformative shifts in governmental power, or reconfigurations in city administrations.

The academic scope of the book

Conservation research has brought attention to the intricate link between conservation and urban development, elucidating how national policies pertaining to urban development have influenced the politics surrounding conservation.[2] The field of conservation has been urged to reconsider its methodologies and strategies in order to strengthen its role and flexibility in response to contemporary urban problems.[3] Given

---

2   Gregory J Ashworth and John E Tunbridge, 'Old Cities, New Pasts: Heritage Planning in Selected Cities of Central Europe', *GeoJournal*, 1999, 105–16; Gregory John Ashworth, 'Conservation as Preservation or as Heritage: Two Paradigms and Two Answers', *Built Environment (1978-)* 23, no. 2 (1997): 92–102; Max Page and Randall Mason, *Giving Preservation a History: Histories of Historic Preservation in the United States* (Routledge, 2004); John Pendlebury, *Conservation in the Age of Consensus* (London: Routledge, 2008).

3   Ashworth, 'Conservation as Preservation or as Heritage: Two Paradigms and Two Answers'; Hans-Rudolf Meier, *Denkmale in Der Stadt--Die Stadt Als Denkmal: Probleme Und Chancen Für Den Stadtumbau* (Dresden: TUD press, 2006); Pendlebury, *Conservation in the Age of Consensus*; Francesco Bandarin and Ron van Oers,

the diversity of national and regional planning contexts, the exploration of case studies is thus imperative to unveil the various scenarios that may emerge during the practical execution of conservation policies.[4]

In studying cultural heritage and conservation policy and practice, researchers have analyzed the discursive processes of significance production and the power dynamics involved in defining heritage and determining what elements are deemed worthy of conservation.[5] While acknowledging the importance of discourse, researchers have emphasized the material aspects of cultural heritage[6] and how empirical fac-

---

Reconnecting the City: The Historic Urban Landscape Approach and the Future of Urban Heritage (Wiley, 2014); Stephanie Ryberg-Webster and Kelly L. Kinahan, 'Historic Preservation and Urban Revitalization in the Twenty-First Century', *CPL Bibliography* 29, no. 2 (2014): 119–39.

4   Randall Mason and Erica Avrami, 'Heritage Values and Challenges of Conservation Planning', in *Management Planning for Archaeological Sites*, ed. Gaetano Palumbo and Jeanne Marie Teutonico (Corinth: Getty, 2002), 13–26; Helaine Silverman, 'Heritage and Authenticity', in *The Palgrave Handbook of Contemporary Heritage Research* (London: Springer, 2015), 69–88; Jeremy C Wells and Barry L Stiefel, *Human-Centered Built Environment Heritage Preservation: Theory and Evidence-Based Practice* (New York: Routledge, 2019).

5   Laurajane Smith, Uses of Heritage (London: Routledge, 2006); David C Harvey, 'The History of Heritage', in The Ashgate Research Companion to Heritage and Identity, ed. Brian J. Graham and Peter Howard (Ashgate Publishing, Ltd., 2008), 19–36; John Pendlebury, 'Conservation Values, the Authorised Heritage Discourse and the Conservation-Planning Assemblage', International Journal of Heritage Studies 19, no. 7 (2013): 709–27, doi:10.1080/13527258.2012.700282; Silverman, 'Heritage and Authenticity'; Heike Oevermann, Eszter Gantner, and Sybille Frank, Städtisches Erbe – Urban Heritage, Informationen Zur Modernen Stadtgeschichte (Berlin, 2016); Christoph Bernhardt, Martin Sabrow, and Achim Saupe, eds., Gebaute Geschichte: Historische Authentizität Im Stadtraum (Göttingen: Wallstein, 2017).

6   Rodney Harrison, 'Conclusion: On Heritage Ontologies: Rethinking the Material Worlds of Heritage', Anthropological Quarterly, 2018, 1365–83; Rodney Harrison et al., Heritage Futures: Comparative Approaches to Natural and Cultural Heritage Practices (UCL press, 2020).

tors such as professional, economic, and educational conditions can influence conservation practices.[7]

This book centres its attention on Iran's historical development of conservation and heritage planning.[8] Within this context, both discursive and material processes involved in conservation and heritage planning are examined, with their dynamics explored across multiple spheres, including the administrative, academic, professional, and social realms. This investigation primarily focuses on research inquiries at the convergence of conservation and urban studies. The book investigates socio-spatial processes of policymaking and practice regarding the maintenance, restoration, and reuse of urban spaces.

Addressing conservation within an urban context gives rise to a fundamental inquiry: What defines urban conservation or urban heritage planning? The UNESCO World Heritage Committee has classified heritage sites according to the physical scale of the built or natural features they cover, including monuments, groups of buildings, or cultural landscapes (settlements of both cultural and natural significance).[9] In practical terms, and notably in large cities of Iran, the conservation of an entire urban area is seldom achievable due to the scarcity of preserved historic

---

7   Wells and Stiefel, *Human-Centered Built Environment Heritage Preservation: Theory and Evidence-Based Practice*.
8   Ashworth distinguishes between conservation and heritage based on their respective objectives, methods of work, selection criteria, and strategies. Accordingly, this book employs the term 'conservation' to describe the preservation of the built environment with the aim of safeguarding its intrinsic value, which includes its age and artistic significance, while adhering to the methodological traditions of the architectural conservation profession. On the other hand, the term 'heritage' is used when approaches in handling the built environment, history, and memory are tailored to meet the current economic and sociopolitical objectives, rather than focusing on the inherent value of specific monuments. See: Ashworth, 'Conservation as Preservation or as Heritage: Two Paradigms and Two Answers'.
9   The World Heritage Committee, 'Operational Guidelines for the Implementation of the World Heritage Convention' (UNESCO World Heritage Centre, Paris, 2021), chap. II.

fabric. Does this suggest that urban conservation or urban heritage planning are almost nonexistent in Iranian cities or similar urban contexts?

Under the Historic Urban Landscape (HUL) approach, the understanding of an urban area has transcended the confines of the conventional categories mentioned above.[10] HUL encompasses the geographical setting, the natural and built aspects, as well as the intangible cultural and socio-economic features of the urban structures under consideration. In my investigation of conservation processes, I adopt a comparable multifaceted perspective. However, to maintain a focused scope, I choose to include only those conservation processes that demonstrate urban-scale significance, thereby avoiding an overly broad perspective that could arise from applying the HUL approach to the notions that I explore in this book. Adopting a relational perspective on the notion of scale thus provides an effective framework for explaining the practices I observed in my research of conservation projects in Tehran. In essence, I focus not on the *size of the objects* being conserved, such as monuments or urban areas, but rather on the *scale of their influence* during or after the preservation process.

Storper and Scott argue that not every phenomenon occurring within a large city can be considered an urban phenomenon. The label of "urban phenomenon" or a constituent element of the city is appropriate only when it "influences urban land nexus dynamics" and contributes to shaping the city's form.[11] For instance, let us consider repurposing a museum. If our concern lies primarily with its internal arrangements, such as interior architecture and structural stability, we are operating within the realm of architectural conservation. However, if we are addressing its placement within the city's socio-economic relationships, including variables such as human and vehicular traffic, parking capacity, the emergence of amenities such as cafes and bookstores, or the utilization of municipal funds that may influence other city projects, we are discussing urban heritage planning. According to this approach,

---

10 WHC UNESCO, 'Recommendation on the Historic Urban Landscape', 2011.
11 Michael Storper and Allen J. Scott, 'Current Debates in Urban Theory: A Critical Assessment', *Urban Studies* 53, no. 6 (2016): 1114–36.

individual buildings, beautified facades, or, as I will discuss in the case study chapter, graffiti art that leaves a socio-spatial mark on the city's engagement with its past can be considered elements of urban heritage planning.

Underlying concepts

Urban heritage assemblage

To fully comprehend the evolution of the academic and professional field of conservation, it is necessary to examine the material role played by historic places, urban spaces, urban infrastructure, and the environment, in addition to analyzing heritage discourses. Within the field of urban planning, scholars have situated heritage planning processes within socio-spatial[12] assemblages.[13] Also, scholars in heritage studies have studied heritage assembled within national and local socio-economic contexts,[14] and as discursive-material processes.[15]

---

12   When assemblage theory is utilized to examine cities and the social processes within them, it takes into account both the social and spatial elements involved. Consequently, it perceives urban processes as socio-spatial processes. See: Manuel DeLanda, *A New Philosophy of Society: Assemblage Theory and Social Complexity* (London & New York: Bloomsbury Publishing, 2006).

13   Jean Hillier, 'More than Meat: Rediscovering the Cow beneath the Face in Urban Heritage Practice', *Environment and Planning D: Society and Space* 31, no. 5 (2013): 863–78; Shulan Fu and Jean Hillier, 'Disneyfication or Self-Referentiality: Recent Conservation Efforts and Modern Planning History in Datong', in *China: A Historical Geography of the Urban* (Springer, 2018), 165–91.

14   Sharon Macdonald, 'Reassembling Nuremberg, Reassembling Heritage', *Journal of Cultural Economy* 2, no. 1–2 (2009): 117–34; Pendlebury, 'Conservation Values, the Authorised Heritage Discourse and the Conservation-Planning Assemblage'.

15   Solmaz Yadollahi, 'Prospects of Applying Assemblage Thinking for Further Methodological Developments in Urban Conservation Planning', *The Historic Environment: Policy & Practice* 8, no. 4 (2 October 2017): 355–71; Harrison, 'Conclusion: On Heritage Ontologies: Rethinking the Material Worlds of Heritage'; Har-

These approaches are grounded in the framework of assemblage[16] and actor-network[17] thinking, which posits that non-human actors also hold agency within social processes. An assemblage can be described as a symbiotic gathering of heterogeneous players, whether human or non-human, co-functioning and forming alliances for a period of time.[18]

In this book, I present the trajectories of conservation and heritage planning in Iran as an assemblage unfolding and changing over time. Like other assemblages, academic and professional fields are historical socio-material entities.[19] Hence, the field of conservation and heritage planning is presented as the evolving assemblage of urban spaces, heritage discourses, communities of practitioners and scholars, organizations, research- and practice-oriented laboratories and workshops, and finally, the common public that engages with urban heritage.

In this context, knowledge of the field comprises two dimensions—'knowing that', acquired through the teaching of conservation theory, and 'knowing how', an embodied knowledge that relies on the material medium and practical experience.[20] The book sheds light on specific sites that, owing to their distinct local material characteristics, have played a pivotal role in shaping the technical know-how of conservation in Iran. These locations have served as workshops and laboratories where the craftsmanship of working with stone and mud brick has been taught and learned. For instance, cities like Isfahan, Yazd, Shiraz, and Bam have been instrumental in training numerous

    rison et al., *Heritage Futures: Comparative Approaches to Natural and Cultural Heritage Practices*.
16 Gilles Deleuze and Felix Guattari, *A Thousand Plateaus*, trans. Brian Massumi (Minneapolis: University of Minnesota Press, 1987); DeLanda, *A New Philosophy of Society: Assemblage Theory and Social Complexity*; Manuel DeLanda, *Assemblage Theory* (Edinburgh: Edinburgh University Press, 2016).
17 Bruno Latour, *Reassembling the Social: An Introduction to Actor-Network-Theory* (Oxford university press, 2005).
18 DeLanda, *Assemblage Theory*.
19 Ibid.
20 DeLanda explores various forms of knowledge and highlights the significance of the material medium in the process of acquiring knowledge. Ibid.

practitioners and scholars who later pursued careers elsewhere in the country. Consequently, the material and discursive contributions of these places have profoundly influenced the preservation of spaces throughout the country. In essence, these sites have co-worked with heritage discourses, influencing the field's scope of interest, as well as its methodological traditions.

To ensure a more coherent and articulated investigation and presentation, the book directs its attention towards distinct domains of where the key players tend to be present. The first domain centres on the overarching socio-economic politics in the state, which operate independently at a higher level than urban planning and heritage policies. The second domain includes the official urban heritage planning policymaking sphere, encompassing the dynamics within the parliament, organizations, and ministries. The third domain pertains to academia, and the fourth domain explores the intersection of official policies with everyday urban life, often involving implemented conservation projects.

Visually thinking (see Figure 1), we can identify how these four key domains intersect at certain areas along their boundaries. These areas serve as arenas where actors from different domains interact. Within these arenas, we often find the presence of players such as places, social media platforms, professionals, and local branches of governmental institutions. Actor-network-inspired policy researchers believe that institutions sometimes use 'boundary objects' to reduce tensions between two or more distinct domains.[21] The arenas in which boundary objects can link actors from different domains to each other are at times intentionally created by the government; at others, they emerge spontaneously as a result of socio-economic and political transformations. Throughout the book, I use the term 'boundary action' to describe

---

21   See: Susan Leigh Star and James R Griesemer, 'Institutional Ecology,Translations' and Boundary Objects: Amateurs and Professionals in Berkeley's Museum of Vertebrate Zoology, 1907–39', *Social Studies of Science* 19, no. 3 (1989): 387–420; Linda Fox-Rogers and Enda Murphy, 'Informal Strategies of Power in the Local Planning System', *Planning Theory* 13, no. 3 (2014): 244–68.

intentional and spontaneous activities occurring within intersecting areas.

For instance, in some sections of the book, I employ this concept to explain the episodic strategies that the government adopts to encourage the participation of non-governmental actors. Boundary action helps to explain how the government tends to employ social media accounts, historic buildings, and local private consultants in non-governmental settings as a means to engage with actors who would normally be sceptical or distrustful of the government.

The concept is also related to a method that I frequently use to investigate the intersection of policymaking and the implementation of projects. Throughout the book, I make references to certain influential scholars as 'bureaucrat-academics', highlighting their dual role within both academic and governmental domains. I attempt to estimate the disparity between theory/policy and practice by triangulating the data obtained from various sources, including academic publications of bureaucrat-academics, their statements in newspapers, on television and radio programmes, academic events, my interviews, and empirical observations of project outcomes in the city. Regarding the term 'bureaucrat-academic', I draw upon sociologist Mohammad Fazeli's concept of the 'sociologist-bureaucrat'.[22] Fazeli employs this term to characterize sociologists who are actively involved in public administration. By identifying as one himself, Fazeli asserts that although these individuals may not possess the freedom to openly criticize the government, they can contribute valuable insights into the intricate workings of the governance system.

---

22 Mohammad Fazeli, *Iran Bar Labe-Ye Tigh, Goftar-Ha-Ye Jameshenasi-Ye Siyasi va Siyasat-e Omumi [Iran, on the Edge of the Blade Essays on Political Sociology and Public Policy]* (Tehran: Rozaneh, 2021).

Figure 1: The overlapping spheres of influence in urban heritage planning

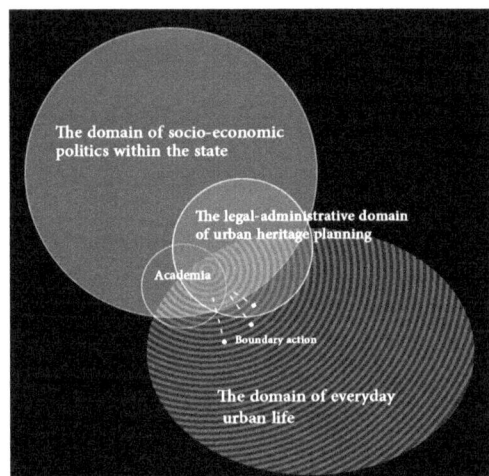

A 'Body Without Organs'

Assemblage theory offers a valuable perspective for comprehending the behaviours and tendencies of socio-material formations while avoiding generalizations. Drawing on the concept of stratified and smooth space introduced by Deleuze and Guattari,[23] Manuel DeLanda contends that in social relationships, including those that shape cities, we can consistently detect variations between organized, coded structures and those that are spontaneous and flexible.[24]

DeLanda proposes a concept involving an imaginary knob that researchers can utilize to describe the level of rigidity observed in socio-material formations.[25] By using this metaphor, I analyze the interplay between various actors, both human and non-human, as they

---

23 Deleuze and Guattari 1987.
24 DeLanda 2016.
25 DeLanda, *A New Philosophy of Society: Assemblage Theory and Social Complexity*.

exert forces either pushing the assemblage towards territorialization or pulling it towards de-territorialization. I focus on examining these behaviours during periods of stability, as well as those of political or economic shock. The underlying notion here is that every assemblage must undergo a process of experimentation to find its optimal position on the knob. In other words, the assemblage needs to strike a balance to avoid the pitfalls of becoming excessively rigid at one end or descending into chaotic disarray at the other.

Another noteworthy proposition of assemblage thinking is that studying the historical behaviour of assemblages (or the recurrent behavioural patterns exhibited by actors within specific contextual circumstances) allows researchers to identify certain habits or tendencies. Understanding these enhances the predictability of behaviours that the socio-spatial assemblage might manifest under similar circumstances in the future.[26]

To illustrate the collective behaviours and tendencies of the administrative, academic, and socio-spatial actors involved in urban heritage planning in Iran, I depict their collective assemblage as a body.[27] When placed in certain circumstances, the metaphorical body undergoes transformative shifts and assumes diverse manifestations. Occasionally, it exhibits flexibility and openness, readily embracing novel forms, while in other instances, it becomes self-destructive and unyielding. It undergoes periods of growth and, alternately, periods of fracture. It can demonstrate cancerous tendencies when the proliferation of rigid structures becomes uncontrollable, much like the uncontrolled proliferation of cancer cells. It can also show a pathological lack of appropriately structured organs to support its proper functioning.

---

26   DeLanda, *Assemblage Theory*; Gert De Roo, Jean Hillier, and Van Wezemael, 'Complexity and Spatial Planning: Introducing Systems, Assemblages and Simulations', in *Complexity and Planning: Systems, Assemblages and Simulations*, ed. Gert De Roo and Jean Hillier (Oxon: Routledge, 2016), 1–36.

27   In A Thousand Plateaus, Deleuze and Guattari occasionally use the term "body" interchangeably with the term "assemblage".

In this conceptual context, a 'Body without Organs' explains a state of openness to new forms of expression and possibilities. This openness should not be confused with pathological chaos or disorder. Deleuze and Guattari suggest that the 'Body without Organs' is a body that is not organized according to pre-existing norms or structures but is nevertheless capable of organizing itself in new and creative ways. In this book, I employ this concept when explaining a historical point where nearly all activities of an assemblage come to a halt, awaiting the emergence of new structures. I specifically emphasize the correlation between the revolutionary socio-political transitions in Iran and the conservation and urban heritage planning assemblage entering a state of a 'Body Without Organs'.

Methods of data collection and analysis: Unravelling the book's structure

In its methodological approach, this book primarily adopts an inductive, empirical stance to explore, explain, and critically analyze the investigated phenomena, which are exemplified through a single embedded case study.[28] Source triangulation serves as a fundamental approach to ensuring the reliability of the collected data and its subsequent results. Nevertheless, when required, method triangulation (or, in this research, triangulation of data collection techniques) is applied to verify and validate qualitative findings.[29] For data analysis, the technique of thematic coding is employed to effectively categorize, cross-check, and triangulate data gathered from various sources, facilitating the interpretation of the research findings.[30]

---

28 Robert K Yin, *Case Study Research: Design and Methods* (Thousand Oaks: SAGE Publications, 2009).
29 For different types of triangulation, see: Ibid.
30 See: H Russell Bernard, Amber Wutich, and Gery W Ryan, *Analyzing Qualitative Data: Systematic Approaches* (Los Angeles: SAGE publications, 2016); Uwe Flick, *An Introduction to Qualitative Research* (Sage, 2009).

While the assemblage-inspired methodology is less commonly utilized in urban heritage research, it is not a new or unproven approach within academic domains like urban studies and urban planning.[31] Elsewhere, I have explored how assemblage thinking can provide valuable methodological tools for addressing inquiries posed by urban heritage research. Methodologically, I am inspired by Baker and McGuirk's 'ethnographic sensibility' in following the interrelationships of human and non-human actors in urban assemblages.[32] It is important to highlight that instead of delving deep into the specific properties of places, ideologies, traditions, natural risks, artistic or political events, artists, and cultural products like songs and films, this research focuses on exploring the role they play within the urban heritage planning assemblage.

Throughout my fieldwork, I gathered research materials through online ethnographic observation[33] of mainstream media and social media platforms, including Instagram, Telegram, and Twitter. Additionally, between 2019 and 2022, I actively participated in urban heritage safeguarding campaigns and attended diverse events aimed at academics, professionals, as well as the general public to closely observe how actors interact and to track the development of projects on the ground.

In Part One, I approach the national conservation and urban heritage planning assemblage in Iran as an ethnographic 'site' of observation.

---

31 For instance, see: Colin McFarlane, 'The City as Assemblage: Dwelling and Urban Space', *Environment and Planning: Society and Space* 29, no. 4 (2011): 649–71; Martin Müller, 'Assemblages and Actor-Networks: Rethinking Socio-Material Power, Politics and Space', *Geography Compass* 9, no. 1 (2015): 27–41; Gert De Roo and Jean Hillier, *Complexity and Planning: Systems, Assemblages and Simulations* (Routledge, 2016); Tom Baker and Pauline McGuirk, 'Assemblage Thinking as Methodology: Commitments and Practices for Critical Policy Research', *Territory, Politics, Governance* 5, no. 4 (2017): 425–42.
32 Baker and McGuirk 2017.
33 Stephen M Lochetto, 'Hybrid Ethnography: Online, Offline, and In Between', 2022.

In a manner akin to ethnographic architectural research,[34] my primary method of data collection is observation. In practical terms, I approach archival and published sources of data, such as legal texts, news, administrative charts and regulations, academic publications, photographs, and maps, with a perspective similar to an ethnographer viewing ethnographic artefacts.

Semi-structured interviews are conducted with academics, practitioners, and the general public, but these are treated as supplementary data sources. This approach is adopted because the human actors themselves are observed as participants within the assemblage. Thus, their viewpoints, while not determinative, are nevertheless influential in shaping the research results. On occasion, data collected from semi-structured interviews is further supported by brief telephone interviews and text/voice message surveys. It is crucial to note that the interviews were all conducted with consent; however, most are not attributed by name to safeguard the anonymity of the interviewees who might otherwise face negative repercussions.

During data analysis, I organized the data concerning different actors into thematic clusters, categorizing them based on the domains wherein they could be found. The more closely two actors shared a theme, the more interconnected they were within the assemblage. By mapping the alliances among actors in each historical period, I depicted the trajectories of the urban heritage assemblage, shedding light on its historical turning points. In the final illustration (see Figure 62), you can see how actors have collectively shaped the urban heritage planning assemblage in Iran through their involvement in territorializing and de-territorializing its structures.

The first part of the book indicates that from the early 1900s to 2022, the evolution of urban heritage planning in Iran is characterized by recurring cycles of struggle to establish an ordered and territorialized official heritage planning system in cities. Yet, with each shift in the political

---

34   Linda Groat and David Wang, *Architectural Research Methods*, 2nd ed. (New Jersey: John Wiley & Sons, 2013).

landscape, the progress made in territorializing heritage planning and conservation experiences setbacks or significant alterations.

Part Two contextualizes and problematizes the national urban heritage assemblage in Tehran. This section places emphasis on examining heritage planning procedures within the area officially outlined as Tehran's official historic zone. It is worth noting that the decision to problematize urban conservation policies in Tehran has several motivations. First, the city offers valuable insights into the diverse challenges that heritage planning encounters in the context of a rapidly developing Iranian megacity. Second, as the capital, Tehran has played a pivotal role in shaping the modern national identity of Iranians and in assembling the structures of the conservation and heritage planning bureaucracy in Iran. Lastly, the risk of losing what little is left of its built heritage positions Tehran as a setting where the consequences of overly practised reconstruction of lost monuments can be contemplated and examined.

Here, the ethnographic research narrows to the local dynamics of urban heritage assemblage in Tehran, encompassing the informal elements integral to this assemblage. Data collection and thematic categorization of the data follow the rationale explained in Part One. The only methodological difference is the inclusion of data collected through ethnographic research in the physical urban setting of Tehran's city centre. The main conclusion of this part is that, situated in a short-term society, the urban heritage assemblage in Tehran has no choice but to turn a blind eye to the long-term and accumulated unresolved economic, spatial, and socio-political conflicts surrounding public space in the city centre.

In the conclusion chapter, the identified tendencies of the investigated assemblage take centre stage, prioritizing insights over recommendations. While the chapter does not offer practical suggestions, the understanding of recurring behaviours provides potential glimpses into the assemblage's future tendencies if the current conditions persist. Amidst the prevailing political and ideological landscape in Iran and the Middle East, the hope of providing urban heritage planning with a sturdy foundation seems to be fading, and this poignant revelation stands as a pivotal finding of this research.

Part One

Urban heritage planning in Iran: Repeated cycles of struggle for territorialization

In the following three chapters, the trajectories of urban heritage assemblage in Iran are diagnostically traced through key examples of national significance, laying out a recurring pattern of territorialization, chaos, and re-territorialization. It is my contention that the academic, legal, and administrative frameworks of conservation and heritage planning have proven inadequate in establishing a solid basis for practical implementation. Using archival research, hybrid ethnography[1] in online and offline settings, semi-structured interviews, and academic literature, the chapters illustrate the struggles of urban heritage assemblage in Iran's turbulent political, economic, and cultural climate from the early 1900s to 2022.

Part One is broken down into three chapters, each covering a cycle. The first cycle starts at the establishment of conservation and heritage bureaucracy in Iran and ends with the 1979 Revolution. The second cycle commences after the 1979 Revolution and the formation of a new heritage administration, which was accompanied by economic and political reforms. These reforms were interrupted when the conservative government assumed power in 2005, bringing with it significant political and administrative upheaval. The third cycle begins with the re-territorialization of urban heritage policy and practice during the second reformist government in 2013. However, this phase is redirected and even-

---

1 Lochetto, 'Hybrid Ethnography: Online, Offline, and In Between'.

tually ended due to the return of unified conservative rule, which commenced in 2018 and was solidified in 2021.

It is noteworthy that the formal and informal relationships among the various actors extend beyond the specific points in time that this book uses to outline the cycles. These historical turning points were identified based on the significant shifts observed in the urban heritage planning context. They are used to illustrate the recurring pattern discussed, rather than to strictly indicate specific time frames.

The first cycle: Assembling the conservation fundaments between two revolutions

With the early 1900s Constitutional Revolution, Iranian society broke with the structures of the past and created a plane of possibilities on which new socio-political structures could emerge. From this plane of possibilities, which Deleuze and Guattari would call a 'Body Without Organs',[2] the governmental, academic, and social assemblage of modern conservation was born in Iran. The legislative-administrative conservation apparatus that developed between 1910 and 1930 was linked to the pre-constitutional socio-political networks[3] around the idea of modern Iranian nationality.[4] Nevertheless, state implementation of conservation as a central policy in Iran began with the establishment of the parliamentary state and its ministries. In this regard, Tehran's

---

2   Deleuze and Guattari, *A Thousand Plateaus*.
3   Elsewhere, I have looked at the transition of Iranian thought from pre-modern handling of old cities to modern conservation. See: Solmaz Yadollahi, 'Reflections on the Past and Future of Urban Conservation in Iran', *Built Heritage* 4, no. 1 (2020): 1–13.
4   For a detailed historical perspective on constructing cultural heritage preservation as part of modernization process in Iran, see: Talinn Grigor, 'Recultivating "Good Taste": The Early Pahlavi Modernists and Their Society for National Heritage', *Iranian Studies* 37, no. 1 (2004): 17–45, doi: 10.1080/0021086042000232929.

material and discursive role in the overarching modernization policies, including conservation, was central.

With the establishment of the Ministry of Knowledge, Awqaf,[5] and Handicrafts [*Vezarat-e Maaref, Awqaf, va Sanaye' e Mostazrefeh*] in 1910, ideas, funds, and human resources were collected in Tehran and distributed to other parts of the country.[6] Western archaeologists also played an important role in laying the foundations for the administrative and academic components of conservation in Iran, for instance by establishing the National Council for Monuments (NCM) [*Anjoman-e Asar-e Melli*] in 1921 and drafting the very first list of national cultural heritage sites.[7] They also played an integral role in drafting the 1930 Antiquities Law[8] and in setting up the College of Fine Arts at the University of Tehran in 1939.[9]

The conservation projects that involved close cooperation with foreign architects and archaeologists were initially undertaken in the mid-1920s and 1930s at Persepolis in Shiraz and the monuments located in the Shah (Naghsh-e Jahan) Square in Isfahan.[10] These sites played

---

5   In Islamic contexts, the term 'Awqaf' refers to donated, inherited, or acquired assets held in trust for charitable social purposes.
6   In 1922, the Parliament approved legislation to allocate funds for the purpose of sending Iranians overseas to attend military schools, with the aim of cultivating domestic human resources essential for the nation. This marked the initiation of subsequent fund allocations administered by the Vezarat-e Maaef. See: Maghsoud Farasatkhah, *The Adventure of University in Iran* (Tehran: Rasa, 2009).
7   I Sadiq, 'Anjoman-e Athar-e Melli', in *Encyclopedia Iranica*, 1985; Grigor, 'Recultivating "Good Taste": The Early Pahlavi Modernists and Their Society for National Heritage'.
8   Parliament of Iran, 'The Law on Antiquities', 1930.
9   The college, led by the French archaeologist André Godard, began as an art school that offered education in architecture, painting, and sculpture.
10 See: Ève Gran-Aymerich and Mina Marefat, 'GODARD, ANDRÉ', *Encyclopaedia Iranica* XI (2001): 29–31; Kishwar Rizvi, 'Art History and the Nation: Arthur Upham Pope and the Discourse on" Persian Art" in the Early Twentieth Century', in *Muqarnas, Volume 24* (Brill, 2007), 45–66; Eugenio Galdieri and Kerāmat-Allāh Afsar, 'Conservation and Restoration of Persian Monuments', in *Encyclopedia Iranica* (New York, 1992).

an important role in shaping the conservation approaches in Iran by providing the technical and material context in which conservation ideas and methods could be examined, learned, and implemented in other sites. Galdieri and Afsar[11] highlight examples of how these sites have contributed to the definition of buffer zones around historic sites and how to use local materials in conservation projects.

Figure 2: Persepolis, Gate of All Nations, photographed during the 1939 excavation season

©The University of Chicago[12]

11 'Conservation and Restoration of Persian Monuments'.
12 Stable URL: https://isac-idb.uchicago.edu/id/91b60f15-5141-4e29-9cb9-2b16f9d224ee

The international debates reflected in the Athens Charter,[13] which advocated the preservation of monuments and the removal of the urban structures surrounding them, were also taken up in Iran during this period. As such, the Antiquities Law relied on expert interpretation of criteria such as artistic, scientific, or historical value (for instance, by listing monuments built before the end of the Zand dynasty in 1794).

At the urban level, the period following the Constitutional Revolution saw the territorialization of land and property within legally defined and registered boundaries of public and private ownership, previously defined by tradition and religion. Technological and demographic changes, widespread automobile use, and increased political control over urban areas led to the proliferation of road-widening projects and redevelopment, as well as the radical replanning of old neighbourhoods in Tehran and other major cities.[14] Together with the Antiquities Law, this urban planning approach led to the development of modern cities in which selected monuments of conservation significance were listed for preservation.

After World War II and the Anglo-Soviet invasion of Iran in 1941, heritage projects were put on hold, pending an environment stable enough to allow for further administrative and on-site conservation measures. Having left the country in the early 1940s due to political instability and war, foreign archaeologists returned to Iran in the postwar period for what was described by Galdieri and Afsar as "the time of the great restoration projects".[15]

Following the revision of the Antiquities Law in 1944, monuments from the Qajar period that were less than a hundred years old became eligible to be classified as historically valuable. The general cultural

---

13 Le Corbusier and CIAM, *The Athens Charter for the Restoration of Historic Monuments* (New York, 1931).
14 EHLERS Ehlers Eckart, 'Modern Urbanization and Modernization in Persia', in *Encyclopedia Iranica*, Cities iv, 1991, http://www.iranicaonline.org/articles/cities-iv; Ali Madanipour, 'Early Modernization and the Foundations of Urban Growth in Tehran', *Fachzeitschrift Des VINI*, 2006.
15 'Conservation and Restoration of Persian Monuments'.

policy reflected, for example, in radio broadcasts[16] and tourism magazines,[17] indicate that the Ashwothian[18] economy-oriented heritage planning was gradually finding a place in urban policymaking. This subtle reorientation is particularly evident in the Law on Municipalities and City Anjomans,[19] on the basis of which the municipalities became responsible for the conservation of urban monuments under the Law on Antiquities. Yet, conservation of monuments remained the primary approach. Cleansing the city fabric surrounding historical monuments in Yazd, Qazvin, Kashan, and Isfahan[20] exemplify interventions resulting from the overlap between administrative and legal systems that operated urban development and conservation.

Assembling and sophisticating conservation in Iranian cities

The period between 1960 and 1970 was characterized by an increase in oil revenue and a corresponding rapid urban development fuelled by a strengthened economy and cooperation with the US.[21] In the progressive and stable political atmosphere after the White Revolution[22] and

---

16   For example, see n. n., 'The Magazin of Radio Tehran [Inja Tehran Ast]', 65 1947, Tehran, National Library of Iran.
17   See 'Revue Du Touring Club de l'Iran [Majale-Ye Jahangardi]', September 1936, Tehran, National Library of Iran; 'Revue Du Touring Club de l'Iran [Majale-Ye Jahangardi]', August 1937, Tehran, National Library of Iran.
18   Ashworth, 'Conservation as Preservation or as Heritage: Two Paradigms and Two Answers'.
19   Parliament of Iran, 'Municipalities and City Anjomans Law [Ghanoon-e Tashkil-e Shahrdari-Ha ve Anjoman-e Sahrha va Ghasabat]', 1949.
20   Asghar Mohammadmoradi, Atossa Amirkabirian, and Hojatollah Abdi Ardakani, *Revitalisation of Historic Urban Fabrics (a Review of Experiences)* (Tehran: University of Tehran, 2017).
21   See: Ehlers, 'Modern Urbanization and Modernization in Persia'; Madanipour, 'Early Modernization and the Foundations of Urban Growth in Tehran'.
22   In 1963, Mohammad Reza Shah initiated his 'White Revolution', which included agricultural and economic reform (for example, the transfer of farmland to peasants), giving women the right to vote, the nationalization of forests, and the mobilization of young men and women in the education, health, and agri-

with the development of the oil economy, the social and administrative structures of conservation began to expand and become more complex, much like other governmental and social formations. Without experiencing a radical break with the past (the legal, administrative, and discursive structure that had emerged following the Constitutional Revolution), the elements of conservation came to be rearranged to form a more complex structure assembled in cities countrywide.

The Ministry of Culture and Art and the Ministry of Development and Housing were both established in 1963 to promote the modernization of cultural and urban development. Although their impact in the cities was quite divergent even to the point of appearing contradictory, their function within a centralized legislative-administrative system nevertheless made the field of conservation more complex and expanded its traditional disciplinary boundaries. Throughout the 1960s and 1970s, government policy and academic publications alike mention conservation of historic urban and rural areas as described in the 1956 Venice Charter,[23] outlining the emerging link between the fields of conservation and urban planning, which respectively fall under the jurisdiction of the two aforementioned ministries. This focus underscores the connection between the domestic urban conservation planning frameworks and the prevailing international discourses of the time.

Some mark the inclusion of settlements such as the City of Damavand and its surroundings and the ancient city of Gorgan in the National Heritage List in 1931 and 1938, respectively, to be the beginning of the drafting guidelines for the conservation of historic cities in Iran.[24] However, aside from documentation of various sites and ongoing discourse

---

cultural corps. Opposed by large landowners and the clergy, the White Revolution led to upheaval that contributed to the 1979 Iranian Revolution. See: Ehsan Yarshater, 'IRAN Ii. IRANIAN HISTORY (2) Islamic Period (Page 6)', *Encyclopaedia Iranica* XIII, no. 3 (2012): 243–46.

23   ICOMOS, *The Venice Charter* (Venice, 1964).

24   Fieldnotes at the expert meeting on experiences of writing guidelines for historic fabrics (the case of Qom presented by Pardaraz Consulting Engineers), organized by Tehran Municipality, Mehraban Historic House, Tehran, 27.01.2020.

at the time, there is no evidence suggesting that before the 1960s, conservation practice in cities went beyond the monument-centred approach represented by the Athens Charter.[25]

Despite theoretical and legal advances, the gap between conservation policy and practice persisted due to the social, political, and economic forces at work in urban areas throughout the 1960s and 1970s, restricting preservation and presentation to select monuments. For instance, municipalities practiced conservation in cities generally based on the 1930 Antiquities Law,[26] which also had a monument-centred approach. The 1968 Law on Acquisition of Land and Property for the Preservation of Historic and Ancient Monuments[27] also provided a legal basis for municipalities and the Ministry of Culture and Art to acquire and remove residential and commercial buildings that 'obscured' outstanding monuments. Also, in 1967, Parliament passed a law whereby a portion of the cement tax went to the NCM for preserving historic buildings.[28] Despite the theoretical acknowledgement of a broader urban perspective, the Master Plans of major cities, influenced by the aforementioned legal-administrative structure and the physical remnants within those cities, indicate a notable emphasis on monuments.

---

25 Le Corbusier and CIAM, *The Athens Charter for the Restoration of Historic Monuments*.
26 Parliament of Iran, 'The Law on Antiquities'.
27 Parliament of Iran, 'Ghanun-e Kharid-e Arazi Abniyeh va Tasisat Baray-e Hefazat Asar Tarikhi va Bastani [Law on Acquisition of Land and Property for the Preservation of Historic and Ancient Monuments]', *The Official Magazine: Rooznameh-e Rasmi-e Keshvar*, 1968.
28 Parliament of Iran, 'Ghanun-e Akhz-e Mablagh-e Bist Rial Avarez Az Har Ton Siman Be Naf-e Anjoman-e Asar-e Melli [The Law on the Taxation of an Amount of Twenty Rials per Ton of Cement for the Benefit of the Anjoman-e Asar-e Melli]' (The Official Magazine: Rooznameh-e Rasmi-e Keshvar, 1968).

In the Master Plan and detailed plans of cities such as Tabriz,[29] Shiraz[30], Isfahan,[31] and Mashhad,[32] interventions in historic areas were placed under the supervision of the Ministry of Culture and Art, and guidelines for specific historic areas were prepared in cooperation with the ministry. While these plans recognized the aesthetic and tourism values of the 'old city', their proposed approach to "integrating them into the cityscape" typically involved visually exposing the historical monuments that were previously obscured by less significant structures.[33] The interventions around the Blue Mosque and Arg-e Alishah are examples of this approach in Tabriz (see Figure 3). The interventions around the Sheikh Safi Shrine in Ardabil and Amir Chakhmagh Square in Yazd are other examples of the spatial manifestation of this policy.[34]

In the fall of 1965, the National Organization for the Preservation of Historical Monuments (NOPHM) [*Sazman-e Melli Hefazat-e Asare Bastani*] was established in Tehran to manage the conservation and promotion of built cultural heritage throughout the country. The organization began its mission by establishing provincial branches and networking with other governmental organizations, such as the Ministry of Development and Housing, municipalities, international institutions, universities,

---

29 The Master Plan for Tabriz was remarkable in that it promoted the revitalization of the socio-spatial fabric of the bazaar and the residential neighbourhoods of the old city. It explicitly referred to the 1930 Antiquities Law for the protection of monuments and the cityscape. But as mentioned earlier, the 1930 Law had a monument-centred approach. See: Moghtader-Andreef, 'Master Plan of Tabriz', 1970.

30 The detailed plan was prepared in 1974–5. See: M. Mansour Falamaki, *Seiri Dar Tajarob-e Marammat-e Shari, as Veniz Ta Shiraz [An Essay on Urban Conservation, From Venice to Shiraz]* (Tehran: Faza Scientific and Cultural Institute, 2005).

31 Organic Engineering Consultancy, 'Detailed Plan of Isfahan' (Ministry of Housing and Urban Development, 1975).

32 Daryoush Bourbour, 'Nosazi-e Atraf-e Haram-e Motahar Hazrat-e-Rza, Mashhad [Projet de Renovation de Haram Hazrat-e-Reza Meched]', *Art and Architecture*, no. 20 (1973): 30–41.

33 For example, see: Moghtader-Andreef, 'Master Plan of Tabriz'.

34 Mohammadmoradi, Amirkabirian, and Abdi Ardakani, *Revitalisation of Historic Urban Fabrics (a Review of Experiences)*.

and national media outlets. NOPHM went on to develop programmes in cooperation with schools, municipalities, radio, television, and cinemas to promote conservation awareness among the general public.[35]

Figure 3: Arg-e Alishah in the Tabriz Master Plan of 1970[36]

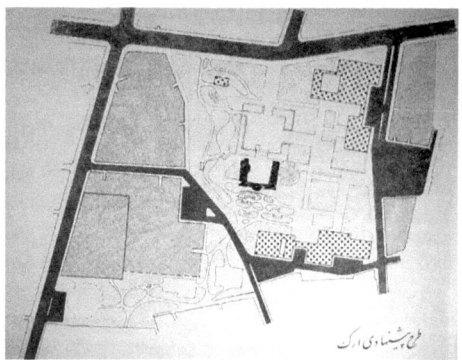

---

35 Agahinameh, *Agahinameh*, vol. 1, 1 (Tehran, 1975); Agahinameh, 'Mosahebe Ba Rais Bakhsh-e Amoozesh Sazman [An Interview with the Director of the Department of Education]', *Agahinameh*, no. 5 (1976); Agahinameh, 'Tashkilat-e Sazman [The Organisation]', *Agahinameh*, no. 23 (1977): 8–9; Art and Architecture, 'News', *Art and Architecture*, no. 15 (1974): 14–17.

36 See: Moghtader-Andreef, 'Master Plan of Tabriz', n.p.

Figure 4: Public exhibitions in Fars (left) and Qazvin (right) on the occasion of the NOPHM's founding anniversary[37]

Backed by generous state funding (made possible due to abundant oil revenue), NOPHM invested in its human resources, benefiting from graduates from the University of Tehran, Farabi University in Isfahan, and Melli University in Tehran. The architecture programmes at these institutions already had a disciplinary interest in architectural and planning history. For example, Hooshang Seyhoun, faculty member and Dean of the College of Fine Arts and Architecture at the University of Tehran in the 1960s and member of Iran-ICOMOS,[38] facilitated a collaboration between the Institute of Archaeology and Iran-ICOMOS to engage architecture students in mapping historic buildings and field trips to historic sites.[39]

---

37   Agahinameh, *Agahinameh*, 1:12–17.
38   The National Committee of the International Council on Monuments and Sites (ICOMOS) in Iran.
39   Mohammad Ghari, 'A Conversation with Hooshang Seyhoin', *Abadi*, no. 48 (2005): 130–34.

Figure 5: Monument Relevé programme for undergraduates, University of Tehran[40]

Later generations of architects, like Falamaki, had a deeper interest in conservation and sought to go beyond architectural and urban history by incorporating conservation into architecture curricula and organizing events such as the 'First Seminar on the Existence and Future of Historic Residential Centres' at the University of Tehran in 1971.[41] The proceedings of the aforementioned event were documented in the first book

---

40 *Nashriyeh-Ye Daneshkadeh-Ye Honarha-Ye Ziba (1341–1343)* [Magazine of the College of Fine Arts 1962–64], vol. 2 (Tehran: University of Tehran, 1964), 13.

41 M. Mansour Falamaki, ed., *Avalin Seminar-e Maremat-e Banaha va Sharhay-e Tarikhi: Vojud va Ayandeye Marakez-e Maskuni-e Tarikhi*[The First Seminar on the Conservation of Historic Cities and Towns: The Existence and Future of Historical Residential Centres] (Tehran: University of Tehran, 1971); M. Mansour Falamaki, Interview with Mr. Mansour Falamaki, interview by Solmaz Yadollahi, 9 October 2019, Tehran.

on urban conservation in Farsi.[42] Falamaki's second book, *Revitalization of Historic Buildings and Cities*, went beyond translating international concepts and discussed the cultural, religious, and geographical factors that affected conservation in Iranian cities.[43]

As the capital, Tehran led the academic discourse on conservation, but Isfahan also played an undeniably crucial discursive-material role in shaping conservation knowledge in Iran. Meidan-e Shah or Naghsh-e Jahan and Chaharbagh Street were the first living urban areas listed as national heritage sites in 1932. Meidan-e Shah in Isfahan was also the first Iranian World Heritage Site listed in 1979 as a well-preserved homogeneous urban complex.[44] The conservation studios of Isfahan, active since the 1930s, were the best places to learn how to conserve. As places where international and Iranian conservation architects and local craftsmen could collaborate and engage with the tangible and intangible facets of local built heritage, these workshops became repositories of practical conservation know-how in Iran.[45]

With the support of the local institutions mentioned earlier, Farabi University in Isfahan pioneered an independent degree program in conservation. Within its administrative and academic network, international institutions,[46] universities, as well as experts from both

---

42   Falamaki, *Avalin Seminar-e Maremat-e Banaha va Sharhay-e Tarikhi: Vojud va Ayandeye Marakez-e Maskuni-e Tarikhi [The First Seminar on the Conservation of Historic Cities and Towns: The Existence and Future of Historical Residential Centres]*.

43   *Baz zendeh sazi-ye banaha ya shahrhaye tarikhi [Revitalization of Historic Buildings and Cities]* (Tehran: University of Tehran, 1977).

44   ICOMOS, 'Advisory Body Evaluation (ICOMOS)' (UNESCO, 1979), Paris, https://whc.unesco.org/en/list/115/documents/.

45   Galdieri and Afsar, 'Conservation and Restoration of Persian Monuments'; Lotfollah Honarfar, 'Meidan-e Naghsh-e Jahan Isfahan', *Honar va Mardom*, no. 104 (1971): 2–28.

46   The first programme of the International Centre for the Study of Conservation and Restoration of Cultural Property (ICCROM) in Isfahan is an example of such collaboration. See: Jukka Jokilehto and Mehr-Azar Soheil, 'Development of ICCROM's Architectural Conservation Training in Reference to Council of Europe Initiatives', *Monumenta* 3 (2015): 104–12, doi:https://doi.org/10.11588/monu.2015.0.42407.

administrative and academic realms of conservation collaborated to shape the contemporary academic and professional discourse and technical expertise in conservation within Iran.

Figure 6: Image captured by Walter Mittelholzer in 1925, showing Naqsh-e Jahan Square in Isfahan[47]

---

47   Obtained from ETH-Bibliothek Zürich, Bildarchiv/Stiftung Luftbild Schweiz (http://doi.org/10.3932/ethz-a-000274599_). This image is in the Public Domain.

Figure 7: An announcement regarding the admission of students to the conservation programme under an agreement between Farabi University and NOPHM.[48] *The third individual from the left is Bagher Ayatollah Zadeh Shirazi, who led the NOPHM's Technical Office in Isfahan during that period. Following the 1979 Revolution, he assumed the directorship of NOPHM until its integration into the Iranian Cultural Heritage Organization.*

---

48 Agahinameh, 'Academic Cooperations between the Farabi University and NOPHM [Hamkarihai Beine Daneshgah-e Farabi va Sazman-e Melli Hefazat-e Asar-e Bastani]', *Agahinameh*, no. 17 (1977): 3; Agahinameh, 'Announcement for Admission of Students for the Program, Conservation of Historic Monuments and Places (Second Phase) for the Academic Year 36–37', *Agahinameh*, no. 18 (1977): 4.

Debating urban heritage planning within the framework of urban renewal

The Fifth National Development Programme (1973–1978), which allocated funds for urban and rural renovation and allowed for private investment in urban renewal, laid the basis for pre- and post-Revolutionary government policies geared toward historic cities. Relying on the overlapping disciplinary boundaries of archaeology, architecture, urban planning, and tourism, the academic and business events of the 1970s raised complex socio-spatial and technical issues related to interventions in historic cities and inadequate synergies in cross-organizational collaboration.[49] The debates of the era transformed monument conservation into urban heritage planning, where questions around preserving monuments and old neighbourhoods were situated in the context of urban socio-economic and spatial concerns.

Figure 8: The Second Symposium of Iranian Architecture in Tehran (1973)[50]

---

49   For instance see: Art and Architecture, 'The Declaration of the Second Symposium of Iranian Architecture-Tehran', *Art and Architecture*, no. 15–16 (1973): 64–66; M. Mansour Falamaki, 'Taghir-e Shekl-e Vahed-Hay-e Memari Dar Baft Shahri [The Architectural Units' Change in Urban Fabrics]', *Art and Architecture*, no. 15–16 (1973): 31–36; Behrouz Habibi, 'Ehya va Negahdari-e Shahr-e Ghadim [Revitalisation and Maintenance of the Old City]', *Art and Architecture*, no. 15–16 (1973): 2–22; Bahman Paknia, 'Masael-e Shahri [Urban Issues]', *Art and Architecture*, no. 15–16 (1973): 23–26.

50   Art and Architecture, *Art and Architecture*, 15–16 (Tehran, 1973), 4–5.

Urban heritage planning in Iran: Repeated cycles of struggle for territorialization   55

The city of Yazd played a crucial role in bringing up issues of urban heritage planning and conservation as concerns involving the materiality of earthen settlements. Iran-ICOMOS organized the first two Terra conferences[51] in Yazd, in 1972 and 1976 respectively, where Iranian and international experts declared that earthen architecture is worth preserving and that earthen settlements could be efficiently preserved using traditional methods and local materials.[52] At these events, scholars such as Reza Kasai argued that the issue of conservation in urban contexts was multidimensional, encompassing economic, technical-constructional, architectural, and social aspects that needed to be considered in city Master Plans.[53] He also stressed that infrastructure deficiencies in old neighbourhoods needed to be addressed through the participation of universities, a broad range of government organizations, and local populations.[54] As a direct consequence of this public discourse—and owing to its intact historic core —Yazd became one of the first cities where conservation zoning and guidelines for intervention in the historic city were proposed to the municipal authorities.[55] Those proposals were not implemented,[56] but looking at the 2017 buffer zone regulations

---

51   International Conference on the Study and Conservation of Earthen Architecture.
52   Agahinameh, 'What Happened During the Second Terra Meeting?', *Agahinameh*, 1976; Art and Architecture, 'News: The First Terra Conference in Yazd', *Art and Architecture*, no. 14 (1972): 78; M Correia et al., 'Terra 2012. 12th SIACOT Proceedings. 11th International Conference on the Study and Conservation of Earthen Architectural Heritage', 2016.
53   'Khesht-e Kham [Mud Architecture}', *Art and Architecture*, no. 14 (1973): 33–41; 'Hefazat va Ehyaye Bafthaye Kheshti [Conservation and Revitalisation of Adobe Urban Fabrics]', *Agahinameh*, no. 5 (1976): 3–5.
54   Agahinameh, 'The Second Terra Conference in Yazd', *Agahinameh*, no. 3 (1976): 4–5; Agahinameh, 'What Happened During the Second Terra Meeting?'; Kasai, 'Khesht-e Kham [Mud Architecture}'.
55   *Revitalisation of Historic Urban Fabrics (a Review of Experiences)*.
56   Parviz Varjavand, 'Acknowledge Yazd Before It Is Too Late [Ta Be Afsoos Nanshesteim, Baft-e Yazd, Takhtgah-e Kavir Ra Daryabim]', *Honar va Mardom*, no. 192–191 (1978): 2–17.

for the World Heritage city of Yazd,[57] traces of the ideas discussed in the 1970s can be seen. Similarly, the notion to create official guidelines for mud brick constructions also had to wait until 2022 to be actualized.[58]

In cities like Tabriz, the government tried to engage the private sector in conservation endeavours. This involved encouraging the economic participation of merchants in conservation projects within the bustling bazaar. The local office of the Ministry of Culture and Art in Tabriz reported submitting a temporary tax programme to the Ministry of Interior to cover the costs of the emergency restoration of the bazaar.[59] The programme was devised following negotiations between conservation authorities, the city council, and the bazaar merchants. These attempts also failed due to the unstable political conditions in the late 1970s, but they arguably inspired ICHHTO's participatory preservation project in the Tabriz Bazaar during the mid-2000s that received an Aga Khan Award.[60]

In the residential neighbourhoods around the bazaars, which neither benefited from the economic wealth and political power of the merchants,[61] nor considered valuable as cultural heritage, conservation was not an option. In most cities, the emerging property economy and housing policies that followed the urban modernization projects and the growth of urban populations made preserving large urban areas a

---

57 ICHHTO, 'Historic City of Yazd, World Heritage Nomination Dossier' (ICHHTO, 2017), 13–14, https://whc.unesco.org/en/list/1544/documents/.
58 Mehr News Agency, 'Sakht-o-Saz Ba Khesht Baray-e Avalin Bar Dar Keshvar Ghanooni Mishavad [Construction with Adobe Will Be Leagalised in Iran for the First Time', *Mehr News Agency*, 2022, mehrnews.com/xY53N.
59 Agahinameh, 'Akhbar: Mosharekat-e Bazarian-e Tabriz Darmored-e Maremat-e Bazar-e Tarikhi-e Shar [News: The Participation of Merchants of Tabriz in the Restoration of the Historic Bazaar of the City]', *Agahinameh*, no. 18 (1977): 19.
60 ICHHTO-East Azerbayjan, '2013 Winning Projects: Rehabilitation of Tabriz Bazaar-Tabriz, Iran' (Aga Khan Award for Architecture, 2013). Also, see my interview with Akbar Tahizadeh in 2010 (Yadollahi, 2017, p. 33, Appendix 2)
61 See: Ahmad Ashraf, 'Bazaar-Mosque Alliance: The Social Basis of Revolts and Revolutions', *International Journal of Politics, Culture, and Society*, 1988, 538–67.

matter of financial impracticality.[62] After the construction of modern boulevards that cut through the old city, commercial activities traditionally located in the bazaars were drawn to the areas along the new access roads, while the areas behind them lost land value.[63] In the new spatial-economic order, the urban gentry and bazaar merchants began to move out of the city centres, settling in modern neighbourhoods and investing in property outside the old city.[64] As the more prosperous populations moved away from the historic centres, the maintenance and redevelopment of buildings and infrastructure in these areas slowed down. In many cities, including Tabriz[65] and Tehran,[66] large parts of residential areas in the old city gradually became the backstage of the bazaar, providing cheap storage and workshop space to serve the bazaar itself, with maintenance efforts limited to serve this utility. This is an indication of the political and economic power of the bazaar merchants, which has always been a decisive factor in conservation and urban planning policies in the bazaar and its surrounding neighbourhoods.

In the case of religious sites, the traditional tendency to prioritize the continuity of religious function over the preservation of material artefacts blended with the ambition to develop and expand sacred

---

62 See Ehlers, 'Modern Urbanization and Modernization in Persia'; Eckart Ehlers and Willem Floor, 'Urban Change in Iran, 1920–1941', *Iranian Studies* 26, no. 3–4 (1 September 1993): 251–75, doi:10.1080/00210869308701802..
63 Ehlers, 'Modern Urbanization and Modernization in Persia'.
64 Ibid.
65 Solmaz Yadollahi, 'The Iranian Bazaar as a Public Place: A Reintegrative Approach and a Method Applied towards the Case Study of the Tabriz Bazaar' (Doctoral thesis, Brandenburg University of Technology, 2017), https://opus4.kobv.de/opus4-btu/frontdoor/index/index/docId/4294.
66 The socio-economic and spatial interaction between the bazaar and the old city centre is discussed in detail in the chapter, Assembling urban heritage in Tehran: Collecting heritage fragments here and there.

places.⁶⁷ The urban renewal plan⁶⁸ for the religious city of Mashhad⁶⁹ in the early 1970s, for example, aimed to transform the Imam Reza shrine into a prominent pilgrimage centre. To achieve this, the plan proposed clearing a large circular area, consisting mainly of residential buildings, around the shrine to show its grandeur. Due to the controversy around the project, three architects were asked to comment on the plan. One of the three, Kamran Diba,⁷⁰ pointed out that, given the religious and political significance of Mashhad, the decision had already been made with the direct support of the Shah. Planning in religious places has always been politically sensitive due to the historical relationships between the clergy and the Iranian states.⁷¹ Mashhad is a telling example of the persistent power relations that have influenced interventions in many historic centres that contain religious sites.

It is worth noting that the aforementioned transformations in major cities like Tehran, Mashhad, and Yazd, and the government policies associated with them triggered the first stirrings of criticism from archaeologists, architects, and planners who argued that the destruction of historic urban fabrics, the erasure of living neighbourhoods, and the clearing of areas around monuments were technocratic, socially unjust, and top-down.⁷² Although the media through which this criticism is car-

---

67 I have described the philosophical and ideological background behind the aforementioned approach here: Yadollahi, 'Reflections on the Past and Future of Urban Conservation in Iran'.

68 Michel Ecochard, 'Rénovation Du Centre de Mashad, Iran', *L'Architecture d'Aujourd'hui* 169 (1973): 58–60; Daryoush Borbor, 'Iran', in *Encyclopedia of Urban Planning*, ed. Arnold Whittick, vol. 29 (Mcgraw-hill New York, 1974).

69 An important pilgrimage site and the burial place of the eighth Shia Imam.

70 Kamran Diba and Reza Daneshvar, *A Garden Between Two Streets* (Paris: Alborz, 2014).

71 For a historical background of the relations of the clergy with the bazaar merchants and the states, see: Ashraf, 'Bazaar-Mosque Alliance: The Social Basis of Revolts and Revolutions'; Homa Katouzian, *Iranian History and Politics: The Dialectic of State and Society*, RoutledgeCurzon / BIPS Persian Studies Series (RoutledgeCurzon, 2003).

72 Varjavand, 'Acknowledge Yazd Before It Is Too Late [Ta Be Afsoos Nanshesteim, Baft-e Yazd, Takhtgah-e Kavir Ra Daryabim]'; 'The Boulevard Disease', *Honar va*

ried out has changed over the years, it very much demonstrates the same approach in present day Iran.

Figure 9: An aerial picture of Tabriz Bazaar and its surrounding neighbourhoods

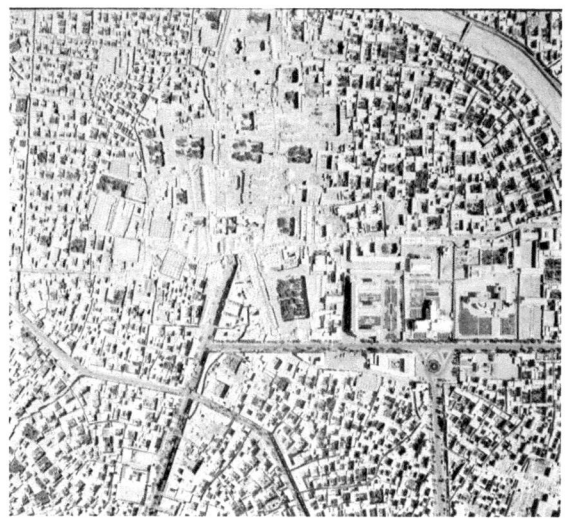

© Iranian Cartography Organization, 1956

Mardom 2, no. 69 (1968): 39–43; Aliasghar Mohtaj, 'An Interview with Keyvan Khosravani about the Sanitation of the Old Urban Fabric of Tehran', *Tamasha*, 1978; Diba and Daneshvar, *A Garden Between Two Streets*.

Figure 10: Dariush Borbor, Architect and Urban Planner, presenting the Urban Renewal of Mashhad City Centre to the Shah, Alam (Ministry of the Royal Court), Eghbal (Chairman of the National Iranian Oil Company), and Valiyan (Governor of Khorasan and Vice-Regent of the Shrine) in Mashhad (1973)[73]

---

73 'Dariush Borbor', in *Wikipedia* (CC BY-SA 4.0, 2023), https://shorturl.at/jkxJ2.

Figure 11: In 1978, Tamasha Magazine published an interview with architect and designer Keyvan Khosravani about protecting Tehran's old neighbourhoods.[74]

---

74   Mohtaj, 'An Interview with Keyvan Khosravani about the Sanitation of the Old Urban Fabric of Tehran'.

Figure 12: A public exhibition of original sketches by architect, Keyvan Khosravani in the Oudlajan neighbourhood of Tehran in the late 1970s, calling on the government to save the neighbourhood[75]

The emergence of a 'Body Without Organs'

The foundations of urban conservation and urban heritage planning in Iran were laid in the 1960s and 1970s, shaped by a central bureaucratic and legal infrastructure, local conservation sites, universities, and the first generation of conservationists who trained later generations. Through my archival research and extensive interviews with 29 conservation professionals, the majority of whom were born in the 1980s or later, it became evident that the infrastructure established in the 1970s has had a profound influence on their theoretical comprehension and technical expertise. Nearly all the interviewees demonstrated familiarity with the conservation theory and history as documented in publications from the 1970s. Even today, conservation architects continue to employ terminology found in literature from the 1960s and 1970s. This can be observed in both conserved sites and those subject to stylistic restoration,

---

75   Keyvan Khosravani, 'Saving Oudlajan', accessed 23 May 2022, https://www.keyvankhosrovani.com/saving-oudlajan/.

where architectural elements are as described in the aforementioned publications and their associated terminology is employed in discussing recent projects. Furthermore, the vast majority of graduates have completed internships or courses focusing on conservation practices in cities such as Shiraz, Isfahan, Bam, and Yazd.

The translation of conservation concepts and technical methods used in European cities such as Bologna, Rome, and Venice in the 1970s[76] led to the emergence of the term 'urban conservation' [*maremmat-e shahri*] in Iran.[77] In this era, conservation and urban heritage planning effected theoretical and technical advancements and geographical expansion to regions far from its governing organs in Tehran and some other influential cities, such as Yazd and Isfahan. However, this transformation failed to make discursive and material-economic connections with a large portion of the Iranian population, many of whom lived in socially and physically declining historic cities.[78] In 1975, a modernity index was created by sociologists from the University of Tehran in a nationwide survey to examine the prevailing attitudes of Iranians.[79] The findings unveiled that a notable segment of Iranian society adhered to strong traditional beliefs

---

76 Keramatollah Afsar, 'Hefz-e Baft Ghadimi Shahrhay-e Tarikhi [Conservation of the Old Fabric of Historic Cities]', *Agahinameh*, no. 34 (1978): 29–30; Falamaki, *Avalin Seminar-e Maremat-e Banaha va Sharhay-e Tarikhi: Vojud va Ayandeye Marakez-e Maskuni-e Tarikhi [The First Seminar on the Conservation of Historic Cities and Towns: The Existence and Future of Historical Residential Centres]*; Falamaki, *Bazzendeh sazi-ye banaha ya shahrhaye tarikhi [Revitalization of Historic Buildings and Cities]*.

77 For instance in: Falamaki, *Baz-zendeh sazi-ye banaha ya shahrhaye tarikhi [Revitalization of Historic Buildings and Cities]*; Afsar, 'Hefz-e Baft Ghadimi Shahrhay-e Tarikhi [Conservation of the Old Fabric of Historic Cities]'.

78 Grigor, 'Recultivating "Good Taste": The Early Pahlavi Modernists and Their Society for National Heritage'; Talinn Grigor, 'The King's White Walls: Modernism and Bourgeois Architecture', in *Culture and Cultural Politics under Reza Shah* (Routledge, 2013), 109–32.

79 Ali Assadi and Marcello L. Vidale, 'SURVEY OF SOCIAL ATTITUDES IN IRAN', *International Review of Modern Sociology* 10, no. 1 (1980): 65–84; Majid Tehranian, 'Communication and Revolution in Iran: The Passing of a Paradigm', *Iranian Studies* 13, no. 1–4 (1980): 5–30.

and did not resonate with the modernization policies implemented by the central government during that period. From the perspective of conservation as an aspect of modernization in Iranian society, I argue that a considerable portion of the Iranian population at that time, as indicated by the aforementioned survey, did not actively embrace conservation initiatives, despite the existence of public awareness-raising campaigns. This assumption is supported by pre-Revolution media coverage, featuring complaints from the public about protracted conservation projects.[80] Ideologically motivated attacks on historic places and numerous court cases against conservation authorities due to clashes between conservation laws and Islamic traditions after the 1979 Revolution also support this contention.[81]

In the tense and unpredictable atmosphere of the late 1970s, urban heritage assemblage, still in its infancy, entered a state of suspense and uncertainty in which progress was slowed or halted altogether. This was due to a major de-territorialization of the academic, legal, and administrative structures established before the Revolution. The diverse entities comprising the urban heritage assemblage, including organizations, laws, individuals, and places, encountered an unpredictable period of transition characterized by what Deleuze and Guattari refer to as a 'Body Without Organs'. Within this state, the assemblage held the inherent capacity to establish new connections and disconnections in response to the socio-political context that unfolded after the Revolution. As the second cycle will explain, cultural heritage and conservation struggled to find its place in the new nexus of ideologies, legislation, and economic forces of post-Revolutionary Iran. In accordance with the emerging order, a new term for territorializing conservation and urban heritage planning had to begin.

---

80 See, for example, the last issue of NOPHM's official journal, *Agahinameh*, for news and commentary on the organization's conflicts with the general public and local organizations. NOPHM, *Agahinameh*, vol. 36 (Tehran, 1978).

81 See the next section.

The second cycle: Re-assembling conservation and heritage planning

An overview of the political landscape in the aftermath of the 1979 Revolution

In the wake of the 1979 Revolution, Iran found itself, for the second time in its contemporary history, as a 'Body Without Organs', which held countless possible socio-political constellations. However, it did not take long for the diverse social and political groups that had participated in and witnessed the event to realize that the Revolution was about to give rise to a new autocratic and theocratic structure with self-destructive tendencies.[82] According to Deleuze and Guattari, such an assemblage can be described as a cancerous body that tends to deny any measure of difference and, by insisting on this tendency, gradually erodes its own organs and resources.[83]

Following the establishment of the Islamic Republic, influential clergy and the political elite set up a political, economic, and military network that ran independently of and in parallel to official governmental bodies.[84] Key players in this network included para-governmental foundations (*bonyads*),[85] which confiscated properties belonging to the former monarchy as well as numerous public and private buildings.[86]

---

82 See: Tehranian, 'Communication and Revolution in Iran: The Passing of a Paradigm'; Ali Assadi and Majid Tehranian, *Sedai Ke Shanide Nashod [The Voice That Was Not Heard]* (Tehran: Nashr-e Nei, 2016).

83 Deleuze and Guattari, *A Thousand Plateaus*.

84 Ali A. Saeidi, 'The Accountability of Para-Governmental Organizations (Bonyads): The Case of Iranian Foundations', *Iranian Studies* 37, no. 3 (1 September 2004): 479–98, doi:10.1080/0021086042000287541; Kazem Alamdari, 'The Power Structure of the Islamic Republic of Iran: Transition from Populism to Clientelism, and Militarization of the Government', *Third World Quarterly* 26, no. 8 (1 November 2005): 1285–1301, doi:10.1080/01436590500336690.

85 Saeidi, 'The Accountability of Para-Governmental Organizations (Bonyads): The Case of Iranian Foundations'.

86 It is nevertheless worth noting that a number of such estates were later used as cultural centres. See for instance: Eskandar Mokhtari Taleghani et al., *Khia-*

They played a key role in the de-territorialization of heritage planning and conservation through their administration of the Awqaf Organization, which was in charge of several religious and non-religious historical properties.[87]

Meanwhile, the war with Iraq and the economic sanctions that began in the 1980s isolated the country economically and politically. In the post-war period and after the passing of the Islamic Republic's charismatic leader, Ayatollah Khomeini, the Islamic Revolutionary network fragmented into multiple power centres that competed not only against each other, but also against official government entities.[88] While these political factions—of informal and formal networks of individuals, groups, and organizations—were loyal to the state as a whole, they had conflicting interests as well as their own economic and cultural agendas.[89] Operating without a political mandate, these diverse factions have been highly influential in preventing meaningful reform in the Islamic Republic.[90]

The multicentric nature of political forces in Iran continued to affect the cultural and economic aspects of conservation and urban heritage planning. The conflict between the political groups intensified after Ayatollah Akbar Hashemi Rafsanjani's[91] attempts at economic decentralization in the 1990s. In response, Islamic Revolutionary networks

---

ban-e Vali-e Asr Miras-e Memari va Shahrsazi-Ye Tehran [Vali E Asr Avenue Tehran's Architectural and Urban Heritage], 2nd ed. (Tehran: Tehran Beautification Organisation, 2019).

87 Alamdari, 'The Power Structure of the Islamic Republic of Iran: Transition from Populism to Clientelism, and Militarization of the Government'.

88 Wilfried Buchta, *Who Rules Iran? The Structure of Power in the Islamic Republic* (Washington: The Washington Institute for Near East Policy and the Konrad Adenauer Stiftung, 2000); Alamdari, 'The Power Structure of the Islamic Republic of Iran: Transition from Populism to Clientelism, and Militarization of the Government'.

89 Eva Rakel, *Power, Islam, and Political Elite in Iran: A Study on the Iranian Political Elite from Khomeini to Ahmadinejad* (Brill, 2008).

90 Ibid.

91 The fourth president of Iran (1989–1997).

redirected the privatization of state-owned enterprises from the private sector to parastatal organizations and other politically influential actors[92]—in an unequal competition with private investors, these became to a large extent the new private sector. During Mahmoud Ahmadinejad's administration, the Islamic Revolutionary Guard Corps (IRGC), as a key parastatal organ, gained enormous power in the economic and political spheres of Iranian society.

Key political scholars also pointed out that the multiplicity of competing formal and informal power centres was the main cause of the incoherence of the post-Revolution Iranian governmental policies.[93] These contradictions emerged and were exacerbated throughout reform-oriented administrations. As we will explore in the upcoming sections, as reformists implemented legal and parliamentary changes to the political system, the Revolutionary network worked in parallel to render their legal mechanisms ineffective. This clash was evident, for instance, in the conflicting dynamics between the tourism and World Heritage policies of the Islamic Republic and its Isolationist measures for national and regional security.

The limitations of the official legal system and elected political organs in the context of Iran's post-1979 political structure was reflected in the weakened impact of the conservation policies that were developed at the time. Mired by a lack of independent and critical academia and autonomous civil society, as well as corrupt administrative practices, the era saw the proliferation of contradictory and short-term cultural and urban planning policies.

---

92 Saeidi, 'The Accountability of Para-Governmental Organizations (Bonyads): The Case of Iranian Foundations'.
93 For instance, Alamdari, 'The Power Structure of the Islamic Republic of Iran: Transition from Populism to Clientelism, and Militarization of the Government'; Saeidi, 'The Accountability of Para-Governmental Organizations (Bonyads): The Case of Iranian Foundations'.

Re-territorializing conservation along the lines of Revolutionary ideological codes

The decade following the 1979 Revolution witnessed the dismantling of the legal and administrative structures that sustained order in urban planning and the conservation of cultural heritage. This was reflected for instance in the unregulated housing actions taken by the Revolutionary para-governmental organizations to bring about social justice[94] and also in the attacks by extremists on historic sites that were considered symbols of the *taghut*[95] and the fallen monarchy.[96] Although the interim government prevented major destruction,[97] media reports,[98] as well as legislation enacted in the early 1980s[99] reflect the government's con-

---

94 This was primarily accomplished by assigning seized assets to the poor. In Tehran alone, approximately 10 million square metres of urban land, located both within the city and its protected zones, were transferred to landless families through a combination of spontaneous seizures and Revolutionary court decisions. See: Ramin Keivani, Michael Mattingly, and Hamid Majedi, 'Public Management of Urban Land, Enabling Markets and Low-Income Housing Provision: The Overlooked Experience of Iran', *Urban Studies* 45, no. 9 (2008): 1825–53.
95 A Quranic word referring to the disbeliever and oppressive rulers.
96 Mehdi Hodjat, 'Cultural Heritage in Iran: Policies for an Islamic Country.' (Doctoral thesis, University of York, 1995), http://etheses.whiterose.ac.uk/2460/1/DX193597.pdf; Shahrzad Shirvani, 'Making Histories of "Sacred" Mausoleums', *Traditional Dwellings and Settlements Review* 29, no. 2 (2018): 55–71.
97 Eskandar Deldam, 'Khaterati az Shaykh Sadegh Khalkhali Givi, bakhsh Dovom [Memories from Shaykh Sadegh Khalkhali Givi, Part Two]', 14 August 2017, shorturl.at/kmxzG.
98 Gholamreza Masoumi, 'Takhrib-e Athar-e Farhangi Tarfand-e Doshmanan-e Enghelab [Destruction of Cultural Properties, a Strategy of the Revolution's Enemies]', *Jomhouri-e Eslami*, 16 January 1982, sec. Farhangi-Honari; 'Gohar-hai Ke Khak Shodand: Masjed-e Mirza Jafar-Mashhad [Jems that turned into Soil: the destruction of Mirza Jafar Mosque-Mashhad]', *Athar* 1, no. 1 (1980): 123–31.
99 Parliament of Iran, 'The Constitution of Islamic Republic of Iran, Article 83' (The Official Magazine: Rooznameh-e Rasmi-e Keshvar, 1979); The Council of the Islamic Revolution, 'Layehey-e Ghanouni-e Raj'e Be Kakhhay-e Niavaran va Saadabad va Nahvey-e Arzyabi va Negahdari-e Amval-e Marboot[The Legal Bill on

cern[100] about ideologically motivated vandalism and the fate of cultural properties confiscated by the *bonyads*.

In June 1982, a UNESCO delegation visited Iran to observe the condition of heritage sites and palaces. Despite the aforementioned domestic concerns, the official journal of NOPHM, *Athar*, wrote: Being convinced that all the news about the destruction of cultural heritage was false, the UNESCO representative committee left Iran with the absolute certainty that Iran's cultural heritage was not in danger.[101] While the national authorities were aware of the real issues and discussed them in Farsi language newspapers, they preferred to keep domestic problems under wraps from outsiders, in this case, the UNESCO representatives. This institutional tendency is reflected in Herzfeld's theoretical framework of 'cultural intimacy',[102] a concept that helps explain the behaviour of the authorities in response to various cases of heritage journalism and activism that are discussed in Part Two.

Territorializing conservation in the Islamic Republic faced ideological challenges particularly following the Islamization of the Constitution, which led to the explicit protection of private property rights.[103] Islamic sharia generally advocates for private property rights and requires the state to allow owners to make optimal use of their property. The Iranian clergy has thus historically opposed urban modernization

---

Niavaran and Saadabad Palaces and The Evaluation and Maintenance of These Properties]', 1980.

100 Article 83 of the Islamic Republic's Constitution mentions the term, 'irreplaceable treasures', referring to properties and objects of national heritage significance that cannot be transferred to the private sector except with the approval of the Islamic Consultative Assembly. The term and the corresponding law later came into conflict with the privatization policies enacted in the mid-1990s.

101 'Mamuriyat-e UNESCO Dar Iran, Kholaseh-Ye Gozaresh-e Bazdid Konandegan-e UNESCO Az Iran [UNESCO's Mission in Iran, a Summary of the UNESCO Visitors' Report]', *Athar* 3, no. 7–9 (1983): 291–96.

102 Michael Herzfeld, 'The European Crisis and Cultural Intimacy', *Studies in Ethnicity and Nationalism* 13, no. 3 (2013): 491–97; Michael Herzfeld, *Cultural Intimacy: Social Poetics and the Real Life of States, Societies, and Institutions* (Routledge, 2016).

103 Parliament of Iran, 'The Constitution of Islamic Republic of Iran' (The Official Magazine: Rooznameh-e Rasmi-e Keshvar, 1979).

policies on the grounds that they interfere with owners' control over their private property.[104] Urban development was to an extent justified on the basis of greater public benefit and social justice,[105] but this attitude did not extend to conservation of cultural heritage. As Mehdi Hodjat, a supervisor of cultural heritage affairs in the interim government and the first director of the later established Cultural Heritage Organization wrote,[106] in the early 1980s, several owners of historic places submitted a complaint to the Guardian Council[107] against the Antiquities Law, which they believed violated their rights to alter or redevelop their properties.[108] The Council decided that some provisions of the Antiquities Law violated sharia law. Consequently, despite cultural heritage conservation continuing to be included in the official policy of the Islamic Republic, the post-Revolutionary legal and administrative system for conservation could face challenges, such as when engaging in negotiations with para-governmental organizations like the Awqaf Organization or regular private owners.

---

104 Mehran Tamadonfar, 'Islam, Law, and Political Control in Contemporary Iran', *Journal for the Scientific Study of Religion* 40, no. 2 (2001): 205–20.

105 For instance see S. Mohammad Beheshti's articles on public ownership in Islam: S. Mohammad Beheshti, 'Malekiyat Dar Eslam (2) [Ownership in Islam (2)]', *Pasdar-e Eslam*, no. 2 (1982): 24–26; S. Mohammad Beheshti, 'Malekiyat Dar Eslam (3) [Ownership in Islam (3)]', *Pasdar-e Eslam*, no. 3 (1982): 28–29. Also see: Tamadonfar, 'Islam, Law, and Political Control in Contemporary Iran'.

106 *Mirath-e Farhangi Dar Iran: Syasat Ha Baray-e Yek Keshvar-e Eslami [Cultural Heritage in Iran, Policies for an Islamic Country]* (Tehran: ICHO, 2001).

107 The Council of 12 Jurists of Islamic law is authorized by the Supreme Leader to monitor the legislation of the Parliament and presidential elections.

108 Such court cases resulting in the delisting of historic buildings decreased in the 1990s, but became more common again in the mid-2000s.

Figure 13: Iraqi war prisoners forming a choral group at Tehran's Evin Prison, performing on a stage that features the monarchy's downfall and the collapse of the pillars of the pre-Islamic historical site, Persepolis

© Jean Gaumy/Magnum Photos, 1986.[109]

Following the reinstatement of the Awqaf trustees in April 1979[110] and the 1984 Awqaf Law,[111] the clergy gained more autonomy in managing the Awqaf. Endowment affairs, which were under the prime minister's authority before the Revolution, were transferred to the Awqaf organization, supervised by the Supreme Leader's representatives. The redevelopment of religious sites and other Awqaf properties in cities like Mash-

---

109 Image used with permission. Copyright [1986]. All rights reserved.
110 Premiership of Iran, 'Layehe-Ye Ghanooni Tajdid-e Gharadad va Ejareh-Ye Amlak va Amvale Mowqufeh va Tajdid-e Entekhab-e Motevalian va Omana Ava Nozar-e Amaken-e Motebarekeh Mazhabi va Masajed [The Bill on the Renewal of the Leasing Contract for Endowment Properties and the Re-Appointment of Administrators of Mosques and Religious Places]' (1979).
111 Parliament of Iran, 'Ghanoun-e Tashkilat va Ekhtiarat-e Sazman-e Awqaf va Omour-e Kheiriyeh [Law of the Establishment of Awqaf Organization]' (The Official Magazine: Rooznameh-e Rasmi-e Keshvar, 1984).

had was a political issue well before the 1979 Revolution.[112] With the Revolution and the new political and executive power of the clergy, the redevelopment of religious sites came to be presented as a political necessity to facilitate public prayers that symbolized the glory and popularity of the Islamic Republic.[113]

The story of the Imam Khomeini Musalla[114] in Tabriz illustrates this political controversy. In the 1980s, Imam Jum'a of Tabriz[115] wrote a book justifying the construction of a *musalla* on the archaeological site and listed the Ilkhanid mosque (Arg-e Alishah),[116] to reuse and revive the ancient mosque. Calling the conservation authorities "ruin-dwelling and ruin-loving owls",[117] he warned them of "disgrace in this world and a mighty punishment in the afterlife".[118] Although the *musalla* was not built according to its initial idealistic plan, which was inspired by the Islamic Republic's emblem (Figure 14), it was eventually built next to the Arg and on top of the archaeological site (Figure 15).[119]

NOPHM's journal, *Athar*, published a report in 1980 on the seminar 'Archaeology in Harmony with the Revolution'.[120] In their coverage of the event, the press emphasized the clear departure from the pre-Revolutionary approach to archaeology and cultural heritage, while embracing a fresh perspective rooted in the principles of the 1979 Revolution and

---

112 See, for instance, the section: Debating urban heritage planning within the framework of urban renewal.
113 For instance see: Moslem Malakouti, *Masjed Masjed Shod [The Mosque Became a Mosque]*, first, vol. 1–2 (Tehran: Shafagh, 1985).
114 *Musalla* is an Arabic word that refers to a typically large area used for congregational prayer, especially at outdoor gatherings or religious events.
115 Malakouti, *Masjed Masjed Shod [The Mosque Became a Mosque]*.
116 Keramatollah Afsar, 'Arg-e 'Alīšāh', in *Encyclopedia Iranica*, 1986, http://www.iranicaoranian Identity III. Medieval Islamic Periodnline.org/articles/arg-e-alisah-remains-of-a-colossal-mosque-built-in-tabriz-completed-1322.
117 *Masjed Masjed Shod [The Mosque Became a Mosque]*, 1–2:588.
118 Ibid., 1–2:3.
119 'Gocaman Tabriz 6: Interview with Mr Akbar Taghizadeh', 2018, shorturl.at/los16.
120 'Seminar-e Bastanshenasi Dar Rasta-Ye Enghelab [Seminar on Archaeology in Line with the Revolution]', *Athar* 2–4, no. 1 (1980): 246–48.

Islam. Over time, however, it became evident that the cultural heritage administrative and academic system had to maintain its dependence on the material and discursive frameworks established during the pre-Revolutionary period.

Figure 14: The initial plan proposed for the musalla was inspired by the Islamic Republic's emblem and covered the historical Arg under its gigantic dome.[121]

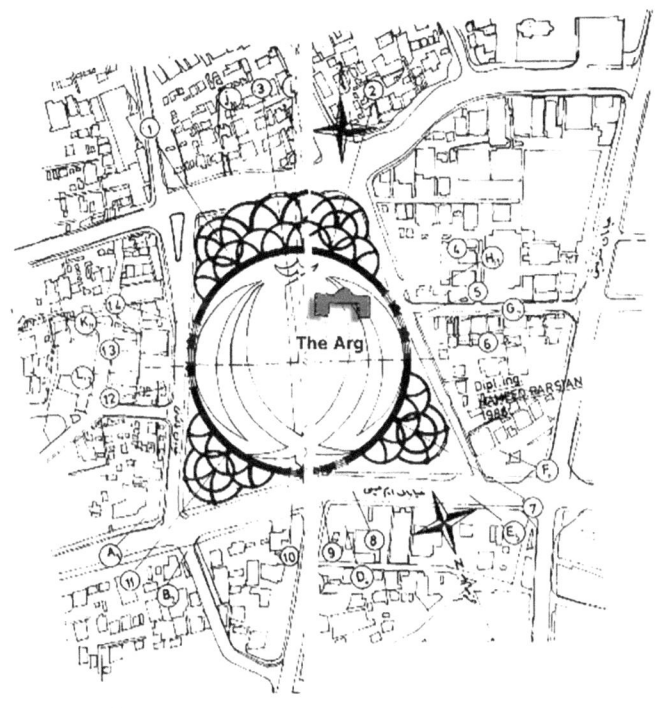

---

121   Malakouti, *Masjed Masjed Shod [The Mosque Became a Mosque]*, 1–2:705–6.

Figure 15: The 'Hello Commander' [Salam Farmandeh] chant[122] *at the gathering ceremony near the Imam Khomeini Musalla and in front of the Arg, Tabriz August 2022*

©ANJA News

Purge committees set up within governmental organizations,[123] and the Cultural Revolution Bureau[124] set up within academic institutions began weeding out staff, professors, and students considered counter-Revolutionary.[125] Farabi University in Isfahan, which had launched a

---

122 A political and ideological song written for the Islamic Republic's younger generations.
123 See: Hooshang Kuklan, 'The Administrative System in the Islamic Republic of Iran: New Trends and Directions', *International Review of Administrative Sciences* 47, no. 3 (1981): 218–24.
124 The Cultural Revolution refers to a series of policies and actions carried out by the government of Iran, under the leadership of Ayatollah Ruhollah Khomeini, who was the Supreme Leader of Iran at that time. It was a project aimed to Islamize Iran's higher education systems. Its Bureau supervised the purging of disloyal students and professors and monitored the ideological environment of universities. See: Saeid Golkar, 'Cultural Engineering Under Authoritarian Regimes: Islamization of Universities in Postrevolutionary Iran', *Digest of Middle East Studies* 21, no. 1 (1 March 2012): 1–23, doi:10.1111/j.1949-3606.2012.00124.x.
125 Ibid.

conservation programme in the late 1970s, was among some 55 higher education institutions that were merged into larger universities.[126] Consequently, the conservation programme in Isfahan that was associated with NOPHM was temporarily suspended until it resumed accepting students in 1983.

Like other public institutions, the Ministry of Culture and Art, NOPHM, and universities in Tehran and Isfahan gradually purged disloyal individuals. The Cultural Revolution caused devastating damage to the country's intellectual resources across many academic fields.[127] My respondents[128] and other senior members of the conservation community[129] who recall the systematic purges of the 1980s in the academic and administrative sectors of conservation believe that the firing of academics and professionals and favouring loyalty over merit caused irreversible damage to the sector. It is also worth noting that the post-Revolution political atmosphere and the Iran-Iraq War that commenced in 1980 led to an unprecedented wave of migration and brain drain from Iran to the United States and Europe.[130]

As *Athar* reported in the early 1980s, conservation activities generally declined due to the instability caused by the Revolution, cooperation among universities ceased due to their closure (following the Cul-

---

126 Farasatkhah, *The Adventure of University in Iran*.
127 Ibid.; Shahrzad Mojab, *The State and University: The"Islamic Cultural Revolution"in the Institutions of Higher Education of Iran, 1980–1987* (University of Illinois at Urbana-Champaign, 1991); LZ Levers, 'Ideology and Change in Iranian Education', *Education in the Muslim World: Different Perspectives*, 2006, 149–90.
128 Anonymous interviews on 9.1.2020 in Tehran and on 19.4.2021 via Skype.
129 See Gocaman Tabriz 6: Interview with Mr Akbar Taghizadeh (in Turkish).
130 Akbar E. Torbat, 'The Brain Drain from Iran to the United States', *Middle East Journal* 56, no. 2 (2002): 272–95; Pooya Azadi, Matin Mirramezani, and Mohsen B Mesgaran, 'Migration and Brain Drain from Iran', *Stanford Iran 2040* (2020): 1–30.

tural Revolution), and international cooperation ended due to political and economic difficulties.[131]

Conservation under Revolutionary austerity

The 1980s were marked by the war with Iraq and the United States' sanctions against Iran. Archival data from this period show no major preservation projects in historic cities and no significant scientific undertakings. However, the institutional and academic elements remaining from the past rallied to build new structures. By the mid-1980s, the government succeeded in bringing the chaotic post-Revolutionary period under control and gradually subordinating the concerns of cultural heritage into the emerging legal and administrative order.

Following the dissolution of the Ministry of Culture and Art in 1980, NOPHM and cultural heritage affairs were placed under the supervision of the newly established Ministry of Culture and Higher Education and the Ministry of Culture and Islamic Guidance. This reflected the new heritage planning bureaucrats who viewed cultural heritage as intricately linked to education and research and believed that aligning it with Islamic values was of utmost importance.[132]

Many state organizations, such as the Iranian Cultural Heritage Organization (ICHO), were established or began operating in 1985.[133] In those years, pre-Revolution plans for historic neighbourhoods in cities

---

[131] Athar, 'Fa'aliat-Ha-Ye Sazman: Kholase-Ye Gozaresh Sale 1358–1359 [Activities of the Organisation: Report of the March 1979-March 1980]', *Athar* 2–4, no. 1 (1980): 185–89.

[132] Mehdi Hodjat, the first Director of the Cultural Heritage Organization, provides an account of this process the rationale behind it. See: Hodjat, 'Cultural Heritage in Iran: Policies for an Islamic Country.'

[133] Parliament of Iran, 'Ghanun-e Tashkil-e Sazman-e Miras-e Farhangi-e Keshvar [Law for the Establishment of the Iranian Cultural Heritage Organisation]' (The Official Magazine: Rooznameh-e Rasmi-e Keshvar, 1986); Parliament of Iran, 'Ghanun-e Asasname-Ye Sazman-e Miras-e Farhangi-e Keshvar [Law of the Statute of the ICHO]' (The Official Magazine: Rooznameh-e Rasmi-e Keshvar, 1986), Tehran.

such as Yazd,[134] Isfahan,[135] and Tehran[136] were revisited by the ICHO, and the Urban Rehabilitation Office[137] sought to establish ties with the municipalities. Parallel to this, a similar office for urban rehabilitation at the Ministry of Housing and Urban Planning (MHUP), also established in 1985, continued the pre-Revolutionary urban renewal projects in the historic neighbourhoods.[138] Thus, both the conservation and urban renewal authorities picked up the former policies. Furthermore, in the face of population growth and the increasing migration of residents from war-torn areas to safer cities, the government had no choice but to invest in projects that would provide for urgent housing needs.

Despite the relative normalization of government affairs, the ownership and management of the irreplaceable treasures inherited from the fallen monarchy remained a problem in the mid-1980s.[139] As highlighted in the introduction of this chapter, a substantial quantity of public and private assets belonging to the previous state and individuals connected

---

134 Mahmoud Tavassoli, 'Baft-e Ghadim, Moghadameh-i Bar Masaleh [The Historic City, an Introduction to the Issue]', in *Kholasehy-e Maghalat: Seminar-e Tadavom-e Hayat Dar Bafthay-e Ghadimi-e Shahrhay-e Iran [The Proceedings of the Seminar on the Continuation of Life in Iran's Historic Cities]* (Tehran: Iran University of Science and Technology, 1993), 5–15.

135 'Gozaresh-e Tarh-e Tajdid-e Nazar Dar Tarh-e Jame va Tafsili-e Esfahan [The Report on the Revision of Isfahan's Master and Detailed Plan]' (Housing and Urban Planning Organisation of Isfahan, 1988).

136 Bagher Ayatollah Zadeh Shirazi et al., 'Samandehi-e Bazaar-e Tehran [The Improvement of the Tehran Bazaar]', *Athar* 1, no. 2 (1980): 9–48; Bagher Ayatollah Zadeh Shirazi et al., 'Behsazi-e Mahaley-e Oudlagan [The Improvement of the Oudlajan Neighbourhood]', *Athar* 1, no. 2 (1980): 55–99.

137 Founded in 1987 by the ICHO.

138 For a detailed background of such projects see: Pirooz Hanachi, Darab Diba, and M. Javad Mahdavinejad, 'Hefazat va Tose'e Dar Iran [Conservation and Development in Iran]' 32 (2007): 51–60; Pirooz Hanachi et al., *Barresi-e Tatbighi-e Tajarob Maremat-e Shahri Dar Jahan va Iran, Ba Negahi Vijeh Be Baft-e Yazd [A Comparative Study Of Urban Preservation Experiences In The World And In Iran, With A Special Focus On The City Of Yazd]*, 1st ed. (Yazd: Sobhan Noor, 2007).

139 Parliament of Iran, 'Ghanoon-e Mohasebat-e Omumi-e Keshvar [The Public Audit Act]' (The Official Magazine: Rooznameh-e Rasmi-e Keshvar, 1987).

to it were seized by the newly established state and parastatal organizations. This resulted in the unregulated exploitation of these assets, which included valuable cultural heritage properties. To regulate the sale and use of such historic properties, the Ministry of Economy and Finance issued an executive order under the Budget Law.[140] The legislation called for the establishment of a steering committee to identify properties of exceptional national value and prevent their privatization. Following the post-war privatization agenda in the 1990s and 2000s, the aforementioned legal instruments and the Steering Committee became the subject of controversy.

Conservation academia in the mid-1980s

With the reopening of universities in 1983, the de-Westernization of academic fields, especially the humanities, was initiated as a continuation of the policies of the Cultural Revolution.[141] The University Crusade [*Jahad-e Daneshgahi*]—a body of Revolutionary academics—pushed the Islamization of universities by monitoring the academic environment and supporting research and scholarly publishing that reflected their agenda.[142] Alongside university presses, the University Crusade formed their own press, which became a platform for academic publications that furthered Revolutionary values. The Annual University Admission [*Konkur*] also facilitated the Islamization and equalization of higher education by adjusting the academic, socio-economic, and political criteria for admission.[143]

Textbooks and teaching content across subjects were also revised under the Cultural Revolution. In the field of conservation, the teaching materials of the 1980s advocated traditionalism, localism, and a

---

140 Ministry of Economic Affairs and Finance, 'Ayin-Nameh-Ye Ejrai-e Tabsareh-Ye (35) Ghanoon-e Budjeh 1368 [Executive Regulations Note (35) of the Budget Law of 1989]', 1989.
141 Universities in Iran had been closed between 1980 and 1983.
142 Levers, 'Ideology and Change in Iranian Education'.
143 Keiko Sakurai, 'University Entrance Examination and the Making of an Islamic Society in Iran: A Study of the Post-Revolutionary Iranian Approach to "Konkur"', *Iranian Studies* 37, no. 3 (2004): 385–406.

postcolonial approach to culture, architecture, and urban planning.[144] One example of conservation teaching material is a syllabus[145] for the architectural conservation module at Shahid Beheshti University.[146] The syllabus encourages students to adopt a critical stance toward Western architectural and conservation theory while applying its practical techniques to promote Islamic values. By questioning "cultural tourism" and "historic landscapes", the syllabus criticizes the Western value system that favours the economic over the spiritual merit of cultural heritage. The text also criticizes Western "bureaucratic management" and "systematic planning", and proposed "jihadi action" drawing on the "successful experience of the Islamic Revolution" and the "Sacred Defence during the war with Iraq"[147] as local, organic solutions for an Islamic Iran. Preservation is deemed to facilitate the return of Islamic society to its authentic identity. With an emphasis on the admonitory value of heritage, referring to the Quranic concept of learning from humanity's mistakes [ibrat], ancient sites such as Persepolis are prescribed a new role as symbols of fallen kings.

I chose this particular syllabus because it was a key text that students had to study to pass the annual *Konkur*, and because it was taught across

---

144   Apart from a few academic dissertations, there were no significant publications dealing with urban conservation in the 1980s. Following the purging of NOPHM, what remained of the organization was merged into the newly formed ICHO, which also took on its predecessor's official journal, *Athar*. In this period, the publication's focus pivoted towards urban and architectural history and archaeology.
145   Ahmad Asgharian Jeddi, Farhad Fakhar Tehrani, and Ghadiri, 'Jozveh-ye Darse Tarh-e Maremmat-e Bana [Subject Transcript for Architectural Conservation]', 1990.
146   The pre-Revolutionary national university of Iran, located in Tehran.
147   The term 'Sacred Defence' emphasizes the perception of the Iran-Iraq war as a just and defensive struggle against Saddam Hussein's aggression. The term has significant cultural and nationalistic meaning in Iran, symbolizing the unity, resilience, and sacrifice of the Iranian nation during the conflict. See: Pedram Khosronejad, *Unburied Memories: The Politics of Bodies of Sacred Defense Martyrs in Iran* (Routledge, 2013); Shabnam J Holliday, *Defining Iran: Politics of Resistance* (London: Routledge, 2016).

Iranian universities until at least the mid-2000s.[148] The position of the authors of this document is also echoed in the Cultural Heritage Law,[149] in the articles of the conservative, pro-state magazine *Keyhan Farhangi*,[150] and in Hodjat's book, *Cultural Heritage in Iran: Policies for an Islamic Country*,[151] showing the overarching ideology ruling the administrative and academic spheres.

Towards the end of the 1980s, despite Revolutionary perseverance, part of the political elite were motivated to end the country's isolation. As political tensions eased, pre-Revolutionary conservationists and scholars returned to the universities and the ICHO as consultants or professors, while others took up teaching posts at the ICHO's Higher Education Centre (HEC), which was established in 1990 to address the organization's lack of staff.[152]

In 1986, the University of Tehran organized an international conference[153] expressing the Islamic Republic's interest in re-starting international cultural and scientific cooperation. At the same time, the conference took a political stand, condemning the destructions in Isfahan and Khuzestan during the war with Iraq as a clear violation of the Hague

---

148 On the basis of personal interviews with conservation graduates from various Iranian universities.

149 Parliament of Iran, 'Ghanun-e Tashkil-e Sazman-e Miras-e Farhangi-e Keshvar [Law for the Establishment of the Iranian Cultural Heritage Organisation]'.

150 Mehdi Hodjat, Bagher Ayatollah Zadeh Shirazi, and Mehdi Chamran, 'Ostad Mohammad Karim Pirnia va Osul-e Memari-e Sonnati [Master Mohammad Karim Pirnia and the Principles of Traditional Architecture]', *Kayhan Farhangi*, 1985; n. n., 'Masjed-e Jame-e Esfahan, Dayeratol-Ma'aref-e Eyni-e Honar-Ha-Ye Eslami [The Jame Mosque of Isfahan, an Encyclopedia of Islamic Architecture]', *Kayhan Farhangi*, 1985.

151 Hodjat, 'Cultural Heritage in Iran: Policies for an Islamic Country.'

152 Here, I draw upon my recollections of studying conservation at the HEC from 2002 to 2006, as well as my examination of the curriculum vitae of various conservation architects whom I have researched or interviewed. Farasatkhah also noted partial reconciliation in national higher education policy in the early 2000s. See: Farasatkhah, *The Adventure of University in Iran*.

153 n. n., 'International Conference on Reconstruction of the War-Damaged Areas, University of Tehran, Iran (6–16 March 1986)', *Athar* 7, no. 12–14 (1987): 97–101.

Convention for the Protection of Cultural Property in the Event of Armed Conflict.[154]

The proceedings of the First Seminar on the Continuation of Life in Iran's Historic Cities, held at Iran University of Science and Technology[155] in Tehran in 1987, also favoured traditionalism,[156] which was seen as a remedy against Western cultural hegemony.[157] However, most of the contributions in the seminar continued the 1970s debates on socio-spatial issues of housing in historic neighbourhoods, essentially pointing to the need for official guidelines for interventions in historic cities. Pointing out that those issues were debated inconclusively some 16 years earlier, with Falamaki,[158] Tavassoli,[159] and Daneshdoost arguing

---

154 UNESCO, 'Convention for the Protection of Cultural Property in the Event of Armed Conflict with Regulations for the Execution of the Convention' (Hague, 1954), https://en.unesco.org/protecting-heritage/convention-and-protocols/1954-convention.

155 The university was founded in 1929 as an engineering school.

156 To read about the connection between a preference for traditionalism and the Islamic Revolutionary ideology in Iran, refer to: Brad Hanson, 'The "Westoxication" of Iran: Depictions and Reactions of Behrangi, Āl-e Ahmad, and Shari'ati', *International Journal of Middle East Studies* 15, no. 1 (1983): 1–23.

157 Mehdi Hodjat, 'Arzesh-Ha-Ye Mojoud Dar Baft-e Tarikhi [Values of the Historic Fabric]', in *Kholasehy-e Maghalat: Seminar-e Tadavom-e Hayat Dar Bafthay-e Ghadimi-e Shahrhay-e Iran [The Proceedings of the Seminar on the Continuation of Life in Iran's Historic Cities]* (Tehran: Iran University of Science and Technology, 1987), 58–65.

158 M. Mansour Falamaki, 'Ayandeh-Ye Baft-Ha-Ye Shahri-Ye Tarikhi-Ye Iran: Padideh-Ha va Badil-Ha [The Future of Urban Historic Fabrics in Iran: Phenomena and Alternatives]', in *Kholasehy-e Maghalat: Seminar-e Tadavom-e Hayat Dar Bafthay-e Ghadimi-e Shahrhay-e Iran [The Proceedings of the Seminar on the Continuation of Life in Iran's Historic Cities]* (Tehran: Iran University of Science and Technology, 1987), 121–32.

159 Mahmoud Tavassoli, 'Baft-e Ghadim, Moghadameh-i Bar Masaleh [The Historic City, an Introduction to the Issue]', in *Kholasehy-e Maghalat: Seminar-e Tadavom-e Hayat Dar Bafthay-e Ghadimi-e Shahrhay-e Iran [The Proceedings of the Seminar on the Continuation of Life in Iran's Historic Cities]* (Tehran: Iran University of Science and Technology, 1987), 5–15.

that the authorities "understand but do not take action",[160] the issue had since been exacerbated by war refugees now housed in economically and physically impoverished historic districts. Falamaki, the organizer of the first seminar on the same topic at the University of Tehran in 1971, told me that after the Revolution, his proposal for organizing a second seminar in the 1980s was rejected. Instead, another 'first seminar' was organized after 16 years, reflecting the new academic system's intent to establish their own conference rather than building on pre-revolutionary discourse. However, despite their efforts, the papers presented at this new conference still showed a clear reliance on pre-revolutionary ideas, highlighting the ongoing dependence of the academic discourse on these earlier concepts.

Post-war recovery and the heritage turn

In 1989, Rafsanjani won the presidential election (and remained in office until August 1997) on an agenda of economic development and reconstruction. During the 1990s, a notable characteristic was the preservation of a limited number of historic buildings, while simultaneously witnessing the widespread demolition of deteriorating historic neighbourhoods. This trend emerged as a response to the post-war reconstruction pressure. Although the High Council for Architecture and Urban Planning (HCAUP)[161] approved urban rehabilitation plans called 'Cultural-historical Axis' plans for selected cities such as Tabriz, Isfahan, Shiraz,

---

160 Yaqoub Daneshdoost, 'Tarhi Bara-Ye Tadavom-e Hayat va Hefz-e Baft-e Tarikhi-Ye Shahr-Ha [A Plan for the Survival and Conservation of Urban Historic Fabrics]', in *Kholasehy-e Maghalat: Seminar-e Tadavom-e Hayat Dar Bafthay-e Ghadimi-e Shahrhay-e Iran [The Proceedings of the Seminar on the Continuation of Life in Iran's Historic Cities]* (Tehran: Iran University of Science and Technology, 1987), 74.

161 A legal body under the Ministry of Housing and Urban Development, the HCAUP was founded in 1966 to define and supervise urban planning policies in Iran.

Kerman, and Hamedan, the plans remained largely unexecuted due to their insufficient integration within urban Master Plans.[162]

The lack of technical coherence in urban Master Plans was partly due to challenges encountered in cross-organizational and cross-sectoral cooperation between parties such as the ICHO, the Ministry of Urban Development, and private urban planning professionals. While not explored extensively within academic literature, diverse experts[163] have spoken openly about official bodies' limitations in dealing with local power-holders, such as governors, influential private or parastatal landowners, and Awqaf managers.[164] As Akbar Taghizadeh,[165] a former cultural heritage official of Eastern Azerbaijan, noted, the HCAUP was politicized from the start, like any other institution in Iran. Thus, its function depended more on the individuals in charge than on legal and administrative mechanisms. Or, as Falamaki noted, the very law that could prevent demolitions in some cities was ineffective in others,

---

162　M. Taghi Rahnamaei and Parvaneh Shah Hosseini, *Process of Urban Planning in Iran*, 2nd ed. (Tehran: SAMT, 2012); Hanachi, Diba, and Mahdavinejad, 'Hefazat va Tose'e Dar Iran [Conservation and Development in Iran]'.

163　Personal fieldnotes at professional meetings, for instance, the First National Symposium on Conservation and Management of Urban Heritage, organized by the Research Centre of Cultural Heritage and Tourism, Tehran, 12–13 February 2022. Also mentioned by the former Deputy Minister of Roads and Urban Development (2013–2019) in a personal interview on 7 January 2020 in Tehran.

164　For example, see the former heritage official, H. Ravanfar's interview with Iranian Students' News Agency (ISNA) about the destruction of the listed Khosrow-agha Bathhouse in Isfahan with the support of the local clerics, the governor and the municipality. See: Shirin Mostaqasi, 'Ravayati Az Takhrib-e Hammam-e Kosrow-Agha [A Narrative of the Demolition of the Khosrow Agha Bathhouse].', *Iranian Students' News Agency*, 9 April 2022, isna.ir/xdMc64.

165　'Gocaman Tabriz 6: Interview with Mr Akbar Taghizadeh'.

especially in religious cities like Mashhad, Qom, and Shiraz.[166] The willingness and power of the authorities to take action against violations of approved plans could thus depend on the national and local political climate.

In the post-war economic atmosphere, the ICHO made a transition from the earlier conservation and research-based approach to an Ashworthian economy-oriented, heritage approach.[167] A pragmatic administration that was in tune with the new politics[168] gradually replaced the early Revolutionary management style that used to distance itself from tourism and saw economic valorization of cultural heritage as a catalyst for Westernization. At the ICHO, Rafsanjani's principle of economic development was manifested by transferring the organisation to the Ministry of Culture and Islamic Guidance, which was responsible for tourism.

The new economic approach also emphasized the adaptive reuse of historic places.[169] A notable example was carried out in Tabriz, where a group of historic houses in the Maghsudiyeh neighbourhood were included in the National Heritage List, acquired, and repurposed as the

---

166 M. Mansour Falamaki, 'Fardai Baray-e Yek Gharn Tajrobeh Maremat-e Shahri Dar Iran [A Future for a Quarter-Century of Urban Conservation Experience in Iran]', in *Proceedings: Hamayesh-e Takhasosi-e Baft-Ha-Ye Shahri, 28–29 Khordad 1376-Mashhad-e Moghadas [Specialized Conference on Urban Fabrics, 18–19 June 1997, Mashhad]* (Specialized Conference on Urban Fabrics, 18–19 June 1997, Mashhad, Mashhad: Ministry of Housing and Urban Development, 1997), 713–34.

167 Ashworth, 'Conservation as Preservation or as Heritage: Two Paradigms and Two Answers'.

168 For instance, see Nasser Pazouki, 'Mabani-e Miras-e Farhangi [Principles of Cultural Heritage]', *Mirath-e Farhangi*, no. 17 (1997): 82–84. An ICHO official argued that in addition to spiritual growth (based on the Revolutionary values), attracting tourism and respecting international conventions could be valuable aims of conservation.

169 ICHO and Ministry of Urban Development and Housing co-published a book on this topic. See: Jasem Ghazbanpour, *Zendegi-e Jadid-Kalbad Ghadim: Gozideh-i Az Bana-Ha-Ye Baarzesh-e Tarikhi [New Life – Old Structure: A Selection of Valuable Historic Buildings]* (Tehran: Ministry of Housing and Urban Development, 1993).

Tabriz University of Islamic Arts. The House of the Constitution in Tabriz was another example of a reuse project.[170]

I interviewed a former manager of the Planning and Budget Organization (PBO) who was appointed Director of the Tehran branch of the ICHO in 1995 to help the PBO find a solution for the ICHO's "never-ending research projects and conservation workshops". He also drew attention to the break in policy directions at the end of one administration and the beginning of another. He said:

> Originally, my assignment at [the] ICHO was temporary. After specializing in cultural heritage, I should have returned to the PBO to establish and manage a cultural heritage office that could supervise the country's cultural heritage economy. With the political changes [the election of President Khatami] in 1997, a new team with new ideas came to power. So; the original plan was cancelled, and I stayed at ICHO.[171]

The repetition of such shifts led to a waste of resources invested not only in projects, but also in training individual personnel and restructuring the administrative infrastructure.

---

170 In the period leading up to the Constitutional Revolution and thereafter, the house served as a meeting point for the movement's leaders in Tabriz.
171 Interview with Ardeshir Oruji former senior advisor to ICHO and former Director General of the ICHO Office for Statistics and Information Planning, 19 April 2021 via Skype.

Figure 16: President Hassan Rouhani visiting the House of the Constitution in Tabriz

©Tasnim News Agency, 2015

Political reform: Territorializing heritage between two identity discourses

The Twenty-Year Vision Document prepared in 2003 depicted Iran in 2025 as an economically and technologically developed country with constructive international relations and an Islamic Revolutionary identity that would serve as an inspiration to the Islamic world.[172] The document legitimized tourism and national identity on the condition that Islamic Revolutionary values were upheld. However, while overarching policy documents such as the Vision Document and national development plans defined the targets, as we will see in the coming sections, a deep gap emerged between those policies and their implementation.

Following the election of Mohammad Khatami[173] and his subsequent attempts at reform, political opposition intensified between factions controlling different state organizations and economic sectors. In particular, when the government launched decentralization and privatization policies in the 1990s, parastatal organizations such as the IRGC[174] became omnipresent players in economic sectors such as banking, housing, and construction.[175] Many important politicians were also members of the abovementioned ideological, economic, and military network.

---

172 The document was prepared by various government entities and experts under the supervision of the Supreme Leader of Iran. Expediency Discernment Council, 'Sanad-e Cheshmandaz-e Jomhuri-e Eslami-e Iran Dar Ofoq-e 1404 [Twenty-Year Vision Document of the Islamic Republic of Iran for 2025]', 2003.

173 In office between 1997 and 2005.

174 For instance, the largest contractor of state development projects is a branch of IRGC, called Khatam-al Anbiya Construction Headquarters. The Kowsar Economic Organization [*Sazman-e Eghtesadi-e Kowsar*], which owns several companies is another actor connected to Bonyad-e Shahid (a para-governmental organization) and Khatam-al Anbia Construction Headquarters.

175 Saeidi, 'The Accountability of Para-Governmental Organizations (Bonyads): The Case of Iranian Foundations'; Kevan Harris, 'The Rise of the Subcontractor State: Politics of Pseudo-Privatization in the Islamic Republic of Iran', *International Journal of Middle East Studies* 45, no. 1 (2013): 45–70, doi:10.1017/S0020743812001250.

This continued into the new millennium, during Mahmoud Ahmadinejad's presidential term from 2005 to 2013, when Islamic Revolutionary networks, including the IRGC, remained the main subcontractors of state organizations or partners of private companies.[176]

Domestic and foreign cultural politics also gave rise to competition between reform-oriented and Revolutionary identity narratives. Holliday described the opposition between reformers and hardliners as a clash between two primary identity discourses, with hardliners emphasizing Islamic values and reformers grounded in Islamic-Iranian values.[177] On one side, media such as the hardline news publication *Keyhan-e Farhangi* promoted Islamist discourse, which demanded a more effective implementation of the Cultural Revolution and warned of the dangers of globalization.[178] On the other, the reformists sought to legitimize President Khatami's slogans of Islamic democracy and dialogue between civilizations within the frame of the Islamic Revolutionary narrative.[179]

As we will see in the following pages, during this period, urban heritage assemblage entered a process of re-territorialization within national and international legal and academic frameworks. However, under the influence of the political struggles mentioned above, most of the processes were halted or redirected in the 2000s.

To ensure the consistency of the ICHO's policies with those of the High Council for the Cultural Revolution, the director of the ICHO became a member of the High Council's Committee for Public Culture

---

176 Harris, 'The Rise of the Subcontractor State: Politics of Pseudo-Privatization in the Islamic Republic of Iran'.
177 Holliday, *Defining Iran: Politics of Resistance*.
178 For example see: Reza Davari et al., 'Shoray-e Ali-e Enghelab-e Farhangi; Masuliat-Ha-Ye Ayandeh [High Council of Cultural Revolution; Future Responsibilities]', *Keyhan-e Farhangi*, 1997; Seyyed Hamid Molana et al., 'Tamadon-Ha; Gofo-Gu va Nazdiki Ya Ruyaruyi va Keshmakesh [Civilisations, Dialogue and Intercession or Confrontation and Conflict]', *Keyhan-e Farhangi*, 1998.
179 For instance, the reactivation of city councils in 1999 was a step toward Islamic democracy. Although city councils had legally functioned in Iran since 1930, they did not involve significant public participation.

in 1998. By 2000, the High Council became the key supervisory body for cultural policy, acting in accordance with the Supreme Leader's official directives. In 2002, the High Council adopted a directive establishing a committee for the preservation of cultural heritage within the framework of the National Security Council.[180] Chaired by the ICHO Director, the committee included representatives from the judiciary, the Awqaf Organization, the IRGC, the Ministry of Intelligence, the Ministry of Economy and Finance, and the police. The aforementioned directives for instance, limited the ICHO's authority over maintenance and conservation plans for Awqaf, aiming to amplify the clergy's role in supervising religious heritage sites.

One of the first projects of the 2000s was the establishment of a political-ideological museum in Jamaran, Tehran. The ICHO made use of the 1973 Law on the National Heritage Listing,[181] which made it possible to define sites as protected national heritage regardless of their construction date, to list Ayatollah Khomeini's house and Hosseineh[182] in Jamaran.[183] Inclusion of the museum in the list was justified based on the criterion of national importance. Another example is the Ibrat Museum (Museum of Admonition), which was set up as a "museum of intangible heritage" in Tehran.[184] Launched in 2001, the project reused the former Pahlavi-era prison under the supervision of the ICHO to narrate the memories of political prisoners of the previous state, including Islamic Revolutionary figures such as Ayatollah Ali Khamenei, Ayatollah Morteza Motahhari, and Ayatollah Naser Makarem-e Shirazi. The preservation of

---

180 High Council of Cultural Revolution, 'Ayin-Nameh-Ye Hefazat Az Miras-e Farhangi-e Keshvar [Iran's Cultural Heritage Conservation Guidline]', 2002.

181 Parliament of Iran, 'Ghanoon-e Sabt-e Athar-e Melli, Aban 1352 [National Heritage Listing Law,1973]', 1973.

182 A Hosseineh is a religious institution or building in Iran primarily used for Shia Islamic rituals and gatherings.

183 Jamaran, situated in the northern part of Tehran city, was the residence of Ayatollah Khomeini.

184 Maryam Azadi and Ghasem Hassanpour, 'Muzeh-Ye Miras-e Gheir-e Malmus [Museum of Intangible Heritage]', *Keyhan-e Farhangi*, 2006.

houses of Revolutionary and historical figures such as Mostafa Chamran[185] in Tehran and Haj Agha Nourollah Najafi[186] in Isfahan and the establishment of museums in these houses was a collaborative activity between municipalities and heritage authorities as part of the state's integrated cultural policies.

Figure 17: Mostafa Chamran's museum-house in Tehran

Author, 2020

---

185 First Defence Minister of post-Revolutionary Iran, commander of paramilitary volunteers in the Iran-Iraq War, killed in that war. He also served as a military participant in the Shia Amal movement in Lebanon.
186 A Shia cleric from Isfahan active in Iran's Constitutional Revolution in the late Qajar period.

The state's overarching identity politics[187] also justified the Setad-e Bazsazi-e Atabat Aliyat's[188] generous donations from public and Awqaf funds for renovating, and redeveloping Shia shrines in Samarra, Karbala,[189] and Najaf[190] in Iraq, as well as religious sites elsewhere outside Iran.[191] In 2006, Shahid Beheshti University engaged in the development plan for the Alavi Shrine in Najaf and its reintegration with the surrounding urban fabric, which was the home of Shia clergy, including Ayatollah Khomeini. With the support of Iran's Supreme Leader, local Shia figures such as Ayatollah Sistani and the Setad-e Bazsazi-e Atabat Aliyat, the project asserted its Shia interests within the power dynamics in Najaf.[192] Under the narrative of Sacred Defence, the project aimed to protect the shrine and revitalize the Shia neighbourhoods destroyed by Saddam Hussein. In separate interviews, two Shahid Beheshti University alumni told me about the strict Islamic ideological and gender criteria for student assistants who were to participate in these projects.

The ongoing resistance to conservation principles in religious places, especially in sites under the administration of the Awqaf clergy, seem to stem partially from conflicting approaches between traditional and

---

187 For instance, the Twenty-Year Vision Document.
188 According to its official website, the headquarters was established in 2003. It is a parastatal organization committed to the reconstruction of shrines and religious places in Iraq and other countries and provides scientific, cultural, educational, health, civil and humanitarian services. See: https://en.atabat.org/en . Khatam-al Anbiya Construction Headquarters has also been involved in the projects.
189 The burial site of Husayn ibn Ali, the iconic Shia Imam, believed to have passed away in the Battle of Karbala.
190 The Shrine of Imam Ali, the first Shia Imam.
191 Sam Dagher, 'Devotion and Money Tie Iranians to Iraqi City', *The New York Times*, 2009, https://www.nytimes.com/2009/05/31/world/middleeast/31karbala.html?smid=url-share.
192 Based on my fieldnotes at the online presentation by Ali Ghaffari (former Director of the Shahid Beheshti University) and Ruhollah Movahedi (a faculty member at Shahid Beheshti University), on Najaf's Story [*Dastan-e Najaf*], organized by the National Contemporary Architecture Centre of Shahid Beheshti University, 27 January 2022.

modern philosophies in dealing with historical ruins.[193] Due to the emphasis placed by sharia law on the continuity of spiritual use, religious sites have traditionally prioritized construction measures that cater to religious functions such as pilgrimage, prayer, or religious education.[194] In terms of heritage planning, the historic shrines and their surroundings are traditionally viewed as containers of Shia religious practice.[195] Therefore, conservation principles such as evidence-based preservation, reversibility, or authenticity of material and architectural form are not prioritized. This has been a continuous tradition at historical religious sites before and after the 1979 Revolution. However, prior to the Revolution, the conservation bureaucracy had stronger enforcement, leading to a less evident conflict. With the Islamization of the state, the underlying philosophical conflicts became more pronounced. In earlier sections, I offered a succinct explanation of this intervention logic, supported by examples like the *musalla* project in Tabriz and Mashhad.[196] In several other cases, such as Shiraz and Najaf, shrine development projects have followed a similar approach.[197]

---

193 See: Yadollahi, 'Reflections on the Past and Future of Urban Conservation in Iran'.

194 For the example of Najaf, see: SK Abid, 'Imam Ali Shrine, Institution and Cultural Monument: The Implications of Cultural Significance and Its Impact on Local Conservation Management', *Structural Studies, Repairs and Maintenance of Heritage Architecture XIV* 153 (2015): 87–98.

195 The same approach can be seen in the case of Arg-e Alishah in Tabriz, discussed in the previous pages. Or the Sadeghiyeh Seminary School in the World Heritage site of Tabriz Bazaar, that I have discussed elsewhere: Solmaz Yadollahi, 'Tracing the Identity-Driven Ambitions of the Iranian Urban Conservation Apparatus', *The Historic Environment: Policy & Practice*, 30 June 2019, 1–20, doi:10.1080/17567505.2019.1637081.

196 Also see: Mohammad Saeid Izadi, 'A Study on City Centre Regeneration: A Comparative Analysis of Two Different Approaches to the Revitalisation of Historic City Centres in Iran' (Doctoral thesis, Newcastle University, 2008), http://hdl.handle.net/10443/759.

197 Also discussed by involved actors at: Ali Ghaffari and Ruhollah Movahedi, 'Najaf's Story (Dastan-e Najaf)' (National Contemporary Architecture Centre of Shahid Beheshti University, 27 January 2022), BTU Cottbus-Senftenberg, Chair

Figure 18: General Qasem Soleimani visiting the Alavi Shrine project in Najaf in 2018[198]

Figure 19: Development plan connecting the holy shrines in Karbala

© Setad-e Bazsazi-e Atabat Aliyat, 2020

---

198 of Urban Management, Fieldnotes; 'Public Discussion: Tajrobe-Ye Mashhad; Ebrat-e Shiraz, Be Name Ziyarat, Dar Barabar-e Tarikh [Mashhad's Experience; Lesson for Shiraz, In the Name of Pilgrimage, Against History]' (Student Union of Architecture Restoration and Urban Planning, 26 February 2022), Fieldnotes. (https://www.nasim.news/fa/tiny/news-2250340)

The religious approach mentioned, together with the economic ambitions of the clergy, has almost always defeated conservation theory in Iranian cities. Falamaki, who was responsible for planning the destroyed area around the shrines in the historic centre of Shiraz, wrote that, following the Revolution, some actors were determined to draw parallel lines connecting two shrines, calling the axis *Beynolharamein* (the sacred path between two shrines).[199] By the time he was commissioned to propose a plan for the area, the shrine development project had already destroyed some 17,000m² of the city's historic fabric between 1995 and 1997.

In parallel, Khatami's reformist government used institutional and legal opportunities to expand and improve international relations. For example, the Third National Development Plan allowed the use of international funds and cooperation with UNESCO and other international institutions.[200] Between 2001 and 2003, Iran ratified the 1954 Hague Convention,[201] reactivated ICOM-Iran, and established ICOMOS-Iran. Despite international NGOs such as ICOMOS playing highly politicized roles in Iran, the resumption of their activities was a sign of relative political openness compared to the early years after the Revolution.

---

199 Falamaki, *Seiri Dar Tajarob-e Maremmat-e Shari, as Veniz Ta Shiraz [An Essay on Urban Conservation, From Venice to Shiraz]*.
200 Parliament of Iran, 'Ghanun-e Barnamey-e Sevom-e Tose-Ey-e Eghtesadi, Ejtemai va Farhangi-e Jomhuriy-e Eslami-e Iran [The Law of the Third Plan of the Economic, Social and Cultural Development of Islamic Republic of Iran]', *The Official Magazine: Rooznameh-e Rasmi-e Keshvar*, 2000.
201 Convention for the Protection of Cultural Property in the Event of Armed Conflict.

Figure 20: The Shahecheragh Development project in Shiraz

© Astan-e Shahecheragh, 2020

Figure 21: Imam Reza Shrine in Mashhad

© Astan Quds Razavi Information Database, n.d.

In 2003, Yazd once again became the host of the Terra Conference, after a span of 27 years. In the same year, after a 24-year hiatus in World Heritage List inscription, Iran submitted a nomination for the inclusion of a site on the World Heritage List.[202] With the inclusion of Bam and its Cultural Landscape on the UNESCO List of World Heritage in Danger in 2004,[203] international cooperation was strengthened at ICHO research centres in Bam and elsewhere. The international workshop on the Recovery of Bam's Cultural Heritage in 2004 proposed the preparation of a comprehensive master plan that took into account the future social and economic development of the city and required the cooperation of governmental and non-governmental institutions and associations at the national and international levels.[204] The ICHO project with the UNESCO/Japan Trust Fund in Tchogha Zanbil was another example of the same approach, reflecting the government's willingness to reform. At the conclusion of the project in 2006, the international project partners, ICHO staff, and students from related disciplines participated in a training workshop on the conservation and management of earthen cultural heritage. Following more than two decades of political and professional isolation, Iranian academics and professionals had been presented with the opportunity for international collaboration.

In a chain of similar international experiences and events, the terminology of the guidelines for the implementation of the World Heritage Convention[205] appeared more and more frequently in academic publications and dissertations in Farsi.[206] This was influenced also by the her-

---

202 Takht-e Soleyman
203 After being largely damaged by the 2003 earthquake.
204 UNESCO-Tehran and ICHO, 'The BAM Declaration and Recommendations' (UNESCO, 2004), https://unesdoc.unesco.org/ark:/48223/pf0000190150.
205 See: https://whc.unesco.org/en/guidelines/
206 For example see. Younes Samadi, *Cultural heritage in domestic and international Law in Iran [Miras-e Farhangi dar Hoghugh-e Dakheli va Benalmelali]* (Tehran: ICHO, 2003); Younes Samadi, *The collection of Laws, Regulations, Guidelines, Circular Notes, and Conventions of the Cultural Heritage Organization [Majmue' Ghavanin, Ayin-nameh-ha, Bakhshnameh-ha va Moahedat-e Sazman-e Mirath-e Frhangi-e Keshvar]* (Tehran: ICHO, 2004); M. Hassan Talebian, 'The Role of Authenticity in Conser-

itage authorities who taught at local universities. Similar to the religious projects in Najaf and Karbala mentioned above, World Heritage nominations and other ICHHTO[207] activities were connected to academic internships and dissertations.

Figure 22: The 2004 International Workshop on the Recovery of Bam's Cultural Heritage[208]

For a certain period in the mid-2000s, the reformist strategy of international conciliation appeared to be relatively successful in World Heritage sites. For example, heritage authorities succeeded in preventing the commercial Jahan Nama Tower from affecting the visual integrity of the Meidan-e Naghsh-e Jahan World Heritage Site.[209] It is worth noting

---

vation of World Heritage Sites the Experiences from Dur-Untash for Authenticity-Based Conservation' (University of Tehran, 2005).
207 The successor to the ICHO.
208 Eskandar Mokhtari Taleghani, ed., *Gozaresh-Ha va Maghalat-e Salaneh-Ye Projeh-Ye Nejatbakhshi-e Miras-e Farhangi-e Bam-(Arg) [Anual Reports and Papers of the Bam Cultural Heritage Recovery Project-(Arg)]*, vol. 1, 2 (Tehran: Research Base of Arg-e Bam, 2005), 257.
209 Feng Jing and Pedro A. Calderon, 'MISSION REPORT / Meidan Emam, Esfahan (Islamic Republic of Iran) (C 115)' (UNESCO World Heritage Centre, 2013), https://whc.unesco.org/en/list/115/documents/.

that the Municipality of Isfahan, a powerful opponent of World Heritage policy at that time, held a significant stake in the Jahan Nama Tower. In Yazd, collaboration between heritage agencies, the private sector, and the municipality resulted in the city's inclusion on the World Heritage List in 2017.[210]

The resurgence of critical heritage journalism[211] was also a result of the heritage planning assemblage that was being formed during the mid-2000s. As in many large cities around the world, the struggles over the preservation of World Heritage sites and development in Tabriz[212] and Tehran[213] consistently made news headlines.

---

210 Not to lose sight of the fact that the mentioned cooperations have led to new problems concerning social justice and fair distribution of the social and economic benefits of the city's World Heritage status. See: Raymond Rastegar, Zohreh Zarezadeh, and Ulrike Gretzel, 'World Heritage and Social Justice: Insights from the Inscription of Yazd, Iran', *Journal of Sustainable Tourism* 29, no. 2–3 (2021): 521–40.

211 See the section on: Debating urban heritage planning within the framework of urban renewal.

212 As reported by the MRUD, for example see: Ministry of Roads and Urban Development, 'Joziyat-e Mosavabeh-Ye Mashroot-e Tarh-e Jame-e Tabriz [In Hanachi's Letter to the Governor of Eastern Azerbaijan; Details of the Contingent Approval of the Tabriz Master Plan]', *MRUD News Service*, 12 August 2016; Ministry of Roads and Urban Development, 'Tey-e Nameh Az Suy-e Moaven-e Vazir-e Rah va Sharsazi Matrah Shod; Takid-e Mojadad Bar Roayat-e Mosavabat-e Shoray-e Ali-e Sharsazi Baray-e Hargooneh Sakht va Saz Dar Javar-e Bazar-e Sabt-e Jahaniy-e Tabriz [In a Letter from the Deputy Minister of Roads and Urban Development; Re-Emphasizing the Need to Comply with the Approvals of the High Council of Urban Planning for All Construction Projects in the Vicinity of the World Heritage Site of Tabriz Bazaar]', *MRUD News Service*, 28 July 2018. And mentioned by Nejadebrahimi, Deputy of Cultural Heritage, Tabriz in an interview with Jam-eJam Eastern Azerbayjan. See: Amin Bilsaz, 'Tabriz Hal Nadarad [Tabriz Is Not Well]', *Jam-e-Jam*, 4 March 2021, https://jamejamonline.ir/005UZg.

213 See: World Heritage Committee, *Decision 38 COM 8B.45* (Doha: UNESCO World Heritage Convention, 2014); ISNA, 'Hokmi Ke Sabt-e Jahaniy-e Kakh-e Golestan Ra Tahdid Mikonad [A Decision That Threatens Golestan Palace's World Heritage Status]', *ISNA*, 9 January 2022, isna.ir/xdKH9P.

In urban planning, the reformists declared their approach for the Ministry of Housing and Urban Development (MHUD) at their 1997 Mashhad Conference.[214] Key terms of the conference were urban identity, civic empowerment, and participation of the private sector, all pictured with a bottom-up planning approach for the future. This coincided with MHUD's establishment of the Housing Development and Construction Company (HDCC) to coordinate the activities of municipalities, state organizations such as ICHHTO, and the private sector in the old urban fabrics. HDCC's comprehensive investigation of the urban management system in deteriorated areas highlighted incoherent and overlapping parallel procedures carried out by diverse organizations and actors.[215]

Figure 23: Yazd, an aerial view

© ICHHTO, 2017

---

214 Seyyed Mohsen Habibi et al., eds., *Proceedings: Hamayesh-e Takhasosi-e Baft-Ha-Ye Shahri, 28–29 Khordad 1376-Mashhad-e Moghadas [Specialized Conference on Urban Fabrics, 18–19 June 1997, Mashhad]* (Mashhad: Ministry of Housing and Urban Development, 1997).

215 Nilpar Honarvar, 'Iranian Experiences Of Urban Restoration', *HaftShahr* 1, no. 3 (2001): 14–31.

Figure 24: The preserved roofscape of Tabriz Bazaar, the 1990s

© ICHHTO-Eastern Azerbaijan

With the goal of integrating policy with a set of practical tools to address urban decay nationwide, HDCC organized cross-sector conferences involving urban planning and heritage authorities, municipalities, universities, developers, and planning consultants.[216] In 2000, HDCC founded *HaftShahr*, an interdisciplinary journal on urban heritage, conservation, and urban regeneration, bringing together actors from the fields of heritage and urban and regional planning. Reflecting the overarching national policies of privatization and decentralization, the

---

216 Haftshahr, 'Gozaresh-e Avalin Hamayesh-e Behsazi va Nosazi-e Baft-Ha-Ye Farsoodeh, Mashhad, 1387 [Report of the First Conference on Regeneration and Revitalisation of Urban Distressed Areas, Mashhad, 2008]', *HaftShahr* 4, no. 43–44 (2014): 145–61; Housing Development and Construction Company and Housing Development and Construction Company-Fars, *Dovomin Hamayesh-e Behsazi va Bazafarini-e Baftha-Ye Tarikhi, Farsoodeh-Ye Shahri va Sokunatgahha-Ye Gheir-e Rasmi, Shiraz, 1389 [Second Conference on the Improvement and Regeneration of Historic, Distressed Urban Fabrics and Informal Settlements, Shiraz, 2010]* (Shiraz: Navid-e Shiraz, 2011).

journal published a series of interviews and roundtables to interconnect values-based conservation and international heritage guidelines with domestic issues of identity, earthquake risk preparedness, and housing.[217] Consequently, urban planners became key players in heritage policy, which had previously been carried out by ICHHTO conservation architects, archaeologists, and architectural historians.

The mentioned interdisciplinary discussions, led by bureaucrat-academics, aligned with the objectives outlined in the Third and Fourth National Development Plans, [218] establishing the conceptual and legal prerequisites for the 2014 National Urban Regeneration Programme.[219] Nevertheless, parallel to administrative and academic efforts to territorialize heritage policy and practice in cities, heterogeneous de-territorializing forces were at work.

At the government level, urban renewal funds became a major factor hindering heritage preservation. In the absence of a clear legal distinction between decayed and historic urban areas, provinces competed to

---

217   For instance: Habib Jabari, ed., 'Modakhele Dar Baft-Ha-Ye Shahri va Masale-Ye Mosharekat [Interventions in Urban Fabric and the Participation Issue]', *HaftShahr* 2, no. 4 (2001): 28–46; Asghar Mohammadmoradi, 'Editor's Note: Zaroorat-e Maremat [The Essentiality of Conservation]', *HaftShahr* 4, no. 12 (2003): 3; Ardeshir Oruji, 'Darshayi Ke Az Zelzeleh-Ye Bam Mitavan Amookht [Lessons to Be Learnt From the Bam Earthquake]', *HaftShahr* 5, no. 17 (2005): 86–89.

218   Parliament of Iran, 'Ghanun-e Barnamey-e Sevom-e Tose-Ey-e Eghtesadi, Ejtemai va Farhangi-e Jomhuriy-e Eslami-e Iran [The Law of the Third Plan of the Economic, Social and Cultural Development of Islamic Republic of Iran]'; Parliament of Iran, 'Ghanun-e Barnamey-e Chaharom-e Tose-Ey-e Eghtesadi, Ejtemai va Farhangi-e Jomhuriy-e Eslami-e Iran [The Law of the Fourth Plan of Economic, Social and Cultural Development of Islamic Republic of Iran]', *The Official Magazine: Rooznameh-e Rasmi-e Keshvar*, 2004.

219   The National Document for Regeneration, passed by the Parliament in 2014 was a result of these activities. Ministry of Roads and Urban Development, 'Sanad-e Melli-e Rahbordi-e Ehya, Behsazi va Nosazi va Tavanmandsazi-e Bafthaye Farsudeh va Nakaramad-e Shahri [The National Strategic Document for Revitalization, Rehabilitation, Renovation, and Reinforcement of Deteriorated and Dysfunctional Urban Fabrics]' (MRUD, 2014).

designate larger areas as decayed urban fabric to receive more renewal funds from the government.[220]

At the municipal level, municipalities began shifting toward economic independence in the late 1990s under the decentralization policies. The process resulted in the phenomenon of density selling.[221] On the one hand, density selling provided a large source of income for the municipalities, fuelling corruption.[222] On the other hand, it provided a solution for housing the growing urban populations and encouraged small- and large-scale redevelopment projects in historic cities. A famous example of this kind was the unregulated increase in density sales capacity in Tehran between 2007 and 2012.[223]

The aforementioned privatization policies in the areas of urban planning and cultural heritage also triggered an influx of investors and developers into the historic districts. Public, private, and para-governmental rent-seeking investors began to invest in construction and

---

220 Naser Bonyadi, Giti Etemad, and Farhad Golizadeh, 'Goftoguyi Dar Khosus-e Siyasat-Ha va Barnameh-Ha-Ye Behsazi va Nosazi-Ye Shahri Dar Iran [A Roundtable Discussion on Urban Improvement and Urban Renewal Policies in Iran]', *HaftShahr*, no. 33–34 (2011): 129–34.

221 Density is understood as floor area ratio of buildings. As part of the post-war economic decentralization policies of the 1990s, the government started to cut municipality funds. To solve the funding shortfall, municipalities were allowed to use private capital by granting density bonuses to property developers. In other words, municipalities could allow developers to build taller buildings if they paid the associated fines. See: Abolghasem Azhdari, Mehdi Alidadi, and Dorina Pojani, 'What Drives Urban Densification? Free Market versus Government Planning in Iran', *Journal of Planning Education and Research*, 2022, 0739456X221126625.

222 Hasan Abedi Jafari et al., *Sanjesh-e Fesad va Salamati Sazmani Shahrdari-e Tehran [Measuring Corruption and Organizational Health of the Municipality of Tehran]* (Tehran: Research and Planning Centre of Municipality of Tehran, 2016).

223 Fieldnotes of the public Clubhouse debate on 'Wounds on Tehran Detailed Plan' held on June 9th, 2021, where urban planners who were involved in the preparation of Tehran's Detailed Plan reviewed illegal changes in the document between 2007 and 2012. Also see: Mahyar Arefi, 'Towards a Conceptual Framework for Urban Management: The Iranian Experience', *City, Culture and Society* 4, no. 1 (2013): 37–48.

housing in Iran.[224] As privatization processes unfolded and conservative hardliners assumed power, historic buildings experienced a dual effect. On the one hand, they gained heightened redevelopment value; on the other, they became less safeguarded by heritage laws. Consequently, from the mid-2000s, the explicit protection of private property in accordance with Islamic sharia—as outlined in the early 1980s Guardian Council decision—regained support.[225]

A study conducted by the Research Institute of the Iranian Judiciary shows that court cases resulting in the delisting of National Heritage properties due to a lawsuit brought by a private plaintiff increased after 2005.[226] The report argues that heritage authorities were unable to win disputes against private owners, except for a few cases with technical issues.[227]

My informal conversations with conservation professionals and Neighbourhood Development Offices (NDOs) in Tehran's historic area confirm that cultural heritage authorities sometimes deliberately failed to meet the conditions for legal protection in exchange for a bribe from

---

224 Ilia Farahani and Shadi Yousefi, 'Public Housing, Intersectoral Competition, and Urban Ground Rent: Iran's First Public Housing Program That Never Was', *Human Geography* 14, no. 1 (2021): 45–61.

225 Also according to: Parliament of Iran, 'Ghanoon-e Mojazat-e Eslami [Islamic Penal Law 5th Vol.]' (The Official Magazine: Rooznameh-e Rasmi-e Keshvar, 1996), art. 569; Parliament of Iran, 'Ghanun-e Divan-e Edalat-e Edari [Law of the Administrative Court of Justice}' (The Official Magazine: Rooznameh-e Rasmi-e Keshvar, 2006), art. 13 (1); Parliament of Iran, 'Ghanun-e Tashkilat va Ain-e Dadresi Divan-e Edalat-e Edari [Law on the Organization and Procedure of the Administrative Court of Justice]' (The Official Magazine: Rooznameh-e Rasmi-e Keshvar, 2013), art. 10.

226 Judiciary Research Institute-Iran, *Malekiyat-e Khosusi Ya Manfaat-e Omumi?: Naghd-e Raviye Shoabe Divane Edalat-e Edari Piramun-e Ebtal-e Tasmim-e Sazman-e Miras-e Farhangi va Tarikhi Dar Fehrest-e Athar-e Melli [Private Property or Public Interest? A Critique of the Administrative Court Branches' Procedure Regarding the Annulment of the Cultural Heritage Organization's Decision in the Listing of National Monuments]* (Tehran: Judiciary of the Islamic Republic of Iran, 2014).

227 For instance, in cases where the plaintiff was not a private owner or the submitted petition was incomplete.

the plaintiff. For instance, the Delgosha commercial centre that became famous for threatening the Golestan Palace World Heritage site's skyline was built on a demolished historic caravanserai (Saray-e Delgosha) in the Tehran Bazaar. The listed caravanserai, which was owned[228] by the para-governmental organizations Bonyad-e Mostazafan and Bonyad-e Shahid[229] and a group of private owners, was removed from the list with judicial approval. Some believe that ICHHTO-Tehran played a determining role in both the delisting of the historic caravanserai[230] and the new building's generous height permission.[231]

---

228 According to the building's National Listing dossier prepared in 2007 (available at ICHHTO-Tehran archive).
229 Bonyad-e Mostazafan (Foundation of the Oppressed) and Bonyad-e Shahid (Foundation for Martyrs' and Veterans' Affairs) were two major Revolutionary bonyads that became economic powers after confiscating the properties of pre-Revolutionaries and Bonyad-e Pahlavi. See: Akbar Karbassian, 'Islamic Revolution and the Management of the Iranian Economy', *Social Research*, 2000, 621–40.
230 Heritage officials' failure to provide complete and timely documents to prevent delisting was mentioned in the legal debates on the case. See: Judiciary Research Institute-Iran, *Malekiyat-e Khosusi Ya Manfaat-e Omumi?: Naghd-e Ravi-ye Shoabe Divane Edalat-e Edari Piramun-e Ebtal-e Tasmim-e Sazman-e Miras-e Farhangi va Tarikhi Dar Fehrest-e Athar-e Melli [Private Property or Public Interest? A Critique of the Administrative Court Branches' Procedure Regarding the Annulment of the Cultural Heritage Organization's Decision in the Listing of National Monuments]*; Abolfath Shadmehri, Ali E'ta, and Seyyed Sadegh Kashani, Seminar-e Chalesh-ha-ye Hoghughi va Modiriyati-e Hefazat az Miras-e Memari-e Moaser [Seminar on Legal Challenges of the Management and Conservation of Contemporary Architectural Heritage], interview by Research and Planning Centre of Municipality of Tehran and Tehran City Council, Aparat-live, 5 October 2021, BTU Cottbus-Senftenberg, Chair of Urban Management, Fieldnotes.
231 Deputy General of Cultural Heritage, the officials of ICHHTO-Tehran and journalists discussed the case in detail in a radio programme. See: 'Meyda-Ne Azadi Live Rado Program' (Tehran: Rado Farhang, 27 April 2019), BTU Cottbus-Senftenberg, Chair of Urban Management, Fieldnotes.

Inefficient administration, corruption and privatization: A recipe for chaos

From the early-2000s, governmental organizations such as the ICHO gradually ceded their functions to private entities and local governments.[232] The national policy in this period, enshrined in documents such as the Third Five-Year Development Plan of Iran (2000–2004)[233] and the Budget Law (March 2003-March 2004),[234] emphasized the role of banks as potential investors in tourism and cultural heritage under the framework of cultural development.

Decentralization and privatization led to structural and functional changes in the ICHO. In 2003 and 2006, its areas of authority were expanded to include tourism and handicrafts. Now called the Iranian Cultural Heritage Handicrafts and Tourism Organization (ICHHTO), the organization was moved from the Ministry of Islamic Guidance to the Presidential Office. On the one hand, this increased the flow of money into the organization. On the other, it made the ICHHTO nearly immune to parliamentary control, giving it a reputation for being the government's backyard.[235] The politicized environment of the organization was also reflected in the frequent replacement of its directors. For example, between 2004 and 2013, the organization saw a turnover of six directors, all of whom had served as vice presidents. My interviews suggest that the allocation of key positions at the ICHHTO were political gestures by presidents toward their formal and informal allies. This is also consistently confirmed by political scientists and media reports.[236]

---

232 See: Parliament of Iran, 'Ghanun-e Barnamey-e Sevom-e Tose-Ey-e Eghtesadi, Ejtemai va Farhangi-e Jomhuriy-e Eslami-e Iran [The Law of the Third Plan of the Economic, Social and Cultural Development of Islamic Republic of Iran]'.
233 Ibid.
234 'Ghanoun-e Budjeh Sal-e 1382 Koll-e Keshvar [Budget Law March 2003-March 2004]' (Parliament of Iran, 2003).
235 For instance see: Hekmatollah Mollasalehi, 'Gereh-Ha-Ye Nagoshudeh-Ye Miras [The Unsolved Knots of Cultural Heritage]', *Etelaat Newspaper*, 16 August 2017, https://www.ettelaat.com/archives/303389#gsc.tab=0.
236 See: Ali M Ansari, *Iran under Ahmadinejad: The Politics of Confrontation* (Routledge, 2017).

These frequent, politically driven changes in organizational structure caused disruption to ongoing administrative processes. Informal reports of alleged corruption within the organization became more prevalent during this period, particularly related to the leasing of historical buildings for cultural tourism and the selection of contractors for conservation and reuse projects. Several conservationists I interviewed spoke of a "conservation mafia", referring to a few consulting firms connected with heritage authorities that were usually awarded project contracts. This was also reflected in an unpublished survey conducted by the University of Tehran that monitored career paths of architectural and urban conservation graduates.[237]

During the 1997–2005 administration, the authorities in charge of cultural heritage entered into negotiations with the World Bank, resulting in the latter's investment in 'Improving Iran's Cultural Heritage Organization Capacity in the Protection, Conservation and Social and Economic Exploitation of National Cultural Patrimony'.[238] I interviewed a senior official who was involved in these negotiations who said the original plan was to establish a Cultural Heritage Development Bank to facilitate private sector participation in the preservation and reuse of historic buildings. The Revitalization and Utilization Fund for Historic Sites was set up in service of this aim.[239] After consulting with several conser-

---

[237] 'Report: Professional Conditions of Graduates of Postgraduate Programs in Conservation and Revitalization of Historic Buildings and Urban Fabrics, First Phase', Unpublished (Tehran: Research Institute of Art and Culture, University of Tehran, 2018).

[238] Anthony Bigio, Rana Amirtahmasebi, and Guido Licciardi, *Culture Counts: Partnership Activities of the World Bank and Italian Development Cooperation on Cultural Heritage and Sustainable Development – Report (English)* (Washington, D.C: World Bank Group, 2013), https://documents.worldbank.org/en/publicati on/documents-reports/documentdetail/180971468163171229/culture-counts-p artnership-activities-of-the-world-bank-and-italian-development-cooperatio n-on-cultural-heritage-and-sustainable-development-report.

[239] ICHHTO, 'Asasnameh-Ye Sandough-e Ehya va Bahrebardari Az Banaha va Amaken-e Tarikhi-Farhangi [Statutes of the Rvitalisation and Utilisation Fund for Historical Places]' (2005).

vation experts, the founders of the fund wanted to initiate a paradigm shift in the revitalization and reuse of historic sites based on international standards such as the principles of integrity and authenticity.[240] But, from the beginning of President Ahmadinejad's administration in 2005, the fund's activities became increasingly opaque. Another former senior ICHO official[241] I interviewed spoke openly of massive corruption in the fund, such as favouritism in the selection of investors[242] and a flexible interpretation of legal documents. A flexible interpretation of the laws on irreplaceable treasures[243] allowed the misappropriation of revitalization projects by a politicized committee of experts that decided on the leasing of historic sites and the selection of private investors.[244] After Ahmadinejad's eight-year presidency, the corruption cases, along with several similar cases at the ICHHTO and other government organizations, were widely discussed in the media, leading Parliament to launch a judicial inquiry.[245]

---

240 Revitalisation and Utilization Fund, *Sanad-e Ehya va Bahrebardari Az Amaken Tarikhi va Farhangi [Guidelines for the Revitalisation and Utilization of Historic and Cultural Places]*, second (Tehran: Gang-e Shayegan, 2009).
241 Interviewed by the author on 3 October 2021 in Tehran.
242 Pooya Azadi, 'The Structure of Corruption in Iran', 2020.
243 See Article 83 of the Islamic Republic's Constitution; and Parliament of Iran, 'Ghanoon-e Mohasebat-e Omumi-e Keshvar [The Public Audit Act]'.
244 Online debate by the Director General of Listing and Zoning Office at ICHHTO, Director General of the Iranian Association of Archaeologists, and a heritage journalist organized by the Tourism Research centre of Imam Sadegh University. See: Mostafa Pourali et al., 'Chalesh-Ha va Masael-e Sabt-e Asar-e Farhangi Dar Keshvar [Challenges and Issues of Listing Cultural Properties in Iran]' (Imam Sadiq University, 2021), Fieldnotes.
245 See IRNA, 'Mohseni Ejeie: Hamid Baghaie Bazdasht Shod [Mohseni Ejeie: Hamid Baghaie Was Arrested]', *IRNA*, 6 August 2015, https://irna.ir/xj9VRT ; Fatemeh Aliasghar, 'Hamid Baghaie Dar Miras-e Farhangi va Dolat-e Ahmadinejad Che Kard? [What Did Hamid Baghaie Do at ICHHTO and Ahmadinejad's Administration?]', *Khabaronline*, 23 February 2017, sec. Jame'e, khabaronline.ir/x7sqm; n. n., 'Asnad-e Fesad-e Hodud-e Nim-Triliard Tomani-e Hamid Baghaie Montasher Shod [Hamid Baghai's Corruption Documents of About Half a Trillion Tomans Were Published]', *Young Journalists Club*, 20 March 2018, https://www.yjc.news/ooRBRd.

In August 2021, the Parliamentary Research Centre published a diagnostic study of the legal gaps in identifying irreplaceable treasures that can only be transferred to the private sector with parliamentary approval.[246] According to the research, the term 'irreplaceable treasures' (or *nafayes*) had not been legally defined. Moreover, the document pointed out that the political and social necessities of the early Revolutionary period, which led to the legislation on *nafayes*, had changed. Therefore, in the absence of a clear legal basis, the expert committee resorted to "experience-based" and "agreement-based" methods, as well as using World Heritage criteria. In order to stop the corruption and irreversible damage to cultural properties caused by the loopholes, the document also proposed a clarification of the term 'irreplaceable treasures' and the establishment of an inter-organizational expert committee for the delegation of properties to private bodies.

Apart from the chaotic state of national heritage, World Heritage is often instrumentalized by governments to polish their cultural image and as proof of high achievement. Of all Iranian presidents, Ahmadinejad's speeches at ceremonies for the listing of Iranian sites on the World Heritage List are the most ironic.[247] In a speech on the occasion of the inclusion of the Tabriz Bazaar Complex in the World Heritage List, he described cultural heritage as a "stepping stone to heights of glories" and then advertised his social housing construction project in the province of

---

246 Deputy of Cultural Studies -Parliament of Iran, 'Asibshenasi-e Jaigah-e Nafayes Melli va Monhaser-Befard Dar Nezam-e Ghanoon-Gozari [A Diagnosis of the Place of National and Irreplaceable Treasures in the Legislative System]' (Parliament of Iran-Research Centre, 2021).

247 His populist use of cultural heritage was distinctive, according to many scholars. See: Ali M Ansari, The Politics of Nationalism in Modern Iran, vol. 40 (New York: Cambridge University Press, 2012); Menahem Merhavy, 'Religious Appropriation of National Symbols in Iran: Searching for Cyrus the Great', Iranian Studies 48, no. 6 (2015): 933–48; Ali Mozaffari, 'Picturing Pasargadae: Visual Representation and the Ambiguities of Heritage in Iran', Iranian Studies 50, no. 4 (2017): 601–34.

East Azerbaijan.[248] Or in the last phase of his term, when he had political conflicts with the Supreme Leader, he gave a speech at the ceremony of World Heritage listing of Golestan Palace, saying that preserving cultural heritage would guarantee the nation's future identity and criticizing the Islamic Revolutionary attitude that considered royal buildings as worthless symbols of fallen monarchies.[249]

Figure 25: Ahmadinejad at the World Heritage listing ceremony for Tabriz Bazaar

© Mehr News Agency, 2010

---

248 IRNA, 'Dar Marasem.e Jashn-e Sabt-e JahaniBazar-e Bozorg-e Tabriz [In the Celebration for Tabriz Grand Bazaar Inscription in the World Heritage List]', 31 July 2011, https://irna.ir/x3fzzW.
249 Mohammad Barikani, 'Nekoodasht-e Sabt-e Jahani-e Kakh-e Golestan Be Onvan-e Nokhostin Banay-e Sabt-e Jahani-e Paytakht [Celebrating Golestan Palace as the Capital's First World Heritage Site]', *Hamshahrionline*, 7 September 2013, hamshahrionline.ir/x3TFx.

Urban heritage in the public sphere and academia of the 2000s

The early years of Khatami's reformist government opened up the public sphere in Iran. In my interview with the reformist Director of the ICHO,[250] Seyyed Mohammad Beheshti Shirazi[251] described it thus: "Society stepped out of the private space and began to position itself in the public sphere, reclaiming the city and expressing identity". Beheshti Shirazi's firm belief was that this opening up was solely due to the government's reforms, but it is worth noting that the internet played a decisive role in shaping the emerging public sphere. More specifically, new technological possibilities that transformed journalism and the free exchange of information played an instrumental role in the emergence of a network of professionals and citizens who criticized the government. Despite the conservative judiciary's efforts in the 2000s to suppress the relatively relaxed environment for public expression that emerged in Khatami's administration, public criticism persisted within the limitations imposed by strict conditions.[252] With the crushing of established reform-oriented newspapers that coincided with the availability of the internet in Iran, blogs and social media provided alternative platforms for repressed voices.[253]

Moreover, the number of university students in Iran grew sharply in the 2000s.[254] This contributed to the emergence of formal and informal heritage journalism across a range of political alignments. Several universities began enrolling students in their architectural conservation programmes, previously offered only at the ICHHTO HEC. Among them were the University of Tehran, Shahid Beheshti University (former Melli University), University of Art-Tehran, Iran University of Science and

---

250 His term at the ICHO was between 1997 and 2003.
251 I conducted an interview with him in Tehran on January 7, 2020.
252 Hossein Shahidi, *Journalism in Iran: From Mission to Profession* (London: Routledge, 2007).
253 Marcus Michaelsen, 'The Politics of Online Journalism in Iran', *Social Media in Iran: Politics and Society After*, 2009.
254 Azadi, Mirramezani, and Mesgaran, 'Migration and Brain Drain from Iran'.

Technology, and a growing number of the private Islamic Azad University's branches.[255] With the introduction of new university programs in the field and in alignment with the government's decentralization strategy, the HEC, which was founded in 1990, was dissolved.

The unfolding socio-technical assemblage created a space for critical heritage action in Iran. The explicitness of this criticism differed from that of the 1980s, which was carefully and anonymously formulated and often raised by heritage officials. In their blogs, university students, NGOs, and even insiders from government organizations commented on historic sites at risk and allegations of corruption at the ICHHTO.

For example, commenting on the organization's mismanagement in 2005, a former ICHHTO official accused the presidential team of irresponsibility, disregard for expertise, rash and illogical actions, ignoring collective wisdom, populist actions, dogmatic thinking, disregard for the rule of law, monopolization, the illusion of a hypothetical enemy, and a lack of accountability.[256] As the ICHHTO was broadly known as the government's backyard, the same blogger supported the idea to transform the organization into a ministry; this would help reduce corruption by placing the organization under parliamentary oversight.[257]

---

255 Recently, Imam Sadiq University, affiliated with the Revolutionary powers of the Islamic Republic and recognized as a training ground for the future political elite, has joined the aforementioned universities in introducing research programs focused on national tourism and heritage policies on a large scale. This institution, formerly known as the Center for Management Studies, served as the pre-revolutionary branch of Harvard University in Iran.

256 Ardeshir Oruji, 'Afat-Ha-Ye Roshd va Tose'e [The Pests of Growth and Development]', *Pajuheshgar-e Miras-e Farhangi, Gardeshgari va Sanay-e Dast [Heritage, Tourism and Crafts Researcher]*, 19 December 2007, http://oroji.blogfa.com/post/91/.

257 Ardeshir Oruji, 'Farayand-e Tadvin-e Ghanoon-e Tashkil-e Sazman-e Miras-e Farhangi va Gardeshgari va Zaroorat-e Baznegari-e An [The Process of Drafting the Law on the Establishment of the Cultural Heritage and Tourism Organization and the Need for Its Revision]', *Pajuheshgar-e Miras-e Farhangi, Gardeshgari va Sanay-e Dast [Heritage, Tourism and Crafts Researcher]*, 30 September 2008, http://oroji.blogfa.com/page/10.aspx; Ardeshir Oruji, 'Zaroorat-e Tashkil-e Vezarat-e Miras-e Farhangi [The Necessity of Establishing the Ministry of Cultural Her-

Even the prevalence of favouritism in the system was addressed online, with one news outlet for example mocking the fact that the ICHHTO Director's English teacher had been appointed Director of the National Museum.[258]

In Isfahan, preventing the Jahan-Nama Tower project and the Metro Line-2 from impacting the World Heritage status of Naghsh-e Jahan Square was backed by the active presence of established newspapers and blogs.[259] Mozaffari researched a similar case of heritage activism in the 2000s around the construction of the Sivand Dam, which threatened the World Heritage site of Pasargadae in Shiraz.[260]

---

itage and Tourism]', *Pajuheshgar-e Miras-e Farhangi, Gardeshgari va Sanay-e Dast [Heritage, Tourism and Crafts Researcher]*, 31 July 2009, http://oroji.blogfa.com/post/142. Mohebali, M. Hassan, another insider at ICHHTO talked about this issue later. See:Mohammad Hassan Mohebali and Maryam Jalilvand, 'Razha-Ye Magooy-e Chehrey-e Mandegar-e Miras-e Farhangi [The Untold Secrets of the Heritage Pioneer about the Cultural Heritage Organisation]', *Seday-e Miras*, 2018, https://www.sedayemiras.ir/1397/05/29/.

258   Shahryar, 'Booy-e Eidi [The Scent of Eidi]', *Irangardi Shahryar Dar Shanbeh*, 3 June 2010, 25.5.2020. The issue was also raised in the official newspapers. See: Mehr News Agency, 'Director of National Museum of Iran Dismissed', *Mehr News Agency*, 7 December 2011, en.mehrnews.com/news/46922/; Aliasghar, 'Hamid Baghaie Dar Miras-e Farhangi va Dolat-e Ahmadinejad Che Kard? [What Did Hamid Baghaie Do at ICHHTO and Ahmadinejad's Administration?]'.

259   Elham Ghasemi and Mojtaba Rafieian, 'Analyzing Conflict of Interest in Large-Scale Participatory Projects with Emphasis on the "Public Private People Partnership" Model (4P) (Case Study: Isfahan Jahannema Citadel Project)', *Motaleate Shahri* 9, no. 34 (2020): 90–104, doi:https://doi.org/10.34785/J011.2021.887; Mohammadreza Azimi, 'Amalkard-e Shahrdari-e Esfahan Dar Tajrobeh-Ye Sakht-e Borg-e Jahan-Nama Dar Harim-e Meidan-e Naghsh-e Jahan [The Role of The Municipality of Isfahan in the Experience of Constructing the Jahan-Nama Tower in Naghsh-e Jahan Square's Buffer Zone]' (Tehran, 22 July 2015), https://chaharrah.tv/mohammadreza-azimi-a-1394-04-31/. Also see several posts by Alireza Afshari at khordegiri.blogfa.com and Shahin Sepanta at drshahinsepanta.blogsky.com.

260   Mozaffari, 'Picturing Pasargadae: Visual Representation and the Ambiguities of Heritage in Iran'.

Urban heritage planning in Iran: Repeated cycles of struggle for territorialization   113

The relative political openness also allowed private academic publishers such as Nashr-e Faza, headed by Falamaki, an active pre-Revolutionary academic and conservation architect, to publish research outside the official academic publishing houses. In 2005, Falamaki published the second edition of his 1978 book on Shiraz, critically reflecting on developments in the field of urban conservation after the 1980s.[261] In the same year and with the same publishing house, he published a book on the protective zoning of cultural assets, in which he criticized policies on tourism and economic decentralization.[262]

Meanwhile, official academic publishing, represented by publishers such as Jahad-e Daneshgahi (University Crusade), Samt, and state university presses, tended to adopt politically neutral and predominantly technical positions. The 2000s saw a wave of technocratic publications authored by bureaucrat-academics with varying political leanings, who held key positions in government and at universities.[263]

In general, academic publications of the time, whether written by the aforementioned bureaucrat-academics or not, were optimistic about and consistent with the economic and cultural policies of the National Development Plans and the Twenty-Year Vision Document and viewed disciplinary conservation concepts through the lens of "expediency and objectivity".[264] The publications mainly focused on translating the first

---

261   Falamaki, *Seiri Dar Tajarob-e Maremmat-e Shari, as Veniz Ta Shiraz [An Essay on Urban Conservation, From Venice to Shiraz]*.
262   M. Mansour Falamaki, *Harimgozari Bar Sarvat-Haye Farhangi-e Iran [Respect of the Cultural Goods of Iran]* (Tehran: Faza Scientific and Cultural Institute, 2005).
263   Sociologist Mohammad Fazeli uses a similar term, 'sociologist bureaucrat', to describe sociologists who also work in public administration, such as himself. He argues that while sociologist bureaucrats cannot freely criticize the government, they can nevertheless explain the complexities of the governing process. See: Fazeli, *Iran Bar Labe-Ye Tigh, Goftar-Ha-Ye Jameshenasi-Ye Siyasi va Siyasat-e Omumi [Iran, on the Edge of the Blade Essays on Political Sociology and Public Policy]*.
264   For instance, see: Pirooz Hanachi, *Maremat-e Shahri Dar Baft-Hay-Ye Tarikhi-e Iran [Urban Restoration in Historic Fabrics of Iran]*, 1st ed. (Tehran: University of Tehran Press, 2012).

world's technical terminology and best practices with the hope of informing domestic academia,[265] policy, and practice.[266]

Communication technologies facilitated the liberal voicing of opinions, but as the crackdown of the Green Movement[267] showed, the same technologies also came in handy for the oppressors.[268] Falamaki's response to my question about the effectiveness of the public sphere in preventing ongoing unlawful acts by national and local powers is an apt conclusion to this chapter. He was not as optimistic as Beheshti Shirazi when asked about the public sphere that began to emerge after the wave of reforms, saying that "awareness has grown, but it has never been strong enough to keep up with the economic and ideological forces that have opposed it". Falamaki also pointed out that "complaining would not be a solution. Our journalism and academia cannot solve our problems because they dare not name the root causes". [269]

---

265 M. Mansour Falamaki, *Nosazi va behsazi-e shahri [Urban improvement and renewal]* (Tehran: SAMT, 2013).
266 Seyyed Mohsen Habibi and Malihe Maghsoodi, *Urban Restoration* (Tehran: University of Tehran, 2002); Hossein Kalantari and Ahmad Pourahmad, *Fonun va Tajarob-e Barnamehrizi-e Maremat-e Baft-e Tarikhi-e Shahrha [Techniques and Experiences in Renovation Planning of Historical Area of Cities]* (Tehran: Jahad-e Daneshgahi, 2005); Hanachi et al., *Barresi-e Tatbighi-e Tajarob Maremat-e Shahri Dar Jahan va Iran, Ba Negahi Vijeh Be Baft-e Yazd [A Comparative Study Of Urban Preservation Experiences In The World And In Iran, With A Special Focus On The City Of Yazd]*; Jukka Jokilehto, *Tarikh-e Hefazat-e Memari [History of Architectural Conservation]*, trans. M. Hassan Talebian and Khashayar Bahari (Tehran: Rozaneh, 2008).
267 The political movement that sprung up in Iran after the June 2009 presidential election that led to Ahmadinejad's second term in office.
268 Saeid Golkar, 'Liberation or Suppression Technologies? The Internet, the Green Movement and the Regime in Iran.', *International Journal of Emerging Technologies & Society* 9, no. 1 (2011).
269 On January 9, 2020, I conducted an interview with him at his office in Tehran.

The third cycle: A renewed endeavour to reform urban heritage assemblage

A glimpse on the political terrain after the conservative government 2005-2013

With the return of a reformist administration in 2013, the unfinished legal processes and urban planning projects of 1997–2005 were resumed. The reformist bureaucrat-academics who had retreated to universities during Ahmadinejad's administration regained their seats in municipalities, city councils, and government organizations. However, throughout its term, the reformist government experienced a sense of déjà vu—their reform initiatives swiftly faced conservative opposition, much like those of the Khatami government in 1997. In 2019, the Revolutionary factions ramped up accusations of corruption to towards the reformists and their projects. At the same time, political escalation with foreign powers and the threat of a power vacuum following the possible passing of the Supreme Leader of the Islamic Republic (82 years old at the time) prompted the state to go on the defensive with further militarization.[270]

Under the "unified rule"[271] that came with the new hardliner government in 2021, seats in the Islamic Parliament and city councils, as well as governor and mayoral appointments, went to IRGC members and former or active military officers. Consequently, the reform-minded bureaucrat-academics who had been working in the Ministry of Urban Development, municipalities, and city councils returned to their academic posts. Some who played influential roles in urban heritage planning and conservation sought to continue their unfulfilled projects through civic

---

270 Mahjoob Zweiri and Aljohara AlObaidan, 'The Second Succession in the Islamic Republic of Iran: Change or Continuity?', *Journal of Balkan and Near Eastern Studies* 23, no. 3 (2021): 473–89.

271 Following Ebrahim Raisi's victory in the presidential elections of 2021, a solidified hardline control over all government branches materialized, referred to as 'hokoomat-e yekdast', which is translated as 'unified rule' in this book.

activities, resulting in the recent active engagement of former bureaucrat-academics in the public sphere.

The urban regeneration programme: An ill-fated attempt to territorialize urban heritage

In 2013, the reformist Ministry of Roads and Urban Development (MRUD)[272] re-initiated the urban regeneration programme as a follow-up to its urban planning policies that had been shelved when President Ahmadinejad took office in 2005.[273] The MRUD Minister described the resumed policies as a reform that would initiate a transition in urban planning to a participatory governance approach. This approach promised to give historic cities a new spatial and economic role through urban regeneration [*bazafarini-ye shahri*].[274] In line with the academic argument that the intertwining of political leadership and urban administration (as a scientific and professional process) is a shortcoming of the Iranian urban planning system,[275] Akhundi, the Minister, pointed to cultural and economic globalization when talking about urban governance,[276] a process in which central governments must allow cities to

---

272 As part of the decentralization policies the two ministries of Housing and Urban Development and Roads and Transportation were merged into the new Ministry of Roads and Urban Development in 2011.
273 I conducted an interview with Mohammad Saied Izadi in Tehran on January 7, 2020.
274 Majid Ghamami, ed., 'Goftegu Ba Doktor Abbas Akhundi [A Conversation with Dr. Abbas Akhundi]', in *Barresi-Ye Vaziyat-e Shahrsazi va Barnamehrizi Shahri va Mantaghei Da Iran-e Moaser [Observations on the State of Urban Planning and Urban and Regional Management in Contemporary Iran]* (Tehran: Afrand Publishing House, 2013), 13–31.
275 Abbas Akhundi et al., 'Asib Shenasi-e Model-e Edarey-e Omur-e Shahr Dar Iran [A Diagnosis of the Model of Urban Management in Iran]', *Pajouheshhay-e Joghrafiai* 40, no. 63 (2007): 135–56.
276 Ibid.

become independent of national economies and develop as economic and socio-spatial entities in their own right.[277]

Akhundi[278] and many other reform-minded bureaucrat-academics[279] acknowledged that, in spite of 'cosmetic policies' towards public participation in Iran, the central state has always resisted its actual implementation. However, they offered no solution to the challenge of Iranian cities seeking economic and cultural independence in a theocracy ruled by a set of state and parastatal power centres.[280]

In support of the regeneration programme, universities and institutions to which these bureaucrat-academics were affiliated became involved in the urban regeneration assemblage. Interviews with several conservation graduates and archival research[281] indicate that the topic of urban regeneration became particularly popular, for instance, at the University of Tehran between 2011 and 2019.[282]

---

277 For background on the concept of urban governance and the challenges of implementing it, see: Ade Kearns and Ronan Paddison, 'New Challenges for Urban Governance', *Urban Studies* 37, no. 5–6 (2000): 845–50.
278 Ghamami, 'Goftegu Ba Doktor Abbas Akhundi [A Conversation with Dr. Abbas Akhundi]'.
279 See, for example, the chapters written by actors in the academic and governmental realms of urban planning in Iran in: *Hokmravai-e Novin Shahri (ruykard-ha, mafahim, masael, va chalesh-ha) [New Urban Governance (approaches, concepts, Issues, and challenges)]*, vol. 1 and 2 (Tehran: Tisa, 2017).
280 See the section: An overview of the political landscape in the aftermath of the 1979 Revolution.
281 Based on the thematic analysis of doctoral and master's dissertations available on the Iranian Research Institute for Information Science and Technology (IranDoc) repository. The Institute is affiliated with the Ministry of Science, Research, and Technology (MSRT), 'IranDoc', 2020, https://en.irandoc.ac.ir.
282 Also see translated academic books such as: Peter Roberts and Hugh Sykes, *Urban Regeneration: A Handbook*, trans. Mohammad Saeid Izadi and Pirooz Hanachi (University of Tehran Press, 2014).

Iranshahr: A short-lived theoretical experiment in urban regeneration[283]

One policy of the reformist MRUD was to invest in the pre-Islamic model of 'Iranshahr' in the belief it would provide a theoretical framework for directing Iran's urban regeneration programme toward urban and regional equilibrium.[284] The concept goes back to the pre-Islamic Sassanid Dynasty (3rd century AD) who used this term for their political territory, which stretched from the Oxus to the Euphrates. In administering Iranshahr, they followed Zoroastrian principles of balance and tolerance in dealing with the various ethnic groups, religions, and natural environments.[285]

Mohammad Saeid Izadi, who held the position of Deputy Minister of MRUD at that point in time said in an interview: [286]

We wanted to start from a solid theoretical basis. So, with the support of the Minister, we proceeded with a theoretical experiment at MRUD. Most of our colleagues at the universities refused to support us, arguing that a Ministry was a place for executing measures and not for theoretical work.

Having said that, it is crucial to note the inherent risks of engaging in theoretical discourse within a ministry, particularly when incorporating the controversial Iranist ideas of philosopher and political theorist Javad Tabatabai. Tabatabai's proposition, advocating for the adoption of the ancient pre-Islamic governance model of Iranshahr as a potential means of harmonizing Iran's present-day ethnic, cultural, and environmental

---

283 Here, I expand on my previously published work on the subject. See: Yadollahi, 'Tracing the Identity-Driven Ambitions of the Iranian Urban Conservation Apparatus'.
284 UDRC, 'Iranian Urban Development And Revitalization Corporation Operation Report (2013–2017)' (MRUD, 2017).
285 See: Touraj Daryaee and Khodadad Rezakhani, *From Oxus to Euphrates: The World of Late Antique Iran*, Ancient Iran Series (H&S MEDIA, 2016).
286 I conducted an interview with Mohammad Saied Izadi in Tehran on January 7, 2020. He was Deputy Minister between 2013 and 2017, Deputy Minister of Architecture and Urban Planning between 2017–2019 and the director of the Applied Research centre of UDRC.

dynamics, came too close to echoing a call to replace the Islamist model of governance.[287]

Public events and newspaper interviews indicate that high-ranking bureaucrat-academics, including the MRUD Minister Abbas Akhundi and his deputies, kept a close eye on Tabatabai's theory.[288] For instance, Akhundi, stated in an interview that "returning to the Iranshahr identity" would be his main approach for urban regeneration.[289] In another interview, he argued that the re-investigation of Iranshahr could facilitate dealing with the crisis of identity, liveability, and mobility in contemporary Iranian cities.[290] He believed that his approach included "Iran, Islam, and modernity all together".[291] Also, Izadi, the Deputy Minister of MRUD and Director of the Urban Regeneration Company of Iran (former HDCC) said that the accurate understanding of Iranshahr could be "the missing link in the chain of [their] previous attempts in dealing with the social and environmental complexities of Iranian cities".[292]

Moreover, the MRUD-associated Urban Regeneration Company of Iran (URC) organized a series of discussions in Tehran, Qazvin, Yazd, Isfahan, and other cities about possible applications of the model to address issues around "good governance", the "liveability of cities", and

---

287 Javad Tabatabai, *Khajeh Nezam-al-Molk* (Tehran: Tarh-e Now, 1996); Javad Tabatabai, 'Iran be onvan-e Iranshahr [Iran as Iranshahr]' (Twenty-fourth Meeting of the Iransharian Thought and Civilization, Tehran, 10 March 2017).

288 He was invited to speak in the 24th session of the lecture series on 'Iranshahr Thought and Civilization' [*Selseleh neshasthay-e Andisheh va Tamaddon-e Iranshahri*], held by the MRUD and UDRC.

289 Abbas Akhundi, 'Barnamey-e Melli-e Baz-Afarini-e Shahri Be Ghalam-e Abbas Akhundi [The National Urban Regeneration Agenda, by Abbas Akhundi]', *UN Habitat-Iran*, 2018, para. 3, http://unhabitat.org.ir/?p=4708.

290 Abbas Akhundi, 'An Interview with the Minister of MRUD', *MRUD News Service*, 2018, http://news.mrud.ir/news/51902/.

291 ibid., para. 33.

292 MRUD News Service, 'A Report of the Meeting Series on The Critique of Architecture and Urban Planning', *MRUD News Service*, 2018, para. 3, http://news.mrud.ir/news/50242/.

"citizenship rights" in contemporary Iran.[293] Abbas Akhundi, Beheshti Shirazi (the former director of the ICHO), Mohsen Habibi, Professor of Urban Planning at the University of Tehran, and Javad Tabatabai were among the speakers. Outside of Iran, historian Touraj Daryaee[294] also published on the concept of Iranshahr[295] and talked about it in news and academic publications and on social media.[296] In line with MRUD's 'good governance' policies, Urban Dialogue Houses were founded in cities like Tehran, Gorgan, and Tabriz[297] to "encourage civic engagement and build public trust" in historic city centres.[298]

The concept of Iranshahr came under fierce attack from conservative thinkers, who accused the reformists of promoting Western views of liberalism that diverge from Islamic Revolutionary ideology.[299] In the midst of the pandemonium of ideological and political disputes and despite lobbying by well-known professionals and academics in urban

---

293 See the reports: UDRC, 'Iranian Urban Development And Revitalization Corporation Operation Report (2013–2017)'.
294 Maseeh Chair in Persian Studies & Culture, History, University of California, Irvine
295 Daryaee and Rezakhani, *From Oxus to Euphrates: The World of Late Antique Iran*.
296 In 2020 and 2021, Daryaee reached out to public audience in several Instagram live streams around the topic of Iranshahr. Also see: Touraj Daryaee, Iranshar Tavahom va Eghragh Nist [Iranshahr is Neither an Illusion nor an Exaggeration], 27 October 2020, Etemad Newspaper.
297 For instance, see: Parliament of Iran, 'Ghanun-e Barnamey-e Chaharom-e Tose-Ey-e Eghtesadi, Ejtemai va Farhangi-e Jomhuriy-e Eslami-e Iran [The Law of the Fourth Plan of Economic, Social and Cultural Development of Islamic Republic of Iran]'.
298 Mohammad Saeid Izadi, 'Rah Andazi-Ye Khane-Ha-Ye Gofteman-e Shahri Rahi Bara-Ye Maremat-e Baft-Ha-Ye Tarikhi [Establishment of Urban Dialogue Houses, an Approach to the Preservation of Historic Cities]', *ISNA*, 19 November 2016, isna.ir/xcY47c.
299 For instance in: Mashregh, 'Ideology-Zodai Az Shahr, Barname-Ye Asli-Ye Eslahtalaban Bara-Ye Tehran/ Chera Hanachi Haman Akhundi Ast? [Ideological Cleansing, the Reformists' Main Program for Tehran / Why Hanachi Is the Very Same as Akhundi?]', *Mashregh News*, 18 October 2018; Mohammad Mohsen Rahemi, 'Iranshahri Mordeh Ast [Iranshahri Is Dead]', *Farhikhtegan*, Islamic Azad University, 20 October 2018, http://fdn.ir/23522.

planning and architecture, and sociology the Urban Dialogue House of Tehran (also known as Vartan House)[300] was labelled a "house of corruption" and was closed down in 2019.[301]

The wider problem of the Iranshahr model was that it ran counter to the metanarrative of the Islamic Republic's cultural policy, which can be found, for instance, in the policies of the High Council of the Cultural Revolution, that aimed at cultural engineering.[302] Cultural engineering was defined as "the process of recognizing, diagnosing, purifying and advancing culture and its directions based on the authentic Islamic-Iranian identity".[303] In a joint decree with Ahmadinejad, a Cultural Engineering Map was issued to provide cultural infrastructure for realizing the goals of Islamic society.[304] Cultural engineering was implemented in the digital and physical public spheres, targeting Iranian citizens, Farsi-speaking societies, state organizations, the Islamic world, neighbouring countries, and allies and enemies of the Islamic Republic of Iran. National measures foreseen by the document included the development of cultural spaces to promote the heritage of Sacred Defence, the country's achievements and progress in science and culture, as well as the works of past and present Iranian scientists.

---

300   After the building's Iranian-Armenian architect, Vartan Hovanessian.
301   Drawing on the author's online and offline ethnographic research related to the campaign against the closure of the Vartan House. The participants (professionals and planners from the Municipality of Tehran and the University of Tehran) preferred to remain anonymous.
302   The High Council of the Cultural Revolution had been pursuing the project of cultural engineering since the mid-2000s in a scholarly journal with the same title.
303   High Council of Cultural Revolution and Mahmud Ahmadinejad, 'Mosavabe-Ye Naghshe-Ye Mohandesi-Ye Farhangi-Ye Keshvar [Decree on the Cultural Engineering Map of the Country]' (Parliament of Iran-Research Centre, 2013), pt. 1 (6), Parliament of Iran-Research Centre.
304   High Council of Cultural Revolution and Ahmadinejad, 'Mosavabe-Ye Naghshe-Ye Mohandesi-Ye Farhangi-Ye Keshvar [Decree on the Cultural Engineering Map of the Country]'.

Figure 26: The courtyard of the Urban Dialogue House of Tehran, also known as Vartan House, decorated with a mural depicting an epic story from the Shahnameh[305] about the legendary Iranian prince, Siavash remembering his homeland, Iranshahr

Author, 2019

The Fifth and Sixth Development Plans also emphasized the role of the High Council of the Cultural Revolution in cultural engineering.[306]

---

305   National epic of Greater Iran, written by Abolghasem Ferdowsi (10th-11th century).

306   Parliament of Iran, 'Ghanun-e Barnamey-e Panjom-e Tose-Ey-e Eghtesadi, Ejtemai va Farhangi-e Jomhuriy-e Eslami-e Iran [The Law of the Fifth Plan of Economic, Social and Cultural Development of Islamic Republic of Iran]', *The Official Magazine: Rooznameh-e Rasmi-e Keshvar*, 2011; Parliament of Iran, 'Ghanun-e Barnamey-e Sheshom-e Tose-Ey-e Eghtesadi, Ejtemai va Farhangi-e Jomhuriy-e

This included the further support of the establishment of 'fame museums' that played a role in strengthening national pride and advancing the heritage of the Sacred Defence.[307] Also the reuse of houses of Islamic and Revolutionary figures such as Ayatollah Akbar Hashemi Rafsanjani,[308] Ali Shariati,[309] and Seyyed Hassan Modarres[310] in Tehran as 'museum-houses' were projects of this kind. With the IRGC's military involvement in post-ISIS Syria, the ideology of Sacred Defence previously applied to the Iran-Iraq war in the 1980s, was extended to the defence of sacred Shia shrines in the region.[311]

One of the sharpest attacks to the Iranshahr model came from a member of the High Council of Cultural Revolution, Hossein Kechuyan, who challenged Tabatabai in a debate to accept that his theory placed Iranian identity above Islamic identity.[312] He suggested that Tabatabai

---

Eslami-e Iran [The Law of the Sixth Plan of Economic, Social and Cultural Development of Islamic Republic of Iran]', *The Official Magazine: Rooznameh-e Rasmi-e Keshvar*, 2017.

307   A guideline for the reuse of public historical properties was issued: The Council of Ministers, 'Ayin-Nameh-Ye Amval-e Farhangi Honari va Tarikhi-Ye Nahad-Ha-Ye Omumi va Dolati [Code for Cultural, Artistic and Historical Properties of Public and State Institutions]' (Parliament of Iran, 2003).

308   One of the founding leaders of the Islamic Republic and the fourth president of Iran from 1989 to 1997.

309   A key Islamic Revolutionary ideologue.

310   The Modarres museum was financed by the property and industry magnate Ali Ansari, one of the founders of Tat Bank during Ahmadinejad's term. The Tat Bank was dissolved due to misappropriation accusations and lack of transparency. Ansari later founded Future Bank, which was also implicated in embezzlement accusations that were denied by Ansari's conservative allies. See: Radio Farda, 'Hame-Ye Janjal-Ha-Ye Iran Mall va Ali Ansari [All the Controversies of "Iran Mall" and Ali Ansari]', Radio Farda, 22 April 2019, https://www.radiofarda.com/a/Iran-mall-controversies/29896562.html.

311   Hassan Ahmadian and Payam Mohseni, 'Iran's Syria Strategy: The Evolution of Deterrence', *International Affairs* 95, no. 2 (2019): 341–64.

312   Tasnim, 'Ezharat-e Kechuyan Darbareh-Ye Monazereh-Ash Ba Seyyed Javad Tabatabai+Film[Kechuyan's Statements on His Debate with Seyed Javad Tabatabai + Video]', *Tasnim News Agency*, 6 January 2014, 29.10.2020, https://tn.ai/387906.

would not admit the logical conclusion of his concept (a nationalist, secular approach to government) for fear of its political consequences. Kechuyan further argued that Iranshahr would be impossible in Iran because its understanding of identity contradicted the metanarrative in the Islamic Republic, which drew its identity from the "defence of the holy shrines". A member of the Institute of Humanities and Cultural Studies, affiliated with the Ministry of Science, Seyyed-Javad Miri, also took a similar position against Tabatabai, accusing him of promoting archaic and nationalistic ideas that were contradictory to the ruling forces in the Islamic Republic.[313] The theoretical conflict was soon followed by major changes in urban planning administration.

Figure 27: Seyyed Hassan Modarres's Museum-house, Tehran

Author, 2021

---

313 Seyyed-javad Miri, 'Seyyed Javad Tabatabai Be Donbal-e Bastangerai Ast [Seyyed Javad Tabatabai Is Goal Is Seeking Archaism]', *The Great Islamic Encyclopedia*, 2016, https://www.cgie.org.ir/fa/news/127659; Ghasem Pourhassan, Seyyed-javad Miri, and Mohammad-Ali Moradi, 'Naghd va Barresi-e Andishey-e Iranshahri [Reflecting on the Iranshahri Thought]' (Institute for Humanities and Cultural Studies, Tehran, 31 October 2017), https://www.aparat.com/v/oJa3t.

Administrative and spatial components of the urban regeneration assemblage

Similar to its theoretical component, the administrative component of urban regeneration also was reinforced or undermined, depending on whether reformists or conservatives were in power. In line with urban regeneration policies, the reform-oriented High Council of Architecture and Urban Planning (HCAUP) called for the revision of 168 cities' Master Plans. For this purpose, and under the Law of Safeguarding the Revitalization, Rehabilitation and Renovation of Decayed and Dysfunctional Urban Fabrics,[314] the National Urban Regeneration Document was prepared by the MRUD, the ICHHTO and the High Council of Provincial Governors.[315] This actually marked the continuation of the unfinished project initiated by HDCC during President Khatami's administration. According to Izadi, the MRUD team insisted on including heritage and conservation in the urban regeneration programme despite the sceptical stance and resistance of most of the organizations involved.[316]

A multi-organizational committee for urban regeneration called the National Headquarters was thus established, and its provincial branches started to operate. Within the framework of the Sixth National Development Plan,[317] the urban regeneration programme aimed to address the "qualitative" social complexities at the neighbourhood level.[318] So-

---

314 Parliament of Iran, 'Ghanun-e Hemayat Az Ehya, Behsazi va Nosai-e Bafthaye Farsudeh va Nakaramad-e Shahri [The Law of Safeguarding the Revitalization, Rehabilitation and Renovation of Decayed and Dysfunctional Urban Fabrics]', 2011, art. 16.

315 Ministry of Roads and Urban Development, 'Sanad-e Melli-e Rahbordi-e Ehya, Behsazi va Nosazi va Tavanmandsazi-e Bafthaye Farsudeh va Nakaramad-e Shahri [The National Strategic Document for Revitalization, Rehabilitation, Renovation, and Reinforcement of Deteriorated and Dysfunctional Urban Fabrics]'.

316 I interviewed him in Tehran, on January 7, 2020.

317 Parliament of Iran, 'Ghanun-e Barnamey-e Sheshom-e Tose-Ey-e Eghtesadi, Ejtemai va Farhangi-e Jomhuriy-e Eslami-e Iran [The Law of the Sixth Plan of Economic, Social and Cultural Development of Islamic Republic of Iran]'.

318 Mentioned by senior directors of Urban Regeneration Company, Izadi and Ashayeri in public interviews, for instance: 'Bazafarini Mavane va Rahkar-Ha

ciologist Parviz Piran cooperated with the MRUD and the Municipality of Tehran to establish the theoretical and administrative imperatives for participative planning at a neighbourhood level.[319] Private urban planning consultants, also known as Neighbourhood Development Offices (NDOs),[320] who were subordinate to the municipalities, were assigned to the historic districts to mediate between the local communities, stakeholders, and the government authorities and to facilitate participatory planning.[321]

As mentioned, the Sixth National Development Plan committed the MRUD and the ICHHTO to work together within the urban regeneration programme. Relying on this partnership, the ICHHTO announced buffer zones across historic urban areas in 2015. This was an exceptional opportunity, as zoning regulations that the ICHHTO had been pushing for since the mid-2000s had not been approved due to opposition from

---

[Bazafarini Obstacles and Solutions]', *Titr-e Emshab-e Khabar [Tonight's Headlines]* (Tehran: IRINN, 30 April 2018), Fieldnotes; Mohammad Saeid Izadi, Interview with Mohamad Saied Izadi in Tehran, 7 January 2020, BTU Cottbus-Senftenberg, Chair of Urban Management.

319 Parviz Piran, *Az Shoma Harekat Az Khoda Barekat, Tose'e-Ye Mosharekat Mabna va Mosharekat Mehvar Dar Iran: Mored-e Tehran [God Helps Those Who Help Themselves: Participatory Local Development in Iran: The Case of Tehran]* (Tehran: Sazman-e Nosazi-e Tehran, 2010); Seyyed Mojtaba Mousavian, 'Gozaresh-e Neshast-Ha-Ye Takhasosi-Ye Sherkat-e Madar Takhasosi-Ye Omran va Behsazi-Ye Shahri-Ye Iran [Seminars in Iranian Urban Development and Revitalization Corporation (Session 3rd & 4th)]', *HaftShahr* 4, no. 47–48 (2015): 138–45.

320 Under the Bazafarini Programme, the role of Tehran Urban Renewal Facilitators, who had been working in Tehran since 2008, was revised. See: Kaveh Hajaliakbari and Amir Shafie, *Tose-Ye Mahalli: Chaharchoobi Bara-Ye Mahalleh-Ha-Ye Nakaramad [Neighborhood Development: A Framework for Dysfunctional Neighborhoods]* (Tehran: Research and Planning Centre of Municipality of Tehran, 2018).

321 During my fieldwork, I had the opportunity to interact with the NDOs in Tehran and Yazd. They were young planners, environmentalists, and social workers who dealt with the everyday problems of the population living and working in the most troubled neighbourhoods. Their task included contributing to the development of guidelines for urban regeneration by submitting their local observations and proposed solutions to the municipal authorities.

the MRUD, municipalities, and provincial governors during the administration term of the conservatives. With the approval of buffer zones in urban Master Plans, heritage authorities hoped to preserve the visual integrity of historic areas by controlling density selling. The enactment of the Law on Promotion of Restoration and Revitalization of Historic-Cultural Urban Fabrics also helped in this regard.[322] Under this law, heritage authorities could mobilize private investors, banks, and even major para-governmental organizations, such as the Housing Foundation of the Islamic Revolution (Bonyad-e Maskan), to invest in the preservation and reuse of historic sites. If implemented, these legal instruments could mark a pinnacle in the territorialization of urban conservation under unified national regulations.

However, the course of events in several cities showed that pro-urban heritage laws and policies were not economically compelling enough to be taken forward by local development forces. The discontent of local administrations and key stakeholders in city centres, such as municipalities, private developers, and Awqaf administrators, had actually been predictable, as many had expressed their opposition during the early negotiations in the drafting of the National Urban Regeneration Document.

With the exception of Yazd, which was a World Heritage tourist city, the legal and administrative assemblage of urban regeneration and the Ministry of Cultural Heritage, Handicrafts and Tourism (MCHHT)[323] proved ineffective in many cities in the face of rising conservation costs and property prices that were subject to hyperinflation.[324] This was later exacerbated by several factors such as the COVID-19 pandemic, as well as the frequent anti-government protests from December 2017 to

---

322 Parliament of Iran, 'Ghanun-e Hemayat Az Maremmat va Ehyay-e Bafthay-e Tarikhi-Farhangi [The Law on Promotion of Restoration and Revitalisation of Historic-Cultural Urban Fabrics]', 2019.
323 The ICHHTO became a ministry in 2019.
324 In 2019, Iran's inflation stood at 39.9 percent, rising to 43.4 percent by 2021. See: International Monetary Fund, International Financial Statistics and data files., 'Inflation, Consumer Prices (Annual %) – Iran, Islamic Rep.' (World Bank), accessed 4 January 2023, https://cutt.ly/N2j1Wok.

September 2022, which caused serious economic and political instability in Iran, impacting both the housing and tourism sectors.[325]

In this political and economic climate, the sudden density selling restrictions shocked municipalities and developers, who argued that heritage zoning laws were merely prohibiting development without offering reasonable solutions. The issue of national heritage status became more than ever a misfortune for the owners of historic buildings and those who owned properties in the buffer zones.

Apart from these economic conflicts, the political and ideological struggles of recent years have also contributed to the de-territorialization of the still embryonic urban heritage assemblage. Following disagreement with President Rohani, MRUD Minister Akhundi resigned in 2018,[326] and the key players in the urban heritage and regeneration assemblage were replaced by new officials who worked in accordance with overarching state policies. In a process of establishing unified rule, the hardliners gradually took over parliamentary seats, as well as ministry and city council appointments between 2019 and 2021.

The Urban Regeneration National Headquarters was dissolved, although the provincial committees continued to operate. By 2021, most of the NDOs were also gradually dissolved. Akhundi was accused of pursuing a personal and political agenda with the Iranshahr model.[327] In par-

---

325   Zahed Ghaderi et al., 'Crisis-Resilience of Small-Scale Tourism Businesses in the Pandemic Era: The Case of Yazd World Heritage Site, Iran', *Tourism Recreation Research*, 2022, 1–7; Fahimeh Hateftabar and Jean Michel Chapuis, 'The Influence of Theocratic Rule and Political Turmoil on Tourists' Length of Stay', *Journal of Vacation Marketing* 26, no. 4 (2020): 427–41.

326   Also, his nomination to run in the 13th presidential elections was rejected by the Guardian Council. See: Abbas Akhundi, 'Matn-e Kamel-e Estefa-Ye Abbas Akhundi [The Complete Text of Abbas Akhundi's Resignation]', *Ensafnews*, 20 August 2018, https://cutt.ly/z2f92PN.

327   Abbas Akhundi, 'Name-Ye Sarih-e Akhundi Be Rohani/ Dar Chenin Fazai Joz Naomidi, Forupashi Hambastegi-Ye Ejtemai va Nazar Shodan-e Iran Ayande-Ye Digari Nemitavan Entezar Dasht [Open Letter from Akhundi to Rouhani/ In Such an Atmosphere, Nothing Can Be Expected but Despair, the Collapse of Social Solidarity, and the Devolution of Iran.]', Khabaronline, 13 June 2021, khabaronline.ir/xgY7W.

ticular, the acquisition and reuse of historic houses was criticized as an opportunity for the high-ranking stakeholders at the reformist MRUD to profit through rents. The former Minister and his team's interest in heritage was therefore deemed as incompatible with MRUD's original mission, which was urban development and housing. Some actors from the heritage sector, the municipalities, and academia believed that urban regeneration projects were not so different from the previous renewal projects in practice.[328]

In the name of protecting private property rights, density selling was once again relaxed in many cities. For instance, in Tehran, although the city council had advocated the enforcement of buffer zone regulations in 2017, the new hardliner city council loosened the regulations after 2021.[329] This brought in massive income for municipalities and parastatal owners of religious areas in historic city centres. Also, in Mashhad[330] and Isfahan,[331] the HCAUP's legal warnings cease illegal demolitions were stonewalled by local players. Many believed that the flexible approach of the new heritage minister towards urban heritage

---

328 Based on fieldnotes at the expert meeting on 'Experiences of Writing Guidelines for Historic Fabrics (the case of Qome presented by Pardaraz Consulting Engineers)', organized by Tehran Municipality, Mehraban Historic House, Tehran, 27 January 2020; And fieldnotes at the 'First National Symposium on Conservation and Management of Urban Heritage', organized by the Research Center of the Ministry of Cultural Heritage and Tourism, Tehran, February 12–13, 2022.
329 I witnessed this shock in Tehran during my field research in the city centre and in my discussions with the Neighbourhood Development Offices.
330 'Hayahoo-Ye Takhrib-e Asar-e Tarikhi Dar Mashhad Nooshdaru-Ye Bad Az Marg-e Sohrab [The Belated Outcry Over the Destruction of Historical Monuments in Mashhad]', *IRNA*, 21 November 2018, https://irna.ir/xjrqFL; Mostafa Sareminia, 'Takhrib-e Baft-e Tarikh-Ye Mashhad Taaroz Bar Hoviyat-e Eslami va Farhang Irani Ast [The Destruction of the Historic Fabric of Mashhad Is an Attack on Islamic Identity and Iranian Culture]', 25 June 2022, isna.ir/xdLTmh.
331 'Belataklifi Bala-Ye Jan-e Baft-e Tarikhi-Ye Shargh-e Meidan-e Naghsh-e Jahan-e Esfahan [Indecision, the Bane of the Historic District East of Naqsh Jahan Square in Isfahan]', *IRNA*, 31 May 2022, https://irna.ir/xjJzhj.

in Shiraz made the city the first piece of the demolition domino that hit cities like Isfahan, Ghazvin, Kerman, and Kashan.[332]

In Shiraz, where the historic centre was heavily influenced by parastatal religious institutions, the local authorities refused to comply with the MRUD's official 2015 order to revise shrine development plans for protecting listed buildings. Although the heritage authorities won the dispute before the National Security Council in 2019 over the demolition of ten registered houses in Shiraz, the project was not halted. In 2021, after President Raisi's first visit to Shiraz, the project was relaunched with the united support of all stakeholders including some heritage authorities.[333]

Student associations and more than 150 university professors wrote letters to the President and the Minister of Cultural Heritage to stop or restrict the shrine development project. Some argued that the Awqaf-supported project, which included a hotel, shopping centre, and meeting hall for the city council in the historic centre, exceeded the definition of development of worship spaces.[334] There was also extensive debate on social media and in mainstream newspapers about the fact that the transformation of large religious courtyards and historic cemeteries had become a profit-making endeavour for the Awqaf through selling lux-

---

[332] M. Mehdi Kalantari, 'Domino-Ye Takhrib-e Baft-Ha-Ye Tarikhi [Domino Destruction of Historic Cities]', *Shargh Newspaper*, 13 March 2022, 4242 edition, magiran.com/n4279124.

[333] See the Twitter posts of Mehdi Hajati, former member of Shiraz City Council (Mar 14, 2018, 11:04 AM) Also: Gholamhossein Memarian et al., 'Online Roundtable: Loder-Ha Be Ziafat-e Baft-e Tarikhi-e Shiraz Miravand? [Will the Loaders Head to the Historic City of Shiraz?]', *Fars News Agency*, 20 January 2022, https://www.aparat.com/v/JL3rQ.

[334] M. Mehdi Kalantari and Mandana Khoramshaghaghi, 'Chalesh-Ha-Ye Hefazat va Tose'e Dar Baft-e Tarikhi-Ye Shiraz [Challenges of Conservation and Development in Shiraz's Historic Fabric]' (Online: Shahid Beheshti University, 24 February 2022), Fieldnotes; 'Public Discussion: Tajrobe-Ye Mashhad; Ebrat-e Shiraz, Be Name Ziyarat, Dar Barabar-e Tarikh [Mashhad's Experience; Lesson for Shiraz, In the Name of Pilgrimage, Against History]'.

ury graves near shrines in Shiraz and other cities.[335] Despite widespread public criticism, President Raisi emphasized the need to address development obstacles caused by cultural heritage preservation "in order to improve the living conditions of the general public".[336]

In this turbulent environment, marked by a tilt toward disorder, even those who typically preferred a restrained approach when criticizing the government started to openly express their concerns. For instance, Hodjat, the director of ICOMOS-Iran and one of the key architects of the post-Revolutionary heritage laws and administrative system, ultimately admitted that these laws could be disregarded in Iran.[337]

In 2023, the MCHHT registered the historic Shiraz in the National Heritage list as a reaction to the shrine development project and the public critique surrounding it. This response of heritage bureaucracy to the demolitions in Shiraz closely paralleled its action in 2006 regarding the case of the Oudlajan neighbourhood in Tehran, which also faced extensive demolition.[338] It is worth noting that ever since the Oudlajan neighbourhood was designated as a national heritage site, it has remained an abandoned area of ruins in the midst of a living neighbourhood. This is primarily because of prolonged disputes among various stakeholders, including the municipality, governmental and

---

335 ISNA, 'Ghabr-Ha-Ye Miliyardi Dar Shahecheragh! [Billion-Tuman Graves in Shahecheragh!]', 27 October 2014, isna.ir/x8sx4k; 'Kaseban-e Akherat [The Merchants of the Afterlife]', *Hamshahrionline*, 10 March 2020, hamshahrionline.ir/x6JPW; *Roundtable: Be Bahaneh-Ye Tose'e-Ye Haram City Center Misazand/ Az Tamallok-e 8 Milliun Tomani Ta Forush-e Maghaber-e 1 Miliard Tomani [Construction of a City Center Under the Pretext of Shrine Development/Land Acquisition for 8 Million Tomans per Square Meter and Its Sale for 1 Billion Tomans as Graves.]* (Tehran: Ensafnews, 2022), http://www.ensafnews.com/366407/.
336 'Tazahom-Ha-Ye Miras-e Farhangi Ra Hal Konid Ta Mardom Nafas Bekeshand [Address Heritage-Related Disturbances so That People Can Breathe a Sigh of Relief]', *Official Website of the President of the Islamic Republic of Iran*, 14 July 2022, https://www.president.ir/fa/138393.
337 Mehdi Hodjat, 'Goftari Dar Bab-e Miras-e Farhangi [A Speech about Cultural Heritage]' (Iran University of Science and Technology, Tehran, 5 July 2023), https://www.aparat.com/v/NjTgD.
338 See Part Two, Urban renewal, the case of Oudlajan.

parastatal entities, and heritage authorities, which have hindered the formulation of a long-term plan for the preservation of the place that is now considered a national heritage site. Given the resemblance in the composition of these stakeholders—both those seeking to territorialize the area under heritage regulations and those aiming to de-territorialize the area from these rules to advance economic objectives—it is plausible that the fate of Shiraz's historical area might follow a trajectory similar to that of the Oudlajan case.

Figure 28: A cartoon of Zarghami, the Minister of Cultural Heritage submitting his approval to General Ghalibaf, the Chairman of the Parliament, for the demolition of historic neighbourhoods, starting with Shiraz and moving on to other cities [339]

© Shargh Newspaper, 2022

---

339   Ibid.

In addition, the implementation of the Productivization Law, despite disagreement from the academic and professional community, provided the public sphere with a glimpse into what would become the standard practice in the years ahead. The crucial element that rendered the Productivization Law arbitrary was the fact that those tasked with enforcing the law were granted judicial immunity for their actions under the framework of the legislation. In November 2022, the Supreme Leader gave his approval for the implementation of the aforementioned law, which allowed the state to acquire and liquidate underutilized properties of ministries, state organizations, and state-owned companies such as the Revitalization and Utilization Fund for Historic Sites and the Urban Regeneration Company.[340] The Productivization Law was intended to ensure that underused public properties were sold to the private sector.

The Productivization Law enabled the transfer of ownership of several historic buildings owned by the Ministry of Cultural Heritage and other state organizations to the private sector in a highly non-transparent process. Interestingly, properties under the ownership of parastatal organizations, such as the Awqaf, remained untouched by the Productivization Law. Here, it is also worth recalling the history of privatization in Iran, which allowed parastatal organizations to become dominant players in the private sector particularly after Ahmadinejad's administration.

---

340 Supreme Council of Chiefs of State and Government for Economic Coordination, 'Mosavabeh-Ye Movaledsazi-Ye Darayi-Ha-Ye Dolat [The Act on the Productivization of State Assets]' (Ministry of Economic Affairs and Finance, 24 November 2020).

Figure 29: The Shahecheragh project in Shiraz [341]

© ISNA, 2022

Moreover, the Productivization Law suspended all conflicting legislation for a period of two years, which allowed legal and private persons involved in the decision-making and implementation of the processes to be exempt from public investigation.[342] Although a large portion of the capital generated would be returned to state organizations, the processes were extremely opaque due to the legal immunity of the executors. Hence, these procedures could, for instance, suspend the 1987 Law on Irreplaceable Treasures that makes the sale of nationally significant cultural properties subject to parliamentary approval.[343] While the 1987 law on *nafayes* was frequently breached in the past, public discussions and legal actions against such violations were not explicitly prohibited before. After the implementation of the Productivization Law, experts could only stand by and witness the acts of impunity in the two-year period.

---

341   Somayyeh Hasanlu, 'Pardebardari Az Yak Ettefagh Dar Baft-e Shiraz [Uncovering an Event in the Historic Shiraz]', *ISNA*, 14 June 2022, isna.ir/xdLQ8W.
342   Ibid., para. 5.
343   Parliament of Iran, 'Ghanoon-e Mohasebat-e Omumi-e Keshvar [The Public Audit Act]'.

Urban heritage in academic discourse and the public sphere: A journey from the 2010s to 2022

For decades, both academic and non-academic government entities sought to codify urban planning for historic cities. This involved the deliberations concerning a potential nationwide framework that would act as a basis for drafting legally binding guidelines tailored to historic cities. After the Fifth National Development Plan (2011–2015),[344] the MRUD and the ICHHTO, along with the latter's university partners, conducted a baseline study to develop guidelines for planning historic cities. Part of this study was published in a book that examined the administrative and legal background of preservation in Iranian cities and advocated for a national charter that took into account the cultural, social, economic, and administrative aspects of urban conservation.[345] The authors suggested that a national charter, if accepted by all experts involved, could be a basis for drafting legally binding guidelines for historic cities.

About a decade before the aforementioned publication, Falamaki had already been commissioned by the MRUD to develop a national charter for conservation in the urban context.[346] Yet, despite the extensive scholarly work done to translate international concepts, an agreement was not reached concerning terms such as 'urban conservation', 'restoration', 'rehabilitation', 'regeneration', or 'authenticity' and 'integrity'.[347] The lack of a common language and the disciplinary divide between the experts was also evident at academic or political events I

---

344 Parliament of Iran, 'Ghanun-e Barnamey-e Panjom-e Tose-Ey-e Eghtesadi, Ejtemai va Farhangi-e Jomhuriy-e Eslami-e Iran [The Law of the Fifth Plan of Economic, Social and Cultural Development of Islamic Republic of Iran]'.
345 Mohammadmoradi, Amirkabirian, and Abdi Ardakani, *Revitalisation of Historic Urban Fabrics (a Review of Experiences)*.
346 M. Mansour Falamaki, *Nazariyehi Bar Manshur-e Maremmat-e Shahri [An Essay on Urban Restoration Charter]* (Tehran: MRUD, 2008).
347 Fieldnotes of the panel discussions (one and two) of officials and academics such as M. Talebian, P. Hanachi, S. M. Beheshti Shirazi, A. Mohammadmoradi, Z. Nikzad, A. Gholinejad Pirbazari, and others at the First National Symposium on Conservation and Management of Urban Heritage, organized by the Research

attended. These events tend to represent the standpoint of one disciplinary group. When different fields come together, urban planners are likely to accuse conservationists of reducing complex urban areas to a group of historic buildings, while conservationists accuse planners of neglecting cultural and historical significance.[348]

Although common ground is critical for urban heritage planning, a national charter would only be beneficial if it can be enforced. And, this would only be possible in a system that respected the rule of law. Of the 29 conservation experts I interviewed, many believe that theoretical concepts endorsed in legal documents and official project reports are often disregarded in practice due to economic constraints and corrupt bureaucratic processes. Thus, although legally binding cultural heritage and urban planning documents are undoubtedly a crucial step towards the territorialization of urban conservation in Iran, they have failed to carry sufficient weight in many of the struggles discussed.

This fact may not be straightforwardly discussed in scholarly publications, but in less formal settings, namely at public events, in newsletters, and on social media, the academic and professional community have shown that they are aware of the underlying problem. The frequent changes in governmental policy due to the constant struggle between political factions, the private or institutional mishandling of urban resources, and the lack of will for conservation throughout the governmental system were among the issues that—while not reflected in scholarly publications—were frequently discussed during my fieldwork.[349]

Center of the Ministry of Cultural Heritage and Tourism, Tehran, February 12–13, 2022.

348 For instance: The expert meeting on experiences of writing guidelines for historic fabrics, organized by Tehran Municipality, Mehraban Historic House, Tehran, 27.1.2020; The First National Symposium on Conservation and Management of Urban Heritage, organized by the Research Center of the Ministry of Cultural Heritage and Tourism, Tehran, February 12–13, 2022;

349 Fieldnotes at: the First National Symposium on Conservation and Management of Urban Heritage, organized by the Research Center of the Ministry of Cultural Heritage and Tourism, Tehran, February 12–13, 2022; Online Seminar on The Ro-

As mentioned, in Iran, public opinion on conservation and urban heritage planning has been historically led by architects, conservationists, and planners. In recent years, criticism in the public sphere has gone beyond complaints about the destruction of historic places and has been directed against systematic corruption and mismanagement. Given that such criticism comes at a price, I have noticed a spectrum of directness in the commentary. At the more conservative end, there are lectures and interviews of former government officials who are now academics and NGO directors, and at the other—more outspoken—end, public outcry on social media.

Some, like Mehdi Hodjat, the head of ICOMOS-Iran, who believes that a conservative "Revolutionary spirit"[350] would work better in Iran, have preferred the carefully worded and secretive 1980s-style critique behind closed doors.[351] Considering the politicized nature of NGOs in Iran, similar bodies have also preferred to work behind the scenes. The act of regarding public criticism as unnecessary and preferring hushed resolutions within organizations is consistent with Herzfeld's notion of cultural intimacy.[352] When I asked a member of Docomomo-Iran[353] about the reason for the institute's conservative public stance, he replied that NGOs in Iran are usually headed by influential officials, which gives them prestige on the one hand and makes them vulnerable on the

---

le of International Organizations in Conservation of Cultural Heritage with Emphasis on Architectural and Urban Heritage,18 April, 2021, organized by NGO of Conservators; Seminar on Contemporary Architecture and Question of Intangible Cultural Heritage, 30 May 2021, organized by the Intangible Cultural Heritage Centre-Tehran, Ministry of Cultural Heritage.

350 'In Conversation with Mehdi Hodjat (TV Show)', *Dastkhat* (Tehran: IRIB-Channel 5, 5 July 2021).
351 'ICOMOS-Iran Meeting, Field Notes: Tehran va Darvazehayash Be Ravayat-e Asnad-e Tasviri Tarikhi [Tehran and Its Gates According to Historical Pictorial Evidence].' (Tehran, 21 May 2022).
352 Herzfeld, 'The European Crisis and Cultural Intimacy'.
353 The International Committee for Documentation and Conservation of Buildings, Sites and Neighbourhoods of the Modern Movement.

other.³⁵⁴ Taking a bold position could even lead to the suspension of such organizations.

Between the two extremes of the mentioned spectrum, some actors who are not part of the government have preferred to join pro-reform administrative and academic assemblage in the hopes of making a difference. They have led campaigns in Tehran, for example, to regain access to the Urban Dialogue House or to enforce restrictions on density selling in the historic districts, or to pedestrianize historic streets.

A few academics have openly spoken of the "systematic looting", practiced by "hubristic authorities".³⁵⁵ Or they have called for "the punishment of the greedy", arguing that "this is not a conservation issue, but an issue of injustice" against rentier-based foundations.³⁵⁶ To avoid being labelled Islamophobic, such activists have sought the support of the clergy or found theological justifications for their arguments in favour of conservation. For example, one conservation architect sought the support of a clergyman to align the theological understanding of social welfare with Lefebvre's concept of the "right to the city"³⁵⁷ to argue against the shrine development project in Shiraz.³⁵⁸

---

354   Interview on 17 July 2021 via Skype.
355   *Roundtable: Be Bahaneh-Ye Tose'e-Ye Haram City Center Misazand/ Az Tamallok-e 8 Milliun Tomani Ta Forush-e Maghaber-e 1 Miliard Tomani [Construction of a City Center Under the Pretext of Shrine Development/Land Acquisition for 8 Million Tomans per Square Meter and Its Sale for 1 Billion Tomans as Graves.].*
356   'Public Discussion: Esfahan-e Faryad, Ba Mozuiyat-e Ehdas-e Mehvar-e Aghanoorollah Najafi [on the CConstruction of Aghanoorollah-e Najafi Street]' (Isfahan: Ivan Cultural Group, 8 December 2019), Fieldnotes.
357   See for example: Mark Purcell, 'Excavating Lefebvre: The Right to the City and Its Urban Politics of the Inhabitant', *GeoJournal* 58, no. 2 (2002): 99–108.
358   Ali Hojjatoleslam Elahi Khorasani and M. Mehdi Kalantari, 'Instagram Live Field Notes: Takhrib-e Baft-e Shiraz va Tose'e-Ye Haram-e Shahecheragh Az Manzar-e Fegh-e Eslami [Demolition of the Historical Urban Fabric of Shiraz and Development of the Shahecheragh Shrine From an Islamic Theological Perspective].' (Student Association for Architecture, Conservation and Planning., 3 August 2022).

Figure 30: ICOMOS-Iran public meeting on tourism

Author, 2022

Figure 31: Public meeting organized by Ivan Cultural Group in Isfahan

© Ivan, 2019

Observing the interaction of the general public with urban heritage

The attitude of the general public toward urban heritage policies is, above all, reflected in the number of court cases against heritage authorities.[359] Nevertheless, as Falamaki once said, the livelihood of people in historic cities, like everyone else's, depends on the economic fluctuations of the property market.[360] Indeed, the public are neither inherently vandals nor lovers of historic buildings. My field research in Tehran[361] and in the Tabriz Bazaar[362] confirms that people tend to be sympathetic to conservation, especially when it does not come at a high cost to them. This sympathy may have various psychological and social motives.[363] Or, as David Lowenthal said, "people tend to yearn for the past out of frustration with their present".[364] Similarly, sociologist Mohammad Fazeli argued that Iranian society's nostalgia for the past is a result of frustration due to being overburdened by accumulated unresolved socioeconomic and cultural problems.[365]

Following the inclusion of the Trans-Iranian Railway on the World Heritage List, Instagram users argued that the project was not an

---

359 Judiciary Research Institute-Iran, *Malekiyat-e Khosusi Ya Manfaat-e Omumi?: Naghd-e Raviye Shoabe Divane Edalat-e Edari Piramun-e Ebtal-e Tasmim-e Sazman-e Miras-e Farhangi va Tarikhi Dar Fehrest-e Athar-e Melli [Private Property or Public Interest? A Critique of the Administrative Court Branches' Procedure Regarding the Annulment of the Cultural Heritage Organization's Decision in the Listing of National Monuments]*.

360 Falamaki, 'Ayandeh-Ye Baft-Ha-Ye Shahri-Ye Tarikhi-Ye Iran: Padideh-Ha va Badil-Ha [The Future of Urban Historic Fabrics in Iran: Phenomena and Alternatives]'.

361 See Part Two.

362 Yadollahi, 'The Iranian Bazaar as a Public Place: A Reintegrative Approach and a Method Applied towards the Case Study of the Tabriz Bazaar'.

363 Jeremy C Wells, 'The Affect of Old Places: Exploring the Dimensions of Place Attachment and Senescent Environments', in *Place Meaning and Attachment* (Routledge, 2020), 1–15.

364 David Lowenthal, 'The Heritage Crusade and Its Contradictions', *Giving Preservation a History: Histories of Historic Preservation in the United States*, 2004,19–43.

365 Fazeli, *Iran Bar Labe-Ye Tigh, Goftar-Ha-Ye Jameshenasi-Ye Siyasi va Siyasat-e Omumi [Iran, on the Edge of the Blade Essays on Political Sociology and Public Policy]*.

achievement of the Islamic Republic, but of the Pahlavi era, with social media comments like "Reza Shah, God bless your soul" and pictures showing the Shah supervising the railroad project or opening stations.

Figure 32: A frequently shared photograph of Reza Shah, which gained significant traction on social media after the Trans-Iranian Railway was added to the World Heritage List. The image captures Reza Shah and his son, the Crown Prince, framed within a train window in 1932.[366]

The cannon firing ceremony near Azadi Tower (Shahyad) on Nowruz 1400 (21 March 2021) evoked a similar reaction from the public. The ceremony was organized by the Municipality of Tehran and the military. Beheshti Shirazi, the former Director of the ICHO and former advisor to the municipality, had co-authored a book on the tradition of cannon firing associated with the Pearl Cannon in late Qajar Tehran as a symbol of

---

366 'Be Bahaneh-Ye 81 Salegi-Ye Rah-e Ahan [On the Occasion of the 81st Anniversary of the National Railroads]', *Tinnews*, 26 August 2019, https://www.tinn.ir/fa/tiny/news-195131.

hope for progress and victory.³⁶⁷ By suggesting that Iranians were on the way to solving their problems, he and his co-authors linked the symbolism of the Pearl Cannon to the hope of a successful nuclear agreement by the reformist government.³⁶⁸ Although Beheshti's role (if any) in the 2021 ceremony remains unclear, his approach to the tradition of cannon firing provides a perspective on the event organized by the (then) pro-reform municipality. On Instagram, Javadi Yeganeh, an official at the Ministry of Culture and Islamic Guidance, posted a video of the ceremony, saying that the municipality and the army wanted to revive a forgotten historical tradition of Tehran.³⁶⁹

Meanwhile, on Instagram and Twitter, there was a range of reactions to the news. Some sympathized with reviving a Qajar tradition, posting pictures of women wearing Qajar-style chadors, and writing, "I feel like this is the year 1299 Hijri".³⁷⁰ Concerned that the cannon would damage the Azadi Tower, some wrote in mainstream newspapers that it would be appropriate to fire a cannon not in Azadi but in a Qajar square in Tehran where cannon firing was practiced in the past.³⁷¹ Some said that the organizers would not mind destroying the Pahlavi heritage (the Shahyad or Azadi tower). And several users took advantage of the online publicity surrounding the subject to express their anger at the incompetence and mismanagement of the IRGC, which had caused a disaster a year earlier. Recalling the downing of Flight 752, which killed all 176 passengers on 8 January 2020,³⁷² they addressed the organizers: "Be careful, the cannons

---

367 Seyyed Mohammad Beheshti Shirazi, Elnaz Najjar Najafi, and Behnam Abutorabian, *Sheikh-e Bahai va Toop-e Morvarid [Sheikh Baha'i and the Pearl Cannon]* (Tehran: Rozaneh, n.d.).
368 Ibid.
369 https://www.instagram.com/tv/CMpeXh5pfCx/?utm_source=ig_web_copy_link (accessed on March 22, 2021)
370 In the Islamic lunar calendar, 1881.
371 Fatemeh Karimi, 'Tarak-Ha-Ye Jadid Tasir-e Shelik-e Toop Tahvil-e Sal Ru-Ye Borj-e Azadi? [New Cracks, the Impact of Cannon Fire on the Azadi Tower?]', *Mehr News Agency*, 28 March 2021, mehrnews.com/xV27b.
372 For details see: Jeff Yaworski, 'The Downing of Ukraine International Airlines Flight 752: Factual Analysis' (Global Affairs Canada, 24 January 2021), https://w

could accidentally be war cannons", or "Be careful that you don't accidentally shoot down a plane", or "What if (another) 'human error' happens", or "If the IRGC is going to shoot, people in the Azadi neighbourhood should be careful, what can you do if they say the gunman made a mistake?".

In a country like Iran, where almost every aspect of citizens' daily lives is militarized and politicized, people tend to take any news, including news about heritage, as an occasion for political confrontation. Instagram users' conversations with Mehdi Hajati, a former member of Shiraz City Council who campaigned against the shrine construction project in 2018, shows that people tend to place heritage concerns within a larger political framework. For instance, in response to Hajati's call to resume the campaign against the project in 2022, one user posted:

I don't think our problem nowadays is limited to the demolition of the historic city... everything has become a confrontation of the nation with the state, a confrontation over the hijab, social freedom and citizenship, economic inflation, poverty, and mismanagement of the natural environment; This has become a battlefield and we should not give up fighting.[373]

Following the 2022 'Woman, Life, Freedom' uprising and in the face of increasing public discontent expressed on social media, the Islamic Parliament proposed criminalizing public criticism against the state.[374] Furthermore, the purge process that began in state organizations and universities brought to mind the atmosphere that prevailed after the 1979 Revolution and following the arrival of the hardline government in 2005.

---

ww.international.gc.ca/gac-amc/publications/flight-vol-ps752/factual_analysis-analyse_faits.aspx?lang=eng.

373 https://www.instagram.com/p/CaFDFSogTty/?utm_source=ig_web_copy_link (accessed 11 March 2022)

374 See: Mohammad Najmi, 'Moraghebe Ezhar-e Nazar-Hayetan Bashid [Watch Your Mouth]', *Etemad Newspaper*, 26 January 2023, https://www.etemadonline.com/tiny/news-593602.

Part Two

Assembling urban heritage in Tehran: Collecting heritage fragments here and there

An introduction to Tehran's historic centre and its spatial-economic setting

Historical and natural sites of touristic and cultural value located within the metropolitan area of Tehran all play a role in the city's socio-spatial urban heritage planning.[1] In this book, I mainly focus on the city centre because of the high density of listed areas[2] and its complex spatial-economic setting that makes it a convenient case for analyzing urban heritage policy and practice in an Iranian metropolis. In addition, this area is home to nationally significant sites that are tied to Iran's political history, notably following the Constitutional Revolution. The approximately 2250-hectare area, located in the current municipal Districts 11 and 12, is identified by policy documents as the historical centre of Tehran, covering the city's development trajectories of the 16th-century Safavid and the 19th-century Qajar periods (Figure 33).

1　According to Tehran's 2007 Master Plan. See: Institute for Research and Preparation of Urban Development Plans of Tehran, 'Tarh-e Rahbordi-Sakhtari-Ye Tose va Omran-e Shahr-e Tehran (Tarh-e Jame Tehran 1386) [Strategic-Structural Plan for the Development of the City of Tehran (Master Plan 2007)]' (MRUD, 2007).

2　In addition to individual monuments, large areas such as the bazaar complex (listed since 1977), the Oudlajan Quarter (listed since 2006) and the Arg Quarter (listed since 2007) are protected by national heritage laws.

Figure 33: The location of the Safavid (red) and Qajar (blue) boundaries in the 1967 development plan of Tehran (yellow)[3]

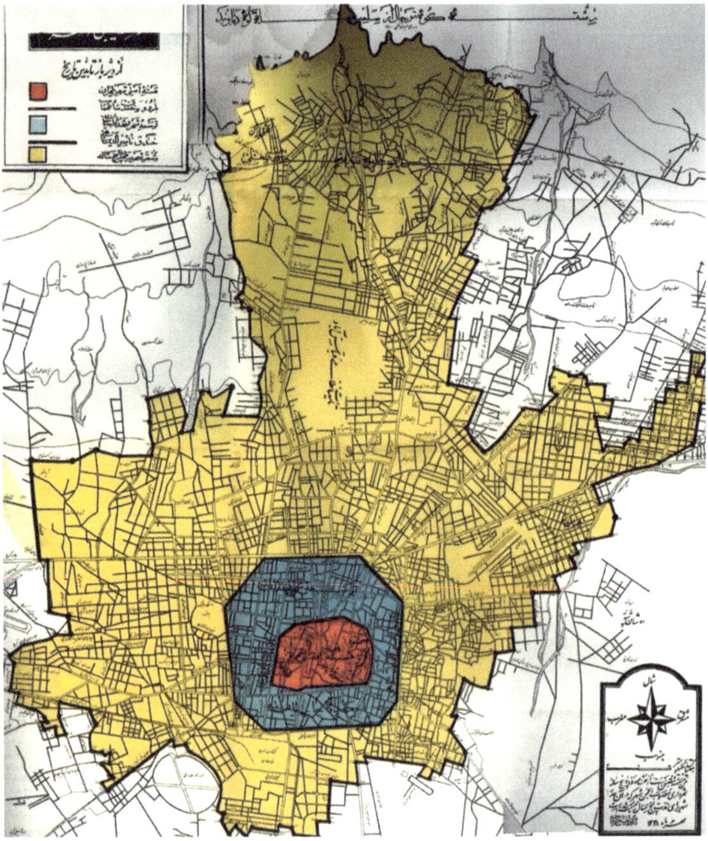

---

3   Reza Shirazian, *Tehran Negari; Bank-e Naghsheh-Ha va Anavin-e Makani-e Tehran-e Ghadim* [Documentation of Tehran; Database of Maps and Place Names of the Old Tehran] (Tehran: Dastan, 2017), 512.

Tehran's first Master Plan[4] and the debates among experts in the early reflect the concerns planners had as early as the 1960s about the future of housing and preservation in the historic city centre.1970s.[5] The underregulated and construction-driven post-Revolutionary policies in Tehran had not been able to overcome the city's long-standing issues.[6] Similarly, neither the pre-Revolutionary modernization projects, nor the Islamic Revolutionary promises for social justice and reform could address the unresolved historical problems of the city centre.[7] In an effort to avoid immediate political and economic risks associated with making concrete decisions for the area, policymakers in Tehran have tended to prevaricate on the issues until they have to be dealt with by future administrations.[8]

The literature on these issues inevitably lands on the dominant actor of the city centre, the Grand Bazaar. As early as the 1970s, scholars warned that the shopping malls mushrooming around the bazaar and the underground railway planned at the time would only aggravate the area's infrastructural precarity.[9] Yet, the decaying and overburdened

---

4   Abdolaziz Farmanfarmaian and Victor Groen Institute, 'Master Plan of Tehran' (Sazman-e Barnameh va Budgeh, 1968).
5   For instance see the proceedings of the Second Symposium of Iranian Architecture-Tehran, 1973: Art and Architecture, *Art and Architecture*, 3–65.
6   Ali Madanipour, 'Urban Planning and Development in Tehran', *Urbanization and the Iranian Revolution* 23, no. 6 (1 December 2006): 433–38, doi:10.1016/j.cities.2006.08.002.
7   Ali Madanipour, *Tehran: The Making of a Metropolis*, World Cities Series (Chichester: John Wiley, 1998); Kian Tajbakhsh, 'The Political Economy of Fiscal Decentralization under the Islamic Republic of Iran', *The Muslim World* 111, no. 1 (2021): 113–37.
8   See, for example, the report prepared by an interdisciplinary team of faculty members at the University of Tehran: Mohammadali Kamrava et al., *Barresi-Ye Tarh-Ha-Ye Nosazi-Ye Baft-e Farsoodeh-Ye Tehran Da Panjah Sal-e Gozashteh [An Overview Of Renovation Projects In Tehran's Decaying Urban Fabric Over The Past Fifty Years]* (Tehran: University of Tehran, Department of Applied Research, 2011).
9   Kazem Vadie, 'Bazaar Dar Baft-e Novin-e Shahri [Bazaar in the Modern Urban Fabric]', in *Avalin Seminar-e Maremat-e Banaha va Sharhay-e Tarikhi: Vojud va Ayandeye Marakez-e Maskuni-e Tarikhi[The First Seminar on the Conservation of Historic*

bazaar in the heart of the city centre continued to expand to take more warehouse and workshop space from its surrounding neighbourhoods. Pointing to the lack of maintenance of the city centre infrastructure (sewage system, electricity, gas, etc.), experts warned that the bazaar and its surroundings had become a time bomb, particularly given the likelihood of the next sizeable earthquake.[10]

Following a fire in the Grand Bazaar in February 2022, former municipal officials, planners, sociologists, and guild representatives discussed how risk preparedness in the bazaar relies on complex spatial politics involving local and national government and para-governmental agencies (*bonyads*), the Awqaf Organization, and the guilds who own a significant share of the religious and commercial units in the bazaar and the city centre.[11]

The historically established influence of the bazaar on national politics,[12] and particularly in the capital,[13] tends to make municipal authorities indulgent when it comes to negotiating space and mobility with those who work in and around it. The spatial politics in the Tehran Bazaar cannot be equated with those of other historical bazaars such as the Tabriz Bazaar, mainly because of the former's political importance. Perhaps this is the reason why the pre- and post-Revolutionary conservation plans for Tehran Bazaar have never materialized,[14] although

---

Cities and Towns: The Existence and Future of Historical Residential Centres], ed. M. Mansour Falamaki (Tehran: University of Tehran, 1971), 89–93.

10   Japan International Cooperation Agency and Tehran Disaster Mitigation and Management Center, 'The Comprehensive Master Plan Study on Urban Seismic Disaster Prevention and Management for the Greater Tehran Area', JICA, 2005.

11   Sociologist, Mohammad Fazeli, guild representative of Tehran Bazaar, Abdollah Esfandyar, former Mayor of Municipal District 12, Alimohammad Saadati, and others were among the speakers at the Clubhouse room for 'Marg Ya Zendegi-e Bazaar-e Tehran' [The Death or Life of the Tehran Bazaar] on 17 February 2022.

12   On the historical background of the bazaar's political alliances in Iran, see: Ashraf, 'Bazaar-Mosque Alliance: The Social Basis of Revolts and Revolutions'.

13   Arang Keshavarzian, *Bazaar and State in Iran: The Politics of the Tehran Marketplace*, vol. 26 (Cambridge University Press, 2007).

14   For instance, the plan proposed by: Ayatollah Zadeh Shirazi et al., 'Samandehi-e Bazaar-e Tehran [The Improvement of the Tehran Bazaar]'.

several state-funded research projects have investigated socio-spatial issues in the area.[15]

My experience walking through Baharestan, Sangeladge, and Oudlajan, areas adjacent to the bazaar, was quite similar. The fenced walls and covered entrances with half-destroyed historic brickwork and covered windows indicate neglected or abandoned houses, warehouses or workshops, some of which were illegal according to local residents. Flyers on the walls also describe common functions for these buildings: "Beginner and professional stickers and shoemakers sought", "Full-time employee with a motorbike wanted", "Skilled workers wanted for wax carving and welding", or "This property (a caravanserai) is for sale". Abandoned usually due to unresolved legal issues, these structures also served as shelters for the homeless, indicated by the scorch marks along the walls. Some buildings, made of materials you could easily knock a hole through, were still inhabited by groups of homeless people. In heavy rain, the softened mud brick structures made it even easier to enter the houses. During the COVID-19 crisis, illegal occupation increased due to the lockdowns, which led to a decrease in on-site monitoring. The frequency of the signs described gradually decreased the further away one walked from the bazaar, and so did the car traffic and the density of motorbikes parked on pedestrian paths (See Figure 34).

---

15 Some of the comprehensive examples of such research projects are: Piran, *Az Shoma Harekat Az Khoda Barekat, Tose'e-Ye Mosharekat Mabna va Mosharekat Mehvar Dar Iran: Mored-e Tehran [God Helps Those Who Help Themselves: Participatory Local Development in Iran: The Case of Tehran]*; Kamrava et al., *Barresi-Ye Tarh-Ha-Ye Nosazi-Ye Baft-e Farsoodeh-Ye Tehran Da Panjah Sal-e Gozashteh [An Overview Of Renovation Projects In Tehran's Decaying Urban Fabric Over The Past Fifty Years]*; Hajaliakbari and Shafie, *Tose-Ye Mahalli: Chaharchoobi Bara-Ye Mahalleh-Ha-Ye Nakaramad [Neighborhood Development: A Framework for Dysfunctional Neighborhoods]*.

Figure 34: The spatial-economic setting of the historic centre of Tehran[16]

16 The map is constructed upon foundational Google Earth imagery (© 2023 Airbus and © 2023 Maxar Technologies) and represents a broad qualitative assessment by the author, intended to elucidate concepts within this book. The evaluation draws from the subsequent sources: Paramadan Engineers Municipality of Tehran, 'Bayaniyeh va sanad-e rahbordi-e modiriyat va hefazat-e baft va banahay-e tarikhi-farhangi-e Tehran [Declaration and strategic document of the management and conservation of the historic-cultural fabric of Tehran]' (Paramadan Engineers, 2014); Bavand Consulting Engineers, 'The Detailed Plan of Tehran's 12th District' (Tehran: Tehran Urban Research and Planning Centre, 2006), Tehran Urban Research and Planning Centre; Institute for Research and Preparation of Urban Development Plans of Tehran, 'Tarh-e Rahbordi-Sakhtari-Ye Tose va Omran-e Shahr-e Tehran (Tarh-e Jame Tehran 1386) [Strategic-Structural Plan for the Development of the City of Tehran (Master Plan 2007)]'.

Assembling urban heritage in Tehran: Collecting heritage fragments here and there 153

Figure 35: The fading remains of a once stately entrance to a historic house in Oudlajan, now under the pressure of the bustling bazaar

Author, 2021

Short stories around renewal, beautification, and place-making in Tehran's historic centre

Urban renewal

Post-Revolutionary urban renewal policy and practice in Tehran continued the course of the 1960s urban modernization projects.[17] Navab was the first large-scale urban renewal project undertaken by the municipality under the state's post-war reconstruction policies in the 1990s.[18] The project brought high financial revenues to the municipality—who could no longer rely on state funding following the post-war decentralization policies—and encouraged further redevelopment ambitions in the city centre.[19] In addition to large-scale projects such as Navab, smaller private redevelopment projects in Tehran's decaying areas such as the city centre also proliferated. Private investors with enough redevelopment capital would put together two or more small properties to develop residential units. Those who did not have the capital would have to stay in the decaying buildings or, in case their property fell under a public project, sell their land to the state, usually at a low price.[20] Whatever the case, the municipality became the primary beneficiary by making property investments or selling urban density to private investors. As

---

17 See: Madanipour, *Tehran: The Making of a Metropolis.*
18 The project revolved around the construction of a new highway that provided a rapid connection between the central and northern districts of the city. Although the Navab project was not located in the historic zone (near its western borders), it has generally influenced urban regeneration practice in Tehran.
19 Ali Madanipour, 'City Profile: Tehran', *Cities* 16, no. 1 (1999): 57–65.
20 Piran conducted field research on the social and economic consequences of such top-down redevelopment policies. See: Piran, *Az Shoma Harekat Az Khoda Barekat, Tose'e-Ye Mosharekat Mabna va Mosharekat Mehvar Dar Iran: Mored-e Tehran [God Helps Those Who Help Themselves: Participatory Local Development in Iran: The Case of Tehran].*

a result, projects like Navab were widely criticized for being socially unjust.[21]

The Oudlajan neighbourhood in the eastern part of Qajar Tehran in particular became a point of contention regarding municipal redevelopment and heritage ambitions. The neighbourhood saw the initial resurgence of heritage activism against top-down urban renewal projects in the 1970s,[22] and has stood as a crucial focal point for numerous urban conservation plans. The dissertation records of Tehran and Isfahan universities since the 1980s show a relatively consistent scholarly interest in this topic, which is addressed as a problem of urban design, urban renewal, urban landscape, and urban regeneration [*bazafarini-ye shahri*]. Pointing to the depth of Oudlajan's socio-spatial dilemma, the mayor of Tehran's District 12 once said in a public meeting: "If we don't save the residential areas in the city centre now, they will be like Oudlajan in ten years".[23]

When an urban conservation specialist I spoke with in Tehran said that roughly half of the professors she knew had already worked on Oudlajan-related projects, she was not exaggerating the amount of academic work in the area. So, why did these studies and plans all fail? Some have concluded that it is a cultural problem—primarily the public's lack of interest in and sense of belonging to the historic city.[24] To that end, many

---

21   Many have argued that it led to substantial changes in the historically evolved social, physical, and functional structure of several neighbourhoods that were affected. See: Madanipour, 'City Profile: Tehran'; Piran, *Az Shoma Harekat Az Khoda Barekat, Tose'e-Ye Mosharekat Mabna va Mosharekat Mehvar Dar Iran: Morede Tehran [God Helps Those Who Help Themselves: Participatory Local Development in Iran: The Case of Tehran]*; H Bahrainy and B Aminzadeh, 'Evaluation of Navab Regeneration Project in Central Tehran, Iran', 2007.

22   See an interview with Keyvan Khosravani, an architect who drew attention to the historic value of the neighbourhood in the 1970s: Keyvan Salimi, 'A Stitch to the Earth, Meeting Keyvan Khosravani', *Memar*, no. 113 (2019): 4–9.

23   On June 3, 2021, a live broadcast took place on the public Instagram account of the District 12 Mayor (asaadati.tehran). The livestream was titled 'Ten Weeks in Tehran's Historic Core' [Dah hafte dar ghalb-e tarikhi Tehran].

24   Naimeh Rezaei and Pirooz Hanachi, 'Mahaleh-Ye Oudlajan, Miras-e Shahri Dar Taghabol Bein-e Sonnat va Modernite [The Oudlajan Neighbourhood, Urban

academics have proposed awareness-raising campaigns to change society's attitude toward cultural heritage. Others have proposed participatory strategies to improve social cooperation with urban conservation projects in the neighbourhood.[25]

I engaged in informal discussions, both online and offline, where stakeholders like heritage activists and professionals were more open and transparent in sharing their insights. These settings provided a platform for candid revelations that diverged from the content typically found in official project reports and academic papers.

In conversations about Oudlajan, almost everyone (journalists, community professionals, artists, conservationists, and scholars) spoke of a deadlock between the heritage authorities, the Municipality, and a bonyad.[26] They narrated the same sequence of events, pointing to an economic interplay of key political actors in the city centre. The story starts in the mid-2000s, when the municipality drew homeless people to certain parts of the neighbourhood and proceeded to reduce those areas' municipal sanitation services. Then, a wave of media reports drew attention to the rising rates of crime in the neighbourhood. Consequently, the police and the municipality, in cooperation with a para-governmental organization called Bonyad-e Taavon-e Naja cleared and acquired an area of about two hectares, intending to use the plot for a joint redevelopment project. Before the project took off, heritage authorities placed the entire area under heritage protection in 2006,

---

Heritage at the Crossroads of Tradition and Modernity]', *Journal of Iranian Architecture Studies* 4, no. 7 (2015): 19–34.

25 Seyyed Mohsen Habibi and Mehran Foroughifa, 'Finding Some Strategies for Encouraging People to Cooperate in Urban Renovation Plans Based on the Game Theory', *Honar-Ha-Ye-Ziba: Memary Va Shahrsazi* 18, no. 19 (2013): 5–14, doi:10.22059/jfaup.2013.51677.

26 Also reflected in the newspapers. For instance see: Maryam Atyabi, 'Bazarcheh-Ye Oudlajan Dar Khatar Ast//Bonyad-e Tavon-e Naja Baft-e Tarikhi Ra Takhrib Mikonad [Oudlajan Bazaar Is in Danger // Bonyad-e Taavon-e Naja Is Destroying the Historical Fabric]', *Honarnews*, 10 December 2011, https://honarnews.com/vdccosq1.2bq1i8laa2.html; ISNA, 'Amadand, Kharab Kardand, va Raftand … [They Came, Destroyed and Left …]', *ISNA*, 25 June 2016, isna.ir/x9QrCW.

halting the project. However, lacking the economic resources necessary for the preservation of such a large urban area and constrained by decentralization policies, the heritage authorities could do nothing else with the site and abandoned it. The fate of the contested land has been on hold to this day.

I visited a part of the demolished area in Borazjan (a smaller neighbourhood within Oudlajan). The atmosphere was intimidating and poetic at the same time. Mirza Hamid's[27] murals on the remains of the demolished houses and the chimneys and staircases exposed to the open space invoked an artistic and melancholic ambience. But, one couldn't help thinking about the residents of the neighbouring houses.

Figure 36: Aerial photos of Oudlajan in 1956*, 2000, and 2007**

*© Iranian Cartography Organization **Google Earth, © 2021 Maxar Technologies

The recent measures of the municipality to clean up the space and organize public events in it have been positive but have had only a short-term impact. I visited the neighbourhood three times—in 2019, 2021, and 2022—and each time noticed the same neglected parking lot, garbage dump, and homeless shelter. Discarded syringes and burn

---

27   Mizra Hamid is a pseudonym for the artist, who is also known as the 'Banksy of Iran'. Mirza's red earth murals can be found on historic and modern buildings in Tehran. His works are popular in historic neighbourhoods such as Oudlajan and Sangeladge. A collection of his works has been exhibited at the New Gallery in Hudson, New York.

marks on the walls hinted strongly at the activities that happen every night.

The social injustice and devastating effects of the demolition and subsequent neglect, which created a wasteland in the middle of the neighbourhood, have been widely criticized. It is worth mentioning that several synagogues and historic houses of Tehran's Jewish community were among the demolished buildings. At the same time, the peaceful coexistence of diverse religious groups with the rich and the poor in Oudlajan has been promoted in heritage projects as the mark of historically developed social tolerance in Tehran. Considering the contradictions, the municipality's heritage projects in other parts of Oudlajan could be seen as an effort to restore its damaged political image after the demolition.

Figure 37: The Borazjan area in Oudlajan and Mirza Hamid's murals on its ruins

Author, 2022

Participatory urban renewal

The emergence of a rhetoric of participatory urban governance in Tehran's urban renewal practices can be attributed to the political reform during the 2010s and the subsequent increase in academic literature influenced by it.[28] The large-scale regeneration project undertaken in the Siroos neighbourhood, a constituent of the historic Chalmeidan Quarter, stands as a less than successful instance showcasing the reformists' application of participatory governance discourse. Despite the pronounced focus on inclusivity, the Siroos regeneration initiative encountered public disapproval due to its parallels with the Navab renovation project. Some felt that since the main investors in the project were linked to or favoured by the state, there was no genuine participation of the private sector and local communities in the project.[29] Residents of the area interviewed in a documentary film said that the authorities acquired as much land as possible and did not start the redevelopment project until more than a decade later when property prices reached a much higher level.[30] I visited the finished project in October 2021. As reported by the newspapers, the result was not so different from that of the Navab project.

From 2013 to 2021, Tehran's urban administration demonstrated a strong focus on reform, much like the government in power during that period. The city administration implemented various measures

---

28 Abbas Akhundi et al., 'Hakemiyat-e Shar-Mantagheh-Ye Tehran: Chlesh-Ha va Ravand-Ha [The Governance Of The City-Region Of Tehran: Challenges And Processes]', *Honar-Ha-Ye-Ziba* 29, no. 29 (2007); Abbas Akhundi and Nasser Barkpour, 'Rahbord-Ha-Ye Esteghrar-e Nezam-e Hokmravai Dar Mantagheh-Ye Kalanshahr-e Tehran [Strategies For Establishing A Governance System In Greater Tehran]', *Rahbord* 57, no. 19 (2010): 297–324.
29 For example, the Director of the Urban Regeneration Company and Vice President of the Parliament's Urban Development Commission discussed this on a television programme. 'Bazafarini Mavane va Rahkar-Ha [Bazafarini Obstacles and Solutions]'.
30 *Siroos, Bood-o-Nabood-e Yek Mahalleh [Siroos,The Existence and Inexistence of a Neighbourhood]*, Documentary, (2014).

to control density selling, advocating for a sustainable long-term perspective in utilizing the city's available space and resources.[31] Some members of the city council attempted to restore urban density regulations in accordance with the approved 2007 Master Plan, reversing the changes made by the conservative government in 2012.[32] Furthermore, in 2014, the reformist Ministry of Roads and Urban Development (MRUD) collaborated with the Tehran City Council to further tighten density regulations. Additionally, heritage authorities introduced new regulations for buffer zones, imposing restrictions on redevelopment activities in historic and touristic areas.

Unsurprisingly, the density restrictions and heritage buffer zone regulations had adverse economic effects on private, state, and parastatal property owners. However, with the subsequent return of the conservative government and city council, conditions began to relax for those property owners who were dissatisfied with the stringent rules. In 2021, the mayor declared that the detailed plan should be reevaluated

---

31   The arguments of key members of the city council and municipality were published in a special issue by the reformist magazine, Shargh at the end of the reformist city administration. Shargh Newspaper, *Vijhenameh-Ye Shahr va Shora-3 [Special Issue: City and Shura-3]*, ed. Mehdi Rahmanian (Tehran: Entekhab Resaneh, n.d.).

32   See: Saied Manavi, 'Taghirat-e Tarh-e Tafsili Che Bar Sar-e Tehran Avard? [What Damage Did the Changes to the Detailed Plan Do to Tehran?]', *Payam-e Ma Newspaper*, 15 May 2021, https://payamema.ir/p/55395; 'Taghirat-e Ahmadinejadi Tarh-e Tafsili-Ye Tehran Hazf Mishavad [Ahmadinejadian Changes in the Tehran Detailed Plan Will Be Removed]', *Alef Analytical News Association*, 5 May 2014; 'Joziyat-e Sabegheh-Ye Tarh-e Tafsili Dar Samaneh-Ye "Tehran-e Man" Montasher Mishavad [Extensive Background Information on the Detailed Plan Was Published in the "Tehran Man" Online System]', *ISNA*, 27 June 2020, isna.ir/xdG7HY.

Assembling urban heritage in Tehran: Collecting heritage fragments here and there   161

and revised.³³ In social media³⁴ and conservative newspapers³⁵ city authorities talked about facilitating private investments in urban renewal, launching mega projects in cooperation with IRGC's Khatam-al Anbia Construction Headquarters, and improving living conditions in decaying neighbourhoods. These fluctuating policy changes are reflected in the inharmonious facades and skyline of the city centre (see Figure 38).

Figure 38: A skyline view of Sangeladge looking west from the rooftop of the Hajrajabali Mosque

Author, 2021

---

33 Fars, 'Zakani: Tarh-e Tafsili Bayad Bazbini Shavad [Zakani: The Detailed Plan Should Be Revised]', *Fars News Agency*, 2 January 2023, http://fna.ir/1u5oxj.
34 For instance, on the City Council's official Instagram page: http://instagram.com/shorashahrtehran
35 Fars, 'Az Tashil-e Sakht-o-Saz Dar Tehran Ta Raf-e Mozal-e Baft-e Farsoodeh [From Facilitating Construction in Tehran to Solving the Problem of Decayed Urban Built Environment]', *Fars News Agency*, 13 September 2021, http://fna.ir/3p3q6.

Perhaps the most positive demonstration of the participation discourse in Tehran was the establishment of Urban Renewal Offices (NDOs) in 2010, which acted as mediators between the neighbourhood residents, municipalities, and state organizations.[36] NDOs played an increasingly active role on-site and on social media, particularly in facilitating post-2013 urban regeneration policies. Part of their duty was to provide neighbourhood development documents as locally informed planning guidelines to be used by the municipal authorities.

To acquire an in-depth understanding of the socio-spatial dynamics in city centre of Tehran, I communicated with the local NDOs and joined some of their civic participation projects. As part of their work involved producing web content and communicating with potential participants through social media, I also followed their activities on Instagram between 2019 and 2022.

In my fieldwork, I witnessed that the trust and cooperation between the local communities and the young professionals working in the NDOs were remarkably higher than any measure of trust gained by government officials. I also found that to gain locals' trust, NDOs sometimes had to blur their boundaries with the officials. During instances of citizen participation initiatives, when NDOs interacted with volunteers, they did not always explicitly mention their administrative affiliation with the municipality.

The very fact that NDO workers did not look like government officials (who, in Iran, follow certain dress codes and administrative protocols) helped them more easily approach and collaborate with ordinary people. Also, the location of the offices (close to the homes or properties of the people concerned) and the absence of formal visitation protocols made NDOs seem more approachable compared to government

---

36 Theorized and implemented in Tehran before the reformist administration, for instance by: Piran, *Az Shoma Harekat Az Khoda Barekat, Tose'e-Ye Mosharekat Mabna va Mosharekat Mehvar Dar Iran: Mored-e Tehran [God Helps Those Who Help Themselves: Participatory Local Development in Iran: The Case of Tehran]*; Hajaliakbari and Shafie, *Tose-Ye Mahalli: Chaharchoobi Bara-Ye Mahalleh-Ha-Ye Nakaramad [Neighborhood Development: A Framework for Dysfunctional Neighborhoods]*.

organizations. It could be argued that the municipality had made a deliberate—and clever—decision in involving NDOs at the intersection between official urban policymaking and everyday urban life. Among actor-network-inspired policy researchers, such strategies apply human and non-human boundary objects to reduce tension between two or more divergent environments.[37] Here, the offices were robust and adaptable enough to be able to function within both the municipal bureaucracy and everyday urban life.

Some NDO professionals even took on additional tasks of their own volition, without the support of further municipal funding.[38] Volunteers similarly became involved in these municipality projects, whether out of personal, professional, or economic interest, or to network with influential municipal authorities. The content produced and collected through the aforementioned activities, as well as the full-time on-site observations of the NDOs were captured in a database at the Urban Renovation Organization of the Municipality of Tehran.

In Sangeladge, for instance, I had the opportunity to witness the progress of the NDO in building a community-based organization (CBO). Through the office, a congenial online/offline environment was created for artists, Instagram influencers, journalists, filmmakers, property agents, investors, tour guides, and skilled volunteers from different fields to address the problems of Sangeladge. Groups connected in diverse ways with the neighbourhood participated, for example, in developing tourism, finding investors to conserve and reuse abandoned historic buildings, and solving environmental problems associated with waste management and the shoe and goldsmith workshops. Following

---

37   Star and Griesemer, 'Institutional Ecology,Translations' and Boundary Objects: Amateurs and Professionals in Berkeley's Museum of Vertebrate Zoology, 1907–39'; Fox-Rogers and Murphy, 'Informal Strategies of Power in the Local Planning System'.

38   Hajaliakbari and Shafie, *Tose-Ye Mahalli: Chaharchoobi Bara-Ye Mahalleh-Ha-Ye Nakaramad [Neighborhood Development: A Framework for Dysfunctional Neighborhoods]*.

the administrative changes in 2021 and after the termination of the office's activities, Sangeladge's CBO remained active.

Not surprisingly, this effective strategy of NDO deployment remained episodic. The NDOs' activities declined after the change in administration in August 2021. The neighbourhood development documents they produced were not applied, at least not during my fieldwork in Tehran. Some of the staff told me in informal conversations that the NDOs' activities were not considered necessary and did not fit into the ideological framework of the new administration. Two of the professionals I met while on the field emigrated to Europe by the end of my research.

Beautification

Progressive decentralization, especially following the Third Development Plan (2000–2005),[39] extended the remit of municipalities to conservation and heritage reuse projects; these had previously been a primary responsibility of the state, namely heritage authorities. Municipal authorities thus set up the Renovation Organization [Sazman-e Nosazi] and Beautification Organization [Sazman-e Zibasazi], which became key implementors of cultural heritage projects. These heritage projects, which were mostly limited in scale and budget, were not as economically rewarding for municipalities as urban renewal projects. However, their value emerged as property investments, considering the annual inflation of land prices and the increase in property values after beautification and reuse.

It has been argued that, in essence, the Renovation Organization focused primarily on urban renewal that was in economic and disciplinary

---

39 Parliament of Iran, 'Ghanun-e Barnamey-e Sevom-e Tose-Ey-e Eghtesadi, Ejtemai va Farhangi-e Jomhuriy-e Eslami-e Iran [The Law of the Third Plan of the Economic, Social and Cultural Development of Islamic Republic of Iran]'.

contradiction to conservation.⁴⁰ The involvement of the Beautification Organization in conservation projects was also criticized for its lack of expertise in cultural heritage. Critics argued that the organization's primary focus on beautifying public spaces and parks through a variety of urban artworks and murals could lead to superficial improvements to places of historic significance.⁴¹ Nevertheless, by the 2010s, as the aforementioned organizations gained experience in adaptive reuse of historic buildings and beautification of historic streets, and established professional links with conservation practitioners, they became key implementing bodies of heritage planning in Tehran. Consequently, the reuse and beautification of historic areas in Tehran was implemented by the administrative and executive structures of urban renewal. Although conservation professionals worked on these municipal projects and heritage legislation was applied to listed buildings, the individuals I interviewed believed that the projects undertaken by the municipality differed from those of Ministry of Cultural Heritage in terms of working procedures and disciplinary and economic preferences. More precisely, although the Ministry of Cultural Heritage was tasked with tourism responsibilities, its legal and administrative structure, since the early 1980s, had been predominantly influenced by archaeology, art history, architectural history, and conservation. On the other hand, the Beautification Organization had its origins in urban renewal, which uses visual urban art and beautification strategies for tourism development and city marketing.

Urban renewal and beautification were tightly interdependent also in terms of the physical marks they left on the city centre.

The renewal projects and the decades-long neglect of the city's built heritage left the municipality with too little to build on when urban heritage planning became a priority. Although planning in a heritage desert was challenging, the municipality's interventions in Tehran showed the

---

40 Mohammadreza Azimi and Yashar Soltani, 'Shahrdari Ba Miras-e Tarikhi Che Khahad Kard? [What Will the Municipality Do with Historic Heritage?]' (Bahamestan-Majma-e Hagh-e Bar Shahr, Tehran, 22 July 2015).
41 Ibid.

potential for rather free-handed beautification and stylistic reconstruction, creating an urban heritage tailored to the spatial-economic structures and political discourses already in place.

The municipality's heritage-related projects in the city centre began in the mid-2000s with the façade beautification programme. An early example that technically informed later projects was carried out in the Marvi commercial axis. The solutions used in Marvi, for instance hiding electricity cables behind structurally independent brick claddings decorated with tile and brickwork,[42] can be found in almost all later projects, for example, in Oudlajan, Khayam, and Naser Khosrow.[43]

---

42 Somayeh Fadaee Nejad, 'Behsazi, Nosazi va Bazsazi Dar Gozar-e Marvi [Rehabilitation, Renovation, and Reconstruction in Marvi Street]', *Honar-Ha-Ye-Ziba* 32, no. 32 (2007): 61–71.

43 Pirooz Hanachi, Mozaffar Farhang, and Yaser Jafari, 'Hefazat Az Manzar-e Shahri Tarikhi Da Jedareh-Ha-Ye Tejari; Tabyin-e Chaharchoob-e Modakheleh Bar Mabnay-e Tajarob-e Behsazi Khiyaban-e Naser Khosrow Tehran [Protection of the Historic Townscape on Commercial Facades; Outlining the Intervention Framework Based on the Experience of the Redevelopment of Naser Khosrow Street in Tehran.]', *Motaleate Shahr-e Irani-Eslami* 8, no. 32 (2018): 77–88.

Figure 39: Examples of beautification works in Marvi, the bazaar neighbourhood, and Khayam Street

Author, 2020–2022

Oudlajan Cluster Bazaar

A widely discussed beautification and reuse project was carried out in the Oudlajan Cluster Bazaar, located in the north of the Grand Bazaar. In 2012, heritage authorities, the District 12 municipality, and shopkeepers signed an agreement to create a traditional handicraft bazaar in the physically declining area. This locale had hitherto accommodated wholesalers and warehouses primarily dealing in construction materials. A byproduct of this agreement was the obligate transformation of the existing businesses, compelling them to alter the nature of their activities. The municipality and University of Tehran supported this agreement and the NDO coordinated the project. The promise that the project would be completed within six months encouraged shopkeepers to participate in the project. Although the formal plan seemed coherent, the project dragged on for more than four years.

I interviewed a professional involved in the project and had the opportunity to talk informally with other practitioners engaged in the project at the events I attended in Tehran. They all put the delays down to the administrative changes in the middle of the project resulting from the major political changes at the ICHHTO in 2012–13. The new heritage authorities had not wanted to continue the project, as one interviewee suggested, "because of a lack of personal interest", which points to the familiar pattern of substantial policy changes during transition periods between administrations.

In the new administration, the project was finished with a beautification of a back alley of the cluster bazaar that also functioned as a storage and workshop area serving the bazaar. The authorities had asked the consultants to quickly design a traditional façade, since much of the original was missing. The project aimed to limit motorbike and vehicle access to the beautified area.

When I visited in 2021 and 2022, motorbikes were still occupying the walkways in the back alley. The handicraft bazaar was not functioning as effectively as the rest of the business district. As per my conversations with the shopkeepers, they were struggling to keep their businesses open. They attributed this struggle to the implementation of a top-down reuse policy for the restored shops, which focused on promoting the sale of traditional handicrafts. The area had failed to gain recognition as a prime location for purchasing high-quality crafts due to its historical role as a wholesale centre for building materials over the course of many decades. One shopkeeper displayed the legally allowed handicraft products in the window and stored the illegal but profit-making wholesale PVC products behind the counter. Some did not even bother to hide the products they were actually selling. Another owner was looking for somebody who could take over the shop and turn it into a handicraft shop.

Figure 40: Oudlajan Cluster Bazaar

Author, 2021

Between 2019 and 2021, I participated in a series of public meetings called 'Wednesdays of Tehran', where projects enacted during the reformist city administration were discussed by experts, celebrities, and the public. The meetings were usually held at the municipality-owned Book Garden in Tehran's Abbasabad district. An event on Oudlajan was organized on Wednesday evening, 15 January 2020, at Sarvestan Hall, a public area near the bookshops. Visitors could join in the discussions or listen to the lectures. Uncharacteristically for a lecture organized by the municipality, the atmosphere was casual and with limited official control.

Figure 41: The beautified back alley of the Oudlajan Cluster Bazaar

Author, 2022

To start, a short film was screened featuring interviews with Pirooz Hanachi, Professor of Conservation at the University of Tehran and Mayor of Tehran during the reformist city council's term, as well as members of the city council, such as Masjed Jamei, former Minister of Islamic Guidance during Khatami's administration. The film gave a positive impression of the Cluster Bazaar project's results, focusing on tourism, and ended with the song 'Khushe-chin' sung by the pre-Revolutionary singer Gholam-Hossein Banan.[44] I noticed that the song was also used at other events organized by the reformist urban government. The lyrics and melody evoked hope and motivation for the development of Iran despite the challenges the country faced. The event,

---

44   Gholam-Hossein Banan (1911–1986) was a prominent Iranian performer and musician. He is considered a pioneer of modern Iranian pop music, which blends elements of traditional Iranian music with Western pop music and jazz.

its location, and its visual and pictorial elements echoed reformist hopes for progress, cultural tolerance, participation, and Islamic democracy.

After the film screening and lectures, some among the audience criticized the project's outcome—a structurally independent brick cladding in front of the existing facades—for being merely decorative and having no social impact. As mentioned, the municipality had experimented with a similar brick cladding solution in previous beautification projects. The consulting planner responded to the critique by arguing that the structure was safer in the event of an earthquake, improved the skyline, and did not interfere with ongoing commercial activities: "We [intentionally] put makeup on this decaying alley in the hope of triggering a change that would stop the blind progression of the bazaar toward other parts of the neighbourhood".

When I asked him about the participatory decision-making that the project claimed, he replied, "our target group for the survey included renowned experts, as well as public and private project stakeholders". Since most of the residents of the neighbourhood have moved out, the property owners are mostly merchants from the bazaar or the owners of the warehouses, workshops and wholesale businesses associated with the bazaar. A filmmaker, who was also invited as a speaker answered the question in a more direct manner, saying: "We all look at the city from above, like Naser al-Din Shah, who viewed this area from the top of Shamsol-emareh".[45] Hinting at the autocratic approach to planning, he said "things had not changed much" since the reign of the Qajar Shah. After these statements, the planner ultimately admitted that building a decorative facade was not necessarily ideal: "We planners and architects are not the ones who set the rules of the game. So what remains up to us is the physical space."

---

45 The Qajar ruler, Naser al-Din Shah, oversaw the construction of Shamsol-emareh, Naser Khosrow Street, and the expansion of Tehran in the mid to late 19th century, solidifying its status as the capital of Iran.

Enghelab-e Eslami Street

One of the early examples of beautification projects in Tehran was carried out by the municipality on Enghelab-e Eslami Street (Enghelab Street).[46] After the establishment of Tehran University in 1939 on this street, located along the northern walls of Qajar City, the area gradually became an intellectual and political hub, housing the City Theatre, several cinemas, publishing houses, bookshops, and cafes.

The beautification project in Enghelab Street included the section between the Ferdowsi and Valia-e Asr junctions, which featured facades typical of Tehran's modern architecture during the 1960s and 1970s. The project drew on the expertise of sociologists, planners, and architects provided by an NDO who worked on the ground with local stakeholders. Relatively speaking, due to the recent construction of buildings in the area and its location at the edge of the Grand Bazaar's sphere of influence, the street had managed to retain some of its residential character. As a result, the Enghelab Street area attracted many private investors for the adaptive reuse of historic buildings compared to the neighbourhoods adjacent to the bazaar. According to the project consultant, new startups and several galleries and cafes were drawn to the area following its beautification and the cafes that already existed on the street since the 1960s became more popular.[47]

As we shall see next, beautification, adaptive reuse, and storytelling have been key themes in Tehran's heritage planning policy over the past decade. And city tours, reuse projects, and beautification measures have materially and discursively included urban spaces like Enghelab in Tehran's urban heritage assemblage. On one of my revisits to Enghelab, I accompanied two young planners from an NDO in Oudlajan who guided a series of city tours called 'Strolling through the veins of

---

46 Before the 1979 Revolution, Enghelab Street was known as Shah Reza Street. The English translation of its present name is "Islamic Revolution Street".
47 Amirmasoud Anoushfar, Maremmat-e Shahri, Nemooneh-ye Khiyaban-e Enghelab [Urban Conservation for the Case of Enghelab Street], interview by Fereydoon Farahani, Instagram Live, 3 March 2021, Anjoman-e Mafakher-e Memari Iran.

Tehran'. When I talked to one of the guides, she said that the idea for the tour came from her master's thesis on strolling in the city, based on Walter Benjamin's concept of the flâneur.[48] She saw the tours as a multipurpose opportunity to pursue her passion for documenting and drawing attention to graffiti art and modern architecture in Tehran. Here we see how ideas and resources from the academic, administrative, and professional realms of urban heritage can come together to assemble and present urban heritage to the public.

But urban heritage assemblage does not always unfold as planned. As demonstrated in the case of the Transnational Railway, or the Azadi Tower, the public is likely to make unpredictable contributions to the urban heritage assemblage. The visitors, of whom only one was not from Tehran, seemed to experience a nostalgic and artistic joy as they passed the corrected facades and were occasionally surprised by the metal tiles on the pedestrian walkways, decorated with heart motifs and lyrics of Mohamadreza Shajarian's popular songs.[49] At certain points during the stroll, tourists recalled and spoke of the November 2019 events[50] in Enghelab and the Girls of Revolution Street.[51] You cannot walk past France Pastry in Enghelab without recalling the public image of the first Girl

---

48 The concept is for example discussed in: Sven Birkerts, 'Walter Benjamin, Flâneur: A Flânerie', *The Iowa Review*, 1982, 164–79; Keith Tester, *The Flâneur* (London: Psychology Press, 1994).

49 Prominent vocalist, Mohammad-Reza Shajarian (1940–2020) was an inspiring figure in the pro-democracy movement in Iran, including the Green Movement of 2009.

50 In November 2019, protests broke out across Iran after the government announced a sudden increase in the price of petrol. The government responded to the protests with a violent crackdown and an internet blackout.

51 See: Faegheh Shirazi, 'The Veiling Issue in 20th Century Iran in Fashion and Society, Religion, and Government', *Religions* 10, no. 8 (2019): 461; '"Girls of Revolution St" Protest Ignites Debate on Iran's Compulsory Hijab', *Center for Human Rights in Iran*, 2018, https://iranhumanrights.org/2018/01/girls-of-revolution-st-protest-ignites-debate-on-irans-compulsory-hijab/.

of the Revolution, Vida Movahed, standing on an electricity box right in front of the bakery with her headscarf tied to a stick.[52]

Like the general public, the interplay between political groups and the unfolding urban heritage is also unpredictable. In August 2021, during the tense presidential election, news and online media reported that France Pastry had been sued for using Pahlavi-era symbols on its pastry boxes.[53] Following the news, pictures of the boxes, especially those showing the Fifth Festival of Arts of 1969 in Shiraz appeared on social media. Some immediately interpreted the event as a sign of the government's fear of reviving any memory of the pre-Revolutionary period. Some posted Vida Movahed's picture in front of the bakery, saying the place was a trigger for distant and near memories. Twitter users posted pictures of pastry boxes depicting a sweepstake by the Iran National Company giving a Paykan buyer a free supply of petrol for seven years, linking it to the crackdown on protests against the November 2019 petrol price increases.[54] Some argued that the temporary closure had nothing to do with the boxes, but was due to the bakery's failure to follow COVID-19 hygiene protocols. Regardless of the actual underlying cause of the event, opinions on social media portrayed a struggle for public space, a struggle that turned brutal in the autumn of 2022.

---

52 RFE/RL's Radio Farda, 'Iconic Iranian Antihijab Protester Jailed For One Year; Human Rights Lawyer's 13-Year Sentence Upheld', *Radio Farda*, 2017, https://www.rferl.org/a/iconic-iranian-antihijab-protester-jailed-for-year/29879887.html.

53 'Qanadi-Ye Faranse Az Mohr-Omum-e Maghazeh-Ye Khod Be Dalil-e 'Tarh-e Ruy-e Jabe'-Hayash Khabar Dar [The French Confectionery Announced the Seal of Its Shop Because of the 'Design on the Boxes It Used']', *BBC-Persian*, 21 August 2021, shorturl.at/jxQ39.

54 In the 1960s, Iran National introduced the Paykan, which was the first domestically manufactured car in Iran.

Figure 42: Examples of beautified facades in Enghelab Street

Author, 2020

Figure 43: Top, Vida Movahed in front of France Pastry[55] and bottom, the bakery

Author, 2022

---

55 Shirazi, 'The Veiling Issue in 20th Century Iran in Fashion and Society, Religion, and Government'.

Figure 44: Tiles with lyrics from Shajarian's popular songs

Author, 2020

Figure 45: Two visitors sitting in front of the bakery's picture of the 1960s

Author, 2022

Figure 46: Pastry boxes of France Pastry, left: Fifth Shiraz Art Festival⁵⁶ and right: Reconstruction of the censored box based on the original posters of the festival

Author, 2023

An unfulfilled place-making dream: Reading Henri Lefebvre and Jane Jacobs in Tehran

Founded in 1851 by Amir Kabir, Darolfonun was a polytechnic college that not only initiated modern higher education in Iran but also played a vital role in the reform of the state apparatus by educating Iranian civil servants. Over a span exceeding ten years, diverse stakeholders, including heritage authorities, the Ministry of Education, Municipality of Tehran, and Iran's National Elites Foundation ⁵⁷(Bonyad-e Melli-e Nokhbegan), had been actively advocating for the formulation of a re-use policy for Darolfonun in alignment with their respective interests. In early 2020, as part of the ongoing struggle on the future use of Darolfonun, the Association of Iranian Architects organized an event called 'Darolfonun, an un-

---

56 'Shirini-Ye Faranse Polomp Shod [The French Pastry Was Sealed]', *Asrshahrvand*, accessed 3 September 2022, https://asrshahrvand.com/?p=283818.

57 National Elites Foundation is a governmental institution under the presidential office.

fulfilled dream' [*Darolfonun, royay-e natamam*].[58] In debating the future of the historic school,[59] leading members of ICOM-Iran and ICOMOS-Iran characterized it as a physical reminder of Qajar Chief Minister Mirza Taqi Khan Amirkabir's dream for state reform, which was disrupted after his assassination. While speakers felt that Amirkabir's plans failed because of his top-down approach to modernization and his neglect of tradition, the underlying struggle to effect any measure of reform in the current Islamic and tradition-oriented state was palpable between the lines. The speakers expressed the desire to preserve the building's identity as a school that would stimulate progressive change and provide an inclusive space for the broader civil society. In the following sections, we will see that the destiny of Tehran's reform-oriented urban assemblage was comparable to that of Darolfonun. Both endured as unfulfilled, half-realized dreams.

Urban heritage assemblage in Tehran, and particularly its place-making elements emerged on the existing administrative and spatial-economic structures of top-down urban renewal and beautification. When the renewal and beautification measures were about to turn into place-making, indicating the possibility of partial convergence with liberal and Western discourses, they were halted or reverted to a purely physically oriented renewal and beautification.

---

58 Seyyed Mohammad Beheshti, former head of the ICHO during President Khatami's term, and Seyyed Ahmad Mohit Tabatabai, Director of ICOM/Iran and former ICHO Deputy also during Khatami's term were two of the speakers. The meeting was organized on Wednesday, 8 January 2020 at Naqsh-e Jahan Art Research Centre, Tehran.
59 See: John Gurney and Negin Nabavi, 'Dār Al-Fonūn', *Encyclopædia Iranica* 6 (1993): 662–68.

During the mid-2010s, Tehran's urban development policy[60] began to prioritize the internationally recognized concept of Historic Urban Landscape (HUL), which incorporates social inclusion.[61] While the beautification approach of the municipality sought to engage stakeholders directly involved in the economic aspects of the projects, the new HUL-inspired urban regeneration projects claimed to reach out to broader social groups. Parallel to the progress of the urban regeneration discourse and HUL in 2010s, academic publications and translations of works on right to the city, walkability, and place-making increased.[62] Most scholarly works—including supervision of dissertations—were conducted by bureaucrat-academics affiliated with the Municipality of Tehran and the MRUD.

---

60   For instance in: Paramadan Engineers Municipality of Tehran, 'Bayaniyeh va sanad-e rahbordi-e modiriyat va hefazat-e baft va banahay-e tarikhi-farhangi-e Tehran [Declaration and strategic document of the management and conservation of the historic-cultural fabric of Tehran]' (Paramadan Engineers, 2014); Islamic City Council of Tehran, 'Barnameh-Ye Panjsaleh-Ye Sevom-e Tose-Ye Shar-e Tehran (1398–1402) [The Third Development Plan of Tehran (2019–2023)]' (Islamic City Council of Tehran, 2018), 46.

61   Tehran's official urban heritage planning policy (see the previous footnote) is strongly influenced by the discourse on Historic Urban Landscape. See: UNESCO, 'Recommendation on the Historic Urban Landscape'.

62   S. Mehdi Moini, 'Afzayesh-e Ghabeliyat-e Piyadehmadari, Gami Be Suy-e Shahri Ensani-Tar [Enhancing Walkability, a Step Towards a More Humane City]', *Honar-Ha-Ye-Ziba* 27, no. 27 (2006); S. Mehdi Moini, *Shahr-Ha-Ye Piyadehmadar [Walkable Cities]* (Tehran: Azarakhsh, 2011); Jan Gehl and Birgitte Svarre, *How to Study Public Life*, trans. Mohammad Saeid Izadi, Samaneh Mohammadi, and Samaneh Kheibari (Tehran: Elm-o-Sanat University Press, 2015); Roberts and Sykes, *Urban Regeneration: A Handbook*; Mohammad Saeid Izadi, 'Sokhan-e Modir Masoul: Tahaghogh-e Gofteman-e Hagh-e Bar Shahr, Shart-e Lazem-e Bazafarini-Ye Paydar [Editorial: The Realisation of the Right to the City Discourse Is the Prerequisite for Sustainable Urban Regeneration]', *HaftShahr* 4, no. 49–50 (2015): 2–3.

Tehran's Third Development Plan placed emphasis on place-making based on collective memory.[63] The assemblage of the policy along with human and non-human actors, including city council members,[64] bureaucrat-academics and their publications,[65] and public spaces in the city centre, sparked a series of formal and informal storytelling initiatives in Tehran.

For example, the city administration involved the neighbourhood councils[66] in events such as the 2019 'Story of Tehran' Festival, where citizens' memories of their neighbourhoods were collected and exhibited as a means of promoting social solidarity.[67] In the space created by

63   Islamic City Council of Tehran, 'Barnameh-Ye Panjsaleh-Ye Sevom-e Tose-Ye Shar-e Tehran (1398–1402) [The Third Development Plan of Tehran (2019–2023)]', para. 46.

64   Ahmad Masjedjamei, *Negahi Be Darvazeh Ghar [A Glimpse of the Darvazeh Ghar]* (Tehran: Sales, 2015); Ahmad Masjedjamei, *Jesm-o-Jan-e Shahr [The Body and Soul of the City]* (Tehran: Rozaneh, 2016).

65   Naser Takmil Homayoun, *Ruydad-Ha va Yadmanha-Ye Tarikhi-Ye Tehran, Az Darolkhelafeh-Ye Naseri Ta Piroozi-Ye Mashrooteh [Historical Events and Monuments in Tehran, from the Naseri Caliphate to the Victory of the Constitutional Revolution]* (Tehran: Cultural Research Bureau, 2015); Seyyed Mohammad Beheshti Shirazi, *Dastan-e Tehran [The Story of Tehran]* (Tehran: Cultural Research Bureau, 2016); Seyyed Mohammad Beheshti Shirazi, *Revitalisation of Tehran, Reflections on the Quality Improvement of Historic Fabric*, Tehran Pajhouhi (Tehran: Cultural Research Bureau, 2017); Seyyed Mohsen Habibi et al., *Khatereh-Ye Shahr, Bazkhani-Ye Sinematografik-e Shahr-e Irani: Dahe-Ha-Ye 1340–1350 [The Memory of the City, a Cinematographic Reencounter with the Iranian City: 1960s-1970s]* (Tehran: Nahid, 2014).

66   *Shorayari-ha* or Neighbourhood Councils operate under the City Council to assist and advise the City Council and the community. Tehran City Council, 'Eslah-e Mavaredi Az Mosavabeh-Ye Tashkil-e Anjoman-Ha-Ye Shorayari-Ye Shar-e Tehran [Amendment of Articles of the Decree on Establishment of Neighbourhood Councils in Tehran]', Pub. L. No. 2560 (2019).

67   As mentioned by a city council member in a meeting with neighbourhood councils. Tehran City Council, 'Ahmad Masjedjamei: Shahr Ra Ba Mosharekat-e Namayandegan-e Mahalat Edare Konim [Masjedjamei: Run the City with the Participation of Local Representatives]', *Councilorship Coordination Headquarters of Tehran Islamic City Council*, 2019, Content code: 4138.

municipality-organized events such as 'Wednesdays of Tehran', celebrities, authors, filmmakers, artists, planners, and architects gathered to discuss municipality projects. During such events, beautification projects were linked to nostalgic views of old Tehran, with its music, films, and history. Although the content presented by the organizers reflected the official communication strategies of the municipality, the selected venues and their atmosphere allowed some degree of informal and critical arguments by the speakers and the audience. I witnessed that at such events actors met and formed informal collaborations and friendships.

In addition, the Fifth and Sixth National Development Plans (effective between 2011–2021)[68] called on government organizations to consider social media and digital technologies in their management strategies. As a result, by the mid-2010s, entities such as the Municipality of Tehran, its sub-organizations, and NDOs had launched their Instagram pages.

In that period, the city administration focused on expanding public spaces and promoting vibrant nightlife in the city centre.[69] The slogan used was "Tehran: A city for all".[70] By the second half of the 2010s, concepts of storytelling and place-making were widely circulated in public and professional events throughout Tehran[71] as well as on Twitter, Insta-

---

68   Parliament of Iran, 'Ghanun-e Barnamey-e Panjom-e Tose-Ey-e Eghtesadi, Ejtemai va Farhangi-e Jomhuriy-e Eslami-e Iran [The Law of the Fifth Plan of Economic, Social and Cultural Development of Islamic Republic of Iran]'; Parliament of Iran, 'Ghanun-e Barnamey-e Sheshom-e Tose-Ey-e Eghtesadi, Ejtemai va Farhangi-e Jomhuriy-e Eslami-e Iran [The Law of the Sixth Plan of Economic, Social and Cultural Development of Islamic Republic of Iran]'.

69   Islamic City Council of Tehran, 'Barnameh-Ye Panjsaleh-Ye Sevom-e Tose-Ye Shar-e Tehran (1398–1402) [The Third Development Plan of Tehran (2019–2023)]', para. 47.

70   Islamic City Council of Tehran, 'Barnameh-Ye Dr. Hanachi [Dr. Hnachi's Program for Mayorship]' (Tehran, 29 April 2018), http://shora.tehran.ir/Portals/0/pdf/go zaresh dar sahn/برنامه دکتر حناچی.pdf.

71   The municipality has reported part of the mentioned debates: Public and International Relations Municipality of Tehran, 'Baztab-e Mehvar-Ha-Ye Goftemani-Ye Modiriyat-e Shahri Da Eghdamat-e Shahrdari-Ye Tehran (1396–1399) [Dis-

gram, and Telegram groups, which I observed during my fieldwork between 2019 and 2021. Tehrani professionals and civil society would talk about the ideas of Henri Lefebvre,[72] Jane Jacobs[73] and Jan Gehl[74] on place and place-making and how these could be translated in the city. The discussions took place for example on the Instagram pages of NDOs and city council members, as well as in the course of online and offline meetings about the recently pedestrianized streets of the city centre.

Considering that many authoritarian political systems favour control and supervision of NGOs, rather than eliminating them altogether, the aforementioned coordination between Tehran's civil society and the city administration is not an unexpected phenomenon.[75] At least during the years I followed the urban heritage assemblage in Tehran, civil society was restrained from exceeding the official policies of the reformist city administration. Civil society thus functioned in cooperation with the official urban politics.

The 2006 Detailed Plan of District 12 envisaged a pedestrian network (see Figure 47) in the city centre that would connect local tourist attractions, including monuments and museums.[76] As Izadi and members of the Tehran professional community who had been advocating

---

course Lines of Urban Management in the Tehran Municipality's Actions between 2017 and 2021]' (Tehran Picture Agency, 2021).
72 Henri Lefebvre and Donald Nicholson-Smith, *The Production of Space* (Wiley, 1991), https://books.google.de/books?id=SIXcnIoa4MwC.
73 Jane Jacobs, *The Death And life of Great American Cities* (New York: Vintage, 1961).
74 Jan Gehl, *Cities for People* (Island press, 2013).
75 David Lewis, 'Civil Society and the Authoritarian State: Cooperation, Contestation and Discourse', *Journal of Civil Society* 9, no. 3 (2013): 325–40.
76 Bavand Consulting Engineers, 'The Detailed Plan of Tehran's 12th District'.

for the project[77] explained at one of the public events,[78] the network would connect the bazaar and the already beautified areas such as Marvi, Naser Khosrow, and Panzdah-e Khordad streets with Si-e Tir, Bab-e Homayoun, Lalehzar, Toopkhaneh Square and Bagh-e Melli. The expanding spatial network would bring together municipal projects with the Tehran tourism sector, the Tehran researchers and historians, several of whom worked part-time in the tourism sector, the NDOs, and the food and leisure services.

Places like Si-e Tir and Bab-e Homayoun, which were originally popular spots for food carts or cafe-vans,[79] who used to inform their customers of their location via social media, gradually became 'food streets'[80] consisting of rows of food stalls that the municipality rented out to small businesses. These food streets received criticism on social media and in public events for undermining the historic value of the city

---

77   Launched in 2017, 'Taraneh-ye Tehran' was perhaps the largest and most active professional group, with more than 1,300 members ranging from students, journalists, architects, and planners from the private sector to (former) ministers and high-ranking heritage and municipal officials. I got to know this group through their campaign to save the Vartan House of Urban Dialogue and joined the Telegram group in December 2019. During my research stays in Tehran, I had the opportunity to attend their in-person meetings. Regular debates at the Vartan House declined due to the COVID-19 lockdowns and the closure of the Vartan House after the resignation of the MRUD minister. Following the political changes in 2021, the group continued its debates on Telegram. However, their links with the city administration decreased significantly.

78   29th Session of Wednesdays of Tehran, Book Garden, 1 January 2020

79   Hamshahri, 'Hoshdar Be Van-Kafe-Ha-Ye Tehran Ke Mojavez Nadarand: Sabr-e Maraje-e Ghanuni Hadi Darad [Warning To Tehran Café-Vans That Don't Have A Licence; Judicial Authorities' Patience Has A Limit]', *Hamshahrionline*, 2 June 2023, hamshahrionline.ir/x8jdG.

80   Amin Rahimi, 'Shabneshini Be Sarf-e Aramesh, Food Street-e Khiaban-e Si-e Tir Patogh-e Shabaneh Baray-Ye Khanevadeh-Ha [Night Stop For Recreation, The Food Street In Si Tir Street Is A Nightly Meeting Place For Families]', *Hamshahri*, 26 May 2018.

centre and causing environmental pollution affecting local residents and public buildings such as hospitals in the area.[81]

Yet, when the city council began to discuss a legal draft concerning the Utilization of Pedestrian Ways, it was met with heavy criticism.[82] The legislation granted the municipality the authority to regulate street vendors in public spaces and lease pedestrian walkways exclusively to qualified business owners. Some justifiably warned that the place-making assemblage was going to gentrify Tehran, arguing that the unsustainable density selling was not so different from selling the streets to the private sector (referring to the reformist city council's measures in limiting density selling on the one hand and passing the bill, on the other).[83]

In short, Tehran's tourism industry and the municipality were the outright winners of pedestrianization and beautification. To have a closer look at the relationships among the actors involved in Tehran's urban heritage assemblage, in addition to online ethnography, I participated in several city tours organized by individuals who collaborated with the city administration. The guides led tourists through the pedestrian areas to collect bits and pieces of the city centre's story linked to the museums and monuments along the way.

---

81 For example, the topic was discussed by Mohammad Saied Izadi, Zahra Taraneh Yalda and the audience in one of Tehran Wednesday events at Abbas Abad Book Garden on 20 October 2019. The same issues were underlined in an online event organized by the Association of Iranian Architects (Anjoman-e Mafakher-e Memari Iran) on 12 August 2020.

82 Tehran City Council, 'Gozaresh-e Tafsili Dar Khosus-e Layehe-Ye 'Tarh-e Bahrebardari Az Piadehro-Ha [Detailed Report on the Bill on the Utilization of Pedestrian Ways]' (Tehran Ciity Council-Archive, 2020).

83 See, for example, the arguments of civil activist M. Karim Asayesh and a former member of the reformist city council here: Sogol Danati, M. Karim Asayesh, and Zahra Nejadbahram, 'Dastandazi Be Piyadehro-Ha [Encroachment on Sidewalks]', *Payam-e Ma Newspaper*, 14 December 2020, 1900 edition, Encroachment on Sidewalks.

Figure 47: *The city centre's pedestrian network as outlined in the 2006 Detailed Plan of District 12*[84]

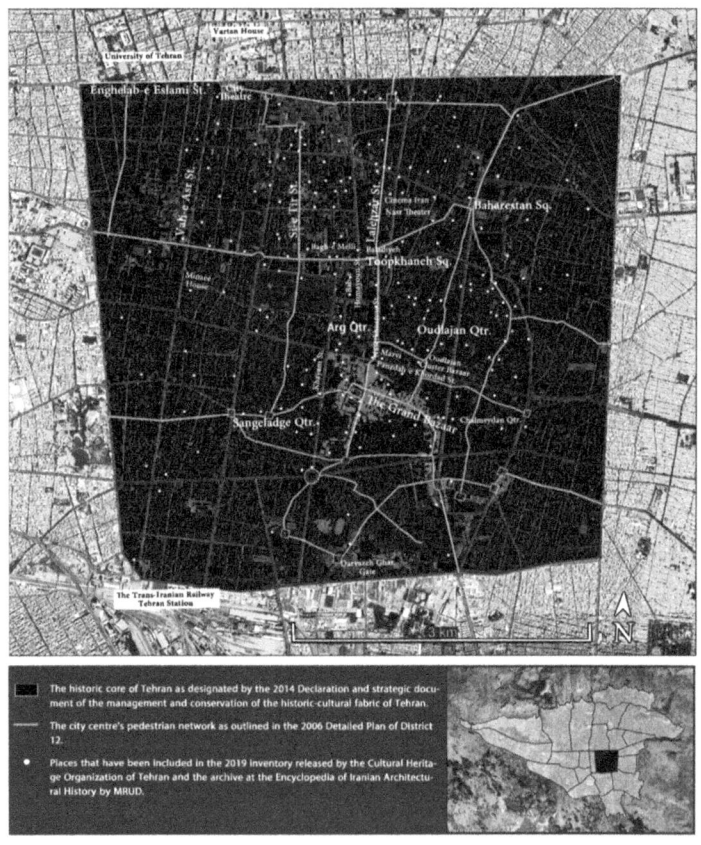

---

84 The map is created on foundational Google Earth imagery (© 2023 Airbus and © 2023 Maxar Technologies) and based on information provided by: Municipality of Tehran, 'Bayaniyeh va sanad-e rahbordi-e modiriyat va hefazat-e baft va banahay-e tarikhi-farhangi-e Tehran [Declaration and strategic document of the management and conservation of the historic-cultural fabric of Tehran]'; Bavand Consulting Engineers, 'The Detailed Plan of Tehran's 12th District'.

Figure 48: Food street in Bab-e Homayoun

Author, 2022

Whether or not they were aware of the official policy navigating storytelling in Tehran, young professionals working in the NDOs, historians, journalists, and architects mixed the official storytelling elements with their own professional and personal areas of interest. Some had a passion for modern architecture and graffiti art, others for Qajar history and architecture. In their informal interaction with the city and the visitors, most of whom were from Tehran, some pointed out places associated with taboo political events. Some organized tours around location tourism [*lokeyshen-gardi*] featured famous shooting locations of pre- and post-Revolutionary films and shows. Others used the tours to monitor and document buildings and to denounce possible damage or vandalism in newspapers and on social media.

Some tour guides, recognized as 'Tehran researchers'—and among them, a few that happen to operate nostalgic cafes and maintain popular Instagram pages—also actively participated in the cultural initiatives organized by the municipality. The city administration's collaboration with local private actors on such initiatives seemed quite consequential. However, what struck me as a native of Tehran was the unprecedented degree of synergy between official and non-official discursive and infrastructural urban elements in their collaboration.

I analyzed the content of the 'Tehranstories' Instagram account, which live-streamed programmes and cultural content for the municipality. Within the fusion of symbols communicated on the account, there was a blending of the official identity discourse with the memories of the ordinary public. On the one hand, the conservative narrative surrounding the war with Iraq in the 1980s intertwined with romantic allusions to the Qajar period, representing the reformist Islamic-Iranian identity discourse. The inclusion of the Golha music programme alongside the above content, on the other hand, tapped into the audience's nostalgic longing for the 1960s and 1970s.[85]

By examining the content of online communications, book publications, and newspaper interviews of the various actors involved—ranging from the city council to the municipality and its affiliated organizations, as well as tourism influencers—I sought to build a picture of the urban heritage model for Tehran they were collectively pursuing. In the urban heritage model that the reformists sought to establish, one could spot the unveiled female harpist of the Nasr Theatre in Lalehzar, an image of the Golha Orchestra with the female singer, Marziyeh[86] sitting in a corner, layered with officially approved icons such as veiled Qajar women and Morteza Ahmadi.[87] Under this model, municipality- and state-owned historic buildings and beautified public spaces in the city centre synergized with private tour agencies and nostalgic cafes. In this model of urban heritage, social media, NDOs, influencers, public events, music, and significant locations and monuments served as boundary objects that had the potential to partially alleviate the strained relationship between citizens and the government.

Similar to the strategy of deploying NDOs at the borders between the urban bureaucracy and everyday urban life, here, tangible and intangible objects were applied to glue together the deeply divided official and non-

---

85   For the history of the programmes see: Jane Lewisohn, 'Flowers of Persian Song and Music: Davud Pirniā and the Genesis of the Golhā Programs', *Journal of Persianate Studies* 1, no. 1 (2008): 79–101.
86   Marziyeh (1924–2010) iconic singer of the 1960s and 1970s.
87   Morteza Ahmadi (1924–2014), Tehranian folk music singer and actor.

official discourses. A wide range of actors participated in the urban heritage assemblage orchestrated by the city administration in accordance with their political affiliation, and the economic and spatial resources available to them.

However, the online content produced by individuals and groups with formal or informal relations with the municipality, as well as the spaces restored by the municipality, show a tendency towards tolerating specific historical periods more than others. As the central arena of Iran's political history since 1786, the capital offered the spatial and discursive possibilities for assembling an urban heritage that would focus on the Qajar[88] and Pahlavi[89] periods. Dealing with Iran's more recent past could put conservative factions of the government on edge. After all, as David Lowenthal noted, drawing on Sigmund Freud, we tend to admire our grandparents' relics while rejecting parental ones, perhaps because the immediate past could mean confronting an uncomfortable heritage.[90] Despite its monarchical identity, Tehran's Qajar background was remote enough to avoid constituting 'uncomfortable heritage'.[91] Instead, it offered traditional and religious features that fit within the framework of the overarching policy that called for the promotion of Islamic-Iranian architecture and urban planning.[92] In addition, the Constitutional Revolution conformed to both the Revolutionary and reformist identities of policymakers. Thus, one could say that the late

---

88 Rulers from 1794 to 1925.
89 Rulers from 1925 to 1979.
90 David Lowenthal, 'Past Time, Present Place: Landscape and Memory', *Geographical Review* 65, no. 1 (1975): 1–36, doi:10.2307/213831.
91 See: John Pendlebury, Yi-Wen Wang, and Andrew Law, 'Re-Using "Uncomfortable Heritage": The Case of the 1933 Building, Shanghai', *International Journal of Heritage Studies* 24, no. 3 (2018): 211–29.
92 Parliament of Iran, 'Ghanun-e Barnamey-e Panjom-e Tose-Ey-e Eghtesadi, Ejtemai va Farhangi-e Jomhuriy-e Eslami-e Iran [The Law of the Fifth Plan of Economic, Social and Cultural Development of Islamic Republic of Iran]'; High Council of Cultural Revolution and Ahmadinejad, 'Mosavabe-Ye Naghshe-Ye Mohandesi-Ye Farhangi-Ye Keshvar [Decree on the Cultural Engineering Map of the Country]'.

Qajar period, including the constitutional movements leading to the Constitutional Revolution until the Pahlavi rule could represent the least uncomfortable heritage for Tehran.

Figure 49: Instances of social media content within the sphere of boundary action, aiming to bridge the gap between collective memories and the established political narrative of Tehran's past [93]

---

[93] Figure 49 displays an assortment of screen captures sourced from public profiles of the Tehran City Council, District 12 Municipality of Tehran, the Vali-e Asr Street Museum, and the Tehranstories' page.

Assembling urban heritage in Tehran: Collecting heritage fragments here and there   191

On several occasions I observed art and architecture from the Qajar period revisited with a more empathetic perspective than the one offered by the modernist Pahlavi reading.[94] Some have seen the revisiting of Qajar architectural heritage as a way to undo the mistakes of the Pahlavis, who were believed to have neglected this period and erased it from Tehran's cityscape.[95] The topic was debated, for example in Telegram group discussions commenting on newspaper articles written by Ahmad Shah Qajar's granddaughter.[96] At professional and public events hosted at Qajar monuments such as the Darolfonun School[97] and the Et-

94 For instance, see: Beheshti Shirazi, *Revitalisation of Tehran, Reflections on the Quality Improvement of Historic Fabric*; Beheshti Shirazi, Najjar Najafi, and Abutorabian, *Sheikh-e Bahai va Toop-e Morvarid [Sheikh Baha'i and the Pearl Cannon]*; Seyyed Mohammad Beheshti Shirazi, 'Tafakor, Hoviyat, Madaniyat [Thought , Identity, Civilisation]', in *Atashgahi Dar Khab-e Atash-Ha [An Aperture To City Planning And Architecture In Iran, A Centennial Experience]*, ed. Ali A. Kiafar (Mashhad: Kasra, 2018), 126–56. The topic was also addressed in depth by Beheshti and Mohit-Tabatabai at 'Darolfonun, an unfulfilled dream', an event held in Tehran in January 2020 at Naqsh-e Jahan Art Research Center of ICOMOS in Tehran.
95 Mohsen Habibi, *Az Shar Ta Shahr [De La Cite a La Ville]* (Tehran: University of Tehran, 1996); Seyyed Mohsen Habibi, 'Shahr, Shahriyat, Shahrsazi Dar Iran [City, Urbanity, Urban Planning in Iran]', in *Atashgahi Dar Khab-e Atash-Ha [An Aperture To City Planning And Architecture In Iran, A Centennial Experience]* (Mashhad: Kasra, 2018), 279–316; Beheshti Shirazi, *Revitalisation of Tehran, Reflections on the Quality Improvement of Historic Fabric*; Hanachi, Diba, and Mahdavinejad, 'Hefazat va Tose'e Dar Iran [Conservation and Development in Iran]'; Sara Mahdizadeh and Pirooz Hanachi, 'The Role of Western Orientalists in Restoration of Historical Buildings during the Pahlavi Era, Iran (1925–1979)', *Honar-Ha-Ye-Ziba: Memary Va Shahrsazi* 21, no. 3 (2016): 5–14.
96 Iran, 'Qajariyeh Be Ravayat-e Tajrobeh/Maryam Farooqi Qajar, Naveh-Ye Ahmad Shah Qajar [Qajar by Experience/ Maryam Farooqi Qajar, Descendant of Ahmad Shah Qajar]', *Iran Newspaper*, 28 February 2019; Maryam Farouqi Qajar, 'Qajar Yek Khanevadeh Nist [Qajar Is Not a Family]', trans. Human Zalpour, *Iran Newspaper*, 24 February 2020.
97 Also mentioned by historians Farzaneh Ebrahimzadeh, who had already appeared as a speaker at events organized by the municipality, and Masud Tareh from the Centre for the Great Islamic Encyclopaedia (Centre for Iranian and Islamic Studies) at an event on 21 January 2020 on the history of education during the Qajar period at the Darolfonun school in Tehran.

tehadiyeh House,[98] Qajar history was mentioned together with the nostalgia of that period reflected in Ali Hatami's films and shows.[99] I could observe the same pattern on the margins of the official and unofficial realms where Tehran's Beautification Organization and the tourism sector interacted. On Instagram, at events such as 'Wednesdays of Tehran' and on city tours, the public was invited to view Tehran's Qajar legacy through a bias-free lens.

Figure 50: Posts of the official Instagram pages of the municipality and city council on reconstruction of demolished Qajar monuments

---

98   'Examining the Historical and Social Development of Tehran House in Dr Mansoureh Ettehadiyeh's Research on Tehran', an event organized by the Tehran Beautification Organization on 9 February 2020 at Ettehadiyeh House (Tehran House).

99   Iranian film director and screenwriter, known for portraying the Qajar period and the Constitutional Revolution of Iran in films and shows such as 'Hajji Washington' (1982), 'Kamalolmolk' (1984), 'Love Stricken' (1992), and 'Hezar Dastan' (1978 to 1987). He was criticized for blending and sugarcoating the uncomfortable Qajar history with a nostalgic narrative. See: Ramin S Khanjani, *Animating Eroded Landscapes: The Cinema of Ali Hatami* (H&S Media, 2014).

Toopkhaneh Square

The reconstruction of Qajar monuments that were destroyed by the Pahlavis is a physical testament to the mentioned policy of sanctioned nostalgia. Some of the city council's proposals, such as the stylistic reconstruction of Takiyeh-Dolat,[100] have remained ideas, but others such as Darvazeh Ghar, one of Tehran's historic gates, have been implemented. The stylistic reconstruction of Baladiyeh, the Qajar municipality building, was the largest and most discussed project of its kind in the city centre. Initiated in 2015, the reconstruction project had been under consideration since the mid-2000s, involving actors from the city administration and universities. In 2016, the municipality and stakeholders from the tourism sector started to promote the project through social media and at public events such as 'Wednesdays of Tehran'.[101]

The project partners used place-making and urban design criteria to justify rebuilding the demolished Qajar building, which aimed at correcting the square's broken geometry. In an Instagram livestream with Zahedi (a filmmaker), for example, the mayor of District 12 said that Baladiyeh defines the boundaries of the square and exemplifies the historical foundations of Tehran's cultural and urban management. In a podcast interview, Mokhtari Taleghani, a former heritage official and current senior advisor to the municipality, echoed a similar viewpoint, contending that the square's geometry was disrupted as a consequence of the demolition of the Baladiyeh and Telegrafkhaneh buildings.[102] According to Mokhtari Taleghani, the Pahlavi government removed Qajar traces such as the gates in Toopkhaneh as part of its beautification programme. Arguing that the reconstruction of Baladiyeh would correct the geometric structure of the square, he suggested that the

---

100 The Takiyeh-Dolat complex in Qajar Tehran was constructed in the mid-19th century as a place of mourning during the month of Muharram, which commemorates the martyrdom of Imam Hussein, the third Shia Imam.
101 The 16th meeting, on 2 October 2019.
102 Ramyar Manouchehrzaseh and Negin Firoozi, 'Meidan-e Toopkhaneh', Radio Nist, accessed 10 April 2022, http://radionist.com/podcasts/ep28-meydantoopkhaneh/.

Qajar Telegrafkhaneh should eventually be rebuilt to replace the existing telecommunications building, which dates back to the early 1970s.

Despite being produced by an independent cultural institute, the podcast adhered to the typical reformist approach to urban heritage. It incorporated interviews from various sources, including municipality advisors, the commissioned planning engineers, as well as academics, Tehran researchers, and social media influencers. The podcast also blended official and unofficial narratives of Tehran's heritage. On the one hand, it featured politically approved accounts of historical events, including the execution of Sheikh Fazlollah Nuri,[103] the demonstrations that sparked the 1979 Revolution, and the terrorist attack in Toopkaneh committed by the Mojahedin-e Khalgh in the early 1980s. On the other hand, memories of the period before the 1979 Revolution were also subtly brought up, with extracts from Radio Iran broadcasts, such as the patriotic song 'Ey Iran', being played in the background. [104]

Similarly, in a *Bukhara*-organized event[105] about Toopkhaneh, Hanachi referred to the documents published by MRUD, according to which Reza Shah intentionally removed reminders of the Qajars from the area. [106] By asking: "Which historical layer is authentic in terms of conservation?", he repeated a question that had already been discussed at the conservation programme of the University of Tehran about a

---

103 Sheikh Fazlollah Nuri (1843–1909), Shia cleric and political leader in the late Qajar period, was a supporter of the Constitution and at the same time an opponent of secularization and modernization.

104 'O Iran' is a song composed by Ruhollah Khaleqi to lyrics by Hossein Gol-e-Golab after the invasion of Iran in World War II. It was first performed by Gholamhossein Banan in 1944 and was used as the opening song for Radio Tehran's morning broadcasts for decades. See: Morteza Hoseyni Dehkordi and Parvin Loloi, 'EY IRĀN', in *Encyclopedia Iranica*, 2000.

105 'Bukhara Evenings' [*Shab-ha-ye Bukhara*], a regular event organized by the *Bukhara* magazine edited by Ali Dehbashi. The event on Toopkhaneh was held on 3 January 2016. Pirooz Hanachi former Deputy MRUD and Mayor of Tehran was one of the speakers.

106 Farokh Mohammadzadeh Mehr and MRUD, *Meidan-e Toopkhaneh-Ye Tehran [Toopkhaneh Square of Tehran]* (Tehran: Payam-e Sima, 2003).

decade earlier.[107] The Baladiyeh project gives a straightforward answer to that question. It seems that the zero hour of Toopkhaneh, according to those involved, was the moment of the demolition of Baladiyeh by the modernist Pahlavi government. Therefore, the authentic historical layer Hanachi was looking for is where the Islamic Republic rebuilds what the Pahlavi administration destroyed.

The project partners' additional ideas, such as the provision of public space, a hall for public discussions on urban issues, as well as a theatre and entertainment centre, mirror other reconstruction projects planned by the municipality, such as the House of Tehran. According to the project's consultant, the building would be an entertainment centre and a dialogue house for the citizens of Tehran to participate in urban governance affairs.[108] A former member of the city council expressed concern about the possible shift in decisions by the new city administration, which could compromise the guarantee of public access to the building.[109] Projects such as the Urban Dialogue House and the House of Tehran, that failed to engage the general public give a clear indication of the fate of the Baladiyeh project. I also observed the trajectory of Ettehadiyeh House, also known as the House of Tehran, as it underwent a series of transformations in terms of reuse concepts and name changes during the transition from a conservative to a reformist government and then back to a conservative one.[110] However, despite these extensive changes, the successive transformations ultimately fell short of their commitments to establish an inclusive "house for the people of Tehran"

---

107 Based on the memories of the author, who was a student of Hanachi at the University of Tehran in the mid-2000s.
108 Manouchehrzaseh and Firoozi, 'Meidan-e Toopkhaneh'.
109 IRNA, 'Negarini-Ye Yek Ozv-e Shora-Ye Shahr-e Tehran Az Enheraf Dar Bahrebardir-Ye "Khane Shahr" [A Member Of The Tehran City Council Is Concerned About The Inappropriate Exploitation Of The "City House"]', *IRNA*, accessed 14 October 2022, https://irna.ir/xjBKWb.
110 Solmaz Yadollahi, 'When Values-Based Conservation Theory Meets Planning Practice in Tehran', in *Conservation Theory and the Urban Realpolitik*, ed. Solmaz Yadollahi, vol. 10, Kulturelle Und Technische Werte Historischer Bauten (Berlin: Birkhäuser, 2024).

or a museum that could effectively compete with international counterparts. It is also worth noting that although the Baladiyeh project aimed to provide the city centre with a theatre and cinema, about 500 metres away, on Lalehzar Street, there are some 18 abandoned historic cinemas and theatre halls that urgently need to be preserved and reused.

Figure 51: Poster of a 'Bukhara Evenings' event about Toopkhaneh Square with the picture of the demolished Telegraph Building (Telegrafkhaneh)

© bukharamag.com

Figure 52: The Municipality of Tehran (Baladiyeh) in 1930s[111]

Figure 53: The ongoing reconstruction project of the Baladiyeh

Author, 2022

---

111   Mostafa Kiani, *Memari-Ye Doreh-Ye Pahlavi-Ye Aval [Architecture During the 1st Pahlavi Dinesty]* (Tehran: Research Institute for Contemporary History of Iran, 2004), 292.

Lalehzar Street

The Qajar-era tulip garden (Lalehzar) became Tehran's—and perhaps even Iran's—gateway to Westernized "high culture and art" in the late 19th and early 20th centuries.[112] With the post-World War II social and political changes in Tehran, the gentrified ambience of Lalehzar Street gradually transformed into a centre for popular entertainment, with several cinemas, hotels, and cabarets offering song and dance, and alcohol.[113] Hung at the entrance of the Hedayat Mosque in the neighbourhood, Ayatollah Taleghani's famous saying—"The trade in unbelief and faith is not without customers, some like this, others that"[114]—described the rather tolerant pre-Revolutionary coexistence of ideologies in the area.

After the 1979 Revolution, all the cabarets and bars, most of the cinemas and some theatres were burnt down or vandalized and the street was gradually handed over to the wholesale electrical appliances and retail guild.[115] With the guild settling in the area, the socio-spatial dynamics in Lalehzar developed in a way similar to those around the Grand Bazaar. Today, the inner parts of the neighbourhood serve as warehouses and workshops for the electrical appliance shops and the textile and fabric businesses located, for example, in the Plasco Tower near Lalehzar.

As of the mid-1990s, the municipality looked into Lalehzar's physical and socio-economic potential for history-oriented beautification, as well as the development of a tourist pedestrian axis.[116] As with other

---

112 Jane Lewisohn, 'The Rise and Fall of Lalehzar, Cultural Centre of Tehran in the Mid-Twentieth Century' (Music Department, SOAS, University of London, 2015).
113 Ibid.
114 'Ayatollah Taleghani Cheguneh Rah-E Behesht Ra Hamvar Mikard? [How Did Ayatollah Taleghani Pave The Way To Heaven?]', *Political Studies and Research Institute*, 6 September 2014, https://psri.ir/?id=q5ol1zfj.
115 Lewisohn, 'The Rise and Fall of Lalehzar, Cultural Centre of Tehran in the Mid-Twentieth Century'.
116 Safamanesh & Co. Engineers, 'Tarh-e Behsazi va Bazsazi-Ye Khiaban-e Lalehzar [Improvement and Reconstruction Plan for Lalehzar Street]' (Tehran Beautification Organization, 1994); Bavand Consulting Engineers, 'The Detailed Plan of Tehran's 12th District'; Rahvan Shahr Consultant Engineers, 'Sanad-e Jame' Mo-

projects, such as Toopkhaneh Square, the period between the late Qajar Constitutional Revolution and the August 1953 coup were considered of historical significance, bringing the Revolutionary and anti-American story of Lalehzar to the fore.[117] At the height of the CIA-organized coup, places like Toopkhaneh and Lalehzar witnessed a political turning point in the development of democracy in Iran; this was also when the intellectual atmosphere of Lalehzar, which was influenced by the Iranian Left Party, began to decline.[118] Lalehzar's political background—associated with the 1905 Constitutional Revolution and the 1953 coup—has been highlighted in post-Revolutionary films and television series,[119] the most famous of which are Ali Hatami's works produced in the Ghazali Cinema Town created by Hatami (Figure 54).

Given its multi-layered and controversial past, the revitalization of Lalehzar has been a contentious subject in Tehran's public sphere. For instance, in a panel discussion entitled 'Revitalising Lalehzar: Bowing to which Past?' participants expressed scepticism about revitalizing the 'maligned' neighbourhood into a cultural centre or converting a profane space into a sacred one.[120]

---

diriyat va Hefazat-e Baft-Ha va Bana-Ha-Ye Tarikhiy-e Tehran [The Comprehensive Document for the Management and Conservation of the Historic Buildings and Urban Fabric of Tehran]' (Tehran: Municipality of Tehran, 2012), Research and Planning Centre of Municipality of Tehran.

117   The coup was planned by the CIA and the British Secret Intelligence Service. See: Donald Newton Wilber, *Regime Change in Iran: Overthrow of Premier Mossadeq of Iran, November 1952-August 1953* (Nottingham: Spokesman Books, 2006).

118   Lewisohn, 'The Rise and Fall of Lalehzar, Cultural Centre of Tehran in the Mid-Twentieth Century'; Wilber, *Regime Change in Iran: Overthrow of Premier Mossadeq of Iran, November 1952-August 1953*.

119   A popular example was the historical drama series 'Shahrzad', directed by Hassan Fathi and released on the Household Entertainment Network in 2015.

120   Speakers of the discussion panel were Zahra Nejad-Baharam (former member of the city council), Ruhollah Nosrati (sociologist from University of Tehran) and Mohammad Atashinbar (from the Nazar Research Center for Art, Architecture & Urbanism). See: Nazar Research Center for Art, Architecture & Urbanism, 'Ruykard-e Ejtemai Lazemeh-Ye Ehya-Ye Khiaban-e Lalehzar [Social Approach as a

Yet, looking at social media and less formal public events about the neighbourhood, one sees all kinds of statements referring to the various past faces of the street. People rave about the lost public spaces such as the Grand Hotel, the theatre halls, cinemas, and luxury fashion shops, but also about the cabarets that staged music and dance and served alcohol. At the first public screening of the film 'Zemestanast' about Lalehzar at the Tehran House of Cinema, I witnessed an instance of the juxtaposition of narratives about the street's past. Upon a scene with a background song by Lalehzar singer Susan, the audience began to clap softly. The hushed clapping seemed to me an expression of taboo nostalgia straining to come out in the open. It revealed that, in the actual assemblage of urban heritage in everyday life, official and non-official narratives remain interwoven with the city. In the public sphere of Tehran, Ali Hatami's political narrative of Lalehzar is as present as ordinary people's memories of oriental dancers and singers in the cabarets of Lalehzar. Moreover, my online and offline ethnographic research confirms that the street has been strongly coded according to its current function in everyday urban life. Most Tehranis immediately associate the name Lalehzar with lamps, cables, and chandeliers.

Prerequisite for the Revitalisation of Lalehzar Street]', *Nazar-Online*, 22 October 2019.

Figure 54: Ghazali Cinema Town, today a Tehran tourist attraction

Author, 2022

Figure 55: A scene featuring Lalehzar from the 'Hezar-dastan' series filmed in the Ghazali Cinema Town [121]

---

121 Mohsen Azarm, 'Shahr-e Farang-e Ali Hatami', *Angah Magazine*, 2020, 43.

Figure 56: A scene from the 'Shahrzad' series featuring the 1953 events in Lalehzar

© shahrzadseries.com

Beautification and place-making in Lalehzar have been much more complicated than the other examples reviewed due to the intertwined ideological and economic conflicts over public space.[122] As mentioned earlier, there were concerns that the beautification of the street would be construed as sympathy for its entertainment-related past. This ideological position has arguably become instrumental in maintaining the existing economic-spatial order in Lalehzar. After all, turning the neighbourhood into a cultural hub very much runs counter to the economic interests of the electrical appliances shops—a sector supported by the neighbourhood's powerful mosque.

---

122 The main conflicts between stakeholders are mentioned in one of the municipality's recent reports on Lalehzar: Bod-e Puya Shahr Engineers, 'Project Report: Samandehi, Behsazi va Nosazi-e Khiaban-e Lalehzar (Had-e Fasel-e Khiaban-e Enghelab Ta Kiaban-e Jomhuri) [Improvement, Reconstruction and Renovation of Lalehzar Street (between Enghelab Street and Jomhuri Street)]' (Municipality of Tehran, Deputy for Urban Planning and Architecture, 2019).

Figure 57: Lalehzar Street in the 1960s[123]

At its core, the relationship between the guild and the mosque in Lalehzar retains the economic and cultural characteristics of the historical alliance between the bazaar and the mosque in Iran.[124] The shop owners, especially the older generation, still participate in the religious ceremonies of Ramazan and Muharram and engage in charity initiatives to strengthen their ties with each other and with the mosque. The informal cooperation between the guild and the Lalehzar mosque was also remarkable during the 2020 COVID-19 crisis. On several occasions during my fieldwork, I witnessed the Lalehzar mosque closely monitoring and critiquing cultural activities in places such as the House of Tehran and the activities of heritage campaigners such as the 'Friends of Lalehzar' group.[125] While the group and the city council members talked about

---

123   Azadeh Moaveni, 'Iran and the US: When Friends Fall Out', *Middle East Eye*, 2022, https://www.middleeasteye.net/big-story/iran-us-uk-oil-friends-fall-apart-cia-coup.
124   See: Ashraf, 'Bazaar-Mosque Alliance: The Social Basis of Revolts and Revolutions'.
125   A group of senior and junior architects and planners, artists, journalists, and students led by urban planner Zahra Taraneh Yalda. The group, which worked informally until 2022, was registered as a Community Based Organisation at the municipality's headquarters for the Empowerment of Non-governmental Organizations.

Lalehzar as a pedestrian zone, the guild continued to use the pavements as regular parking for goods transport and motorbikes that are the most convenient vehicles in the busy inner city. And while the campaigners spoke of future cafes and active cinemas and theatres and more residential areas in the neighbourhood, the guild kept using historic theatres and cinemas and houses as warehouses and workshops. In addition, the variety of ownership types (public,[126] private, and Awqaf), sometimes in the same building, could make changing the status quo in the area extremely complicated.

More recently, cinema owners have attempted to convert their properties into commercial buildings. Even after the reopening of some cultural centres in the 1980s, some cinemas and theatres of Lalehzar remained closed due to the post-Revolutionary cultural policies and the development of online media and streaming services that affected the general cinema sector. Several cinemas in Lalehzar have thus been inactive since the 1990s.

One of the oldest cinemas in the country, Cinema Iran,[127] is a widely debated case in which the owner successfully challenged the heritage protection laws in the Administrative Court of Justice.[128] With the approval of the Ministry of Islamic Guidance and the MRUD[129] to alter the registered use classification of the cinema and the defeat of the Ministry of Cultural Heritage in court, a demolition order was issued in 2020. When the court's decision was published in the media in April 2021, a campaign was launched, addressed to the Minister of Cultural Heritage, to prevent the destruction by listing the cinema. Arguing that the demolition of Cinema Iran would have a domino effect that would threaten

---

126 After the Revolution, several cinemas, theatres, and cabarets were confiscated by parastatal organizations.
127 At its present location, the cinema dates back to the 1930s.
128 For more detailed information about the role of the Administrative Court of Justice see the section on: Political reform: Territorializing heritage between two identity discourses.
129 The Article Five Commission of the HCAUP is the legal body responsible for issuing such permits.

other cinemas of Lalehzar,[130] members of the city council called on the Ministry of Cultural Heritage to list all 18 of the historic cinemas in the area.[131] However, once the reformist city councillors as well as the Minister of Cultural Heritage were out of office in August 2021, media attention for the campaign drastically decreased. At the time of writing, the owner's conflict with heritage activists and heritage authorities is ongoing.

Despite the controversy, the city administration beautified and pedestrianized the northern section of the street in the spring of 2020 and promised free parking space for motorbikes. Unsurprisingly, the beautified pedestrian walkways were immediately claimed by motorbikes. In November 2021, a member of the newly elected city council posted a monitoring report on District 12, calling projects like Lalehzar "theories good for academic books" and "a disaster that has caused a great deal of trouble for the guild and its clients".[132] In response to the criticism, the former mayor of District 12 tagged the council in an Instagram post, arguing that the Lalehzar project was a long-term and social project.[133] For me, this dialogue was another bitter reminder of the short-term nature of Iranian reform, which sooner or later is thwarted by entrenched processes.

---

130 Mojgan Ansari, 'Takhrib-e Cinema Iran-e Lalehzar, Shoru-e Takhrib-e Seriyali-e Cinema Ast [The Destruction Of Cinema Iran In Lalezar Signals The Beginning Of A Series Of Destructions Of Cinemas]', *ISNA*, 29 December 2020, isna.ir/xdHnbz.

131 Mehr News Agency, 'Darkhast-e E'ta Bara-Ye Sabt-e Meli-e Hamzaman-e 18 Cinema-Ye Lalehzar [E'ta's Request for Simultaneous National Registration of 18 Cinemas in Lalezar]' (Mehr News Agency, 1 May 2021), mehrnews.com/xTvqZ.

132 See @mozafar.meysam Instagram post on 28 November 2021, accessed on 29.3.2023.

133 See @amsaadati_official Instagram post on 30 November 2021, and [Stories Highlights: Lalehzar], accessed on 29.3.2023.

Figure 58: Cinema Iran

Author, 2022

Figure 59: An example of the beautified areas in Lalehzar

Author, 2022

Tehran's socio-spatial urban heritage assemblage

Reform-oriented players in Tehran advocated beautification and place-making projects and the creation of a network of pedestrian walkways linking tourist and cultural hubs in the city centre. These nodes include some 195 listed buildings spread across the area.[134] Some, such as the Mostofi-ol-mamalek House in Sangeladge and the Nasirol-molk House in Oudlajan, have been neglected due to lack of funding and irregular administration cycles. Nevertheless, some examples, such as the conversion of a historic house in Oudlajan into a cultural centre called Khaneh-ye Ordibehesht, show that the transfer of ownership to the private sector through the government's 'Build Operate Transfer' (BOT) programme has resulted in remarkable social and economic contributions to the neighbourhood.

An example of the municipality's attempt to include individual buildings to Tehran's urban heritage network is the museum-houses project. Tehran's museum-houses were established in under the national

---

134 According to the records of the Cultural Heritage Organization of Tehran, 32 objects are located in District 11 and 163 objects in District 12.

culture policy of the mid-2000s, which required public institutions to preserve and reuse their cultural assets, especially to promote historical figures of national significance. Museum-houses of figures of the Constitutional Movement and the 1979 Revolution such as Mostafa Chamran and Seyyed Hassan Modarres together with houses of popular anti-Pahlavi figures such as the poet Nima Yushij[135] and the writers Simin Daneshvar[136] and Jalal Al-e Ahmad[137] give a somewhat romantic and nostalgic impression of Tehran's revolutionary past. In the reuse and restoration projects of cases like the Ettehadiyeh House, priority has been given to the Qajar layers of the buildings, while memories of the place associated with a popular 1970s TV series faded out.[138] Similarly, in the case of the War University Museum (Teymourtash's Mansion), the personality of the historical owner[139] was overlooked, placing focus

---

135 Moḥammad Ali Nuri Esfandiari (1897–1958) was a poet known for his pivotal role in shaping modern Persian poetry and his critical reflections on Iran's political environment in the 1940s and early 1950s.

136 Iranian academic and novelist, known for her highly popular novel *Suvashun* (1969). Some have seen implicit references in the novel to the socio-political situation that led to the coup d'état of 28 Mordad 1332 Sh./19 August 1953, planned by the British secret service and executed by the CIA. See: Mas'ud Ja'fari Jazi, 'SUVASHUN' (Encyclopædia Iranica, 2011), https://www.iranicaonline.org/articles/suvashun#prettyPhoto[content]/0/; Mark J. Gasiorowski, 'COUP D'ETAT OF 1332 Š./1953' (Encyclopædia Iranica, 1993).

137 Daneshvar's husband. He is best known for his work 'Gharbzadegi', which has been translated into English as 'Weststruckness', where he makes a harsh critique of Western technology and civilization. His message was favourably received by Ayatollah Khomeini and later by others sympathetic to the 1979 Iranian Revolution. See: Iran Chamber Society, 'Persian Language & Literature Jalal Al Ahmad' (Iran Chamber Society, 2023 2001), https://www.iranchamber.com/literature/jalahmad/jalal_al_ahmad.php.

138 Due to its prominent appearance in the popular television series 'Daie Jan Napoleon', based on the novel by Iraj Pezeshkzad with the same name, the house has been given the nickname 'Daie-jan Napoleon's House' by the general public. See: Yadollahi, 'When Values-Based Conservation Theory Meets Planning Practice in Tehran'.

139 Abdolhossein Teymourtash (1883–1933), a modernist politician of the late Qajar and early Pahlavi period and Court Minister of Reza Shah.

instead on the belongings of the post-Revolutionary users of the house, who were martyrs of the Iran-Iraq War. In a series of public debates, policymakers argued that in such cases it is the physical monument that represents the heritage value, not the dark character of the historical figures associated with them.[140]

However, my field research during several city tours in Tehran has shown that visitors do not necessarily follow the official discursive lines. Visitors often relate to places through their own perspectives on the near and distant past associated with those locations. And observing the reformist city administration's strategy of using boundary objects to soften tensions between official and non-official discourses, I have come to believe that heritage planners have recognized the autonomy of the public in interpreting cultural heritage.

Activities around Vali-e Asr Street (previously known as Pahlavi Street and Mosadeq Street in different political eras) also epitomize the efforts of Tehran's cultural policymakers to reconcile the memories of ordinary people with the values of the government.[141] Minaee House or Vali-e Asr Street Museum located in a section of Vali-e Asr Street that crosses Qajar City in District 11 was an element of the preparation of the street for World Heritage nomination. The Tehran Beautification Organization initiated several pedestrian improvement projects along the street in 2011. At the city council's suggestion, the street was added to the National Heritage List and later to UNESCO's tentative list. The city administration has tried to present the street as a place associated with the memories of Tehranis, a garden street and a 17.2-kilometre-

---

140 For instance in: Cultural Spaces Development Company Municipality of Tehran et al., 'Webinar: Sevomin Webinar-e Barresi-e Tajarob-e Ehyay-e Khaneh-Muzeh-Ye Mashahir-e Tehran [The Third Webinar on the Experiences of Revitalising Houses of Famous Figures in Tehran]' (Instagram Live, 2 December 2020); Cultural Spaces Development Company Municipality of Tehran et al., 'Webinar: Barresi-Ye Tajarob-e Ehya Khaneh Moozeh Mashahir-e Tehran [Reflections on Revitalisation Experiences in the Famous Houses of Tehran]' (Instagram Live, 17 February 2021).

141 After the 1979 Revolution, the street was renamed as a tribute to the 12th Shia Imam.

long plane tree route connecting architectural landmarks from different eras.¹⁴²

I learned about this project through the Instagram livestream of professional workshops held at the Minaee House as a cooperation between the museum and the municipality's Beautification Organization and NGOs such as the Tehranology Association.¹⁴³ In the workshops, interdisciplinary groups of mostly young participants sought to trace and revisit—as Hanachi put it—the social, cultural, physical, and environmental values of the street.¹⁴⁴ Or, as the leader of the workshops wrote, they aimed to find fragments of stories here and there to create a present-day story of the street.¹⁴⁵

From the publications associated with the project,¹⁴⁶ the museum's Instagram account, and the exhibitions at Minaee House, it is clear that policymakers managed to navigate the uncomfortable fact that the street's founder was Reza Shah Pahlavi by placing the street's past

---

142 See: Mokhtari Taleghani et al., *Khiaban-e Vali-e Asr Miras-e Memari va Shahrsazi-Ye Tehran [Vali E Asr Avenue Tehran's Architectural and Urban Heritage]*. And UNESCO's Tentative List: Submitted by: and Iranian Cultural Heritage, Handicrafts and Tourism Organization, 'Vali-e Asr Street' (UNESCO World Heritage Centre, 2019), https://whc.unesco.org/en/tentativelists/6387/.

143 The Tehranology Association [*Anjoman-e Tehran-shenasi*] was established in 2019 with the endorsement of the city council.

144 Pirooz Hanachi, 'Yaddasht-e Shrdar [Mayor's Note]', in *Khiaban-e Vali-e Asr (AJ); Tarrahaneh Andishidan [Vali-e Asr (AS) Street; Thinking Designerly]*, ed. Vahid Ghasemi, Bahra Aqil, and Syyedeh Pegah Hashemi Dogaheh (Tehran: Guya Culture & Art House, 2021), 7.

145 Vahid Ghasemi, 'Molaghat Ba Khiaban (an-e) Dramatik-e Shahr [A Visit to the Street from a Dramatic Angel]', in *Khiaban-e Vali-e Asr (AJ); Tarrahaneh Andishidan [Vali-e Asr (AS) Street; Thinking Designerly]*, ed. Vahid Ghasemi, Aghil Bahra, and Syyedeh Pegah Hashemi Dogaheh (Tehran: Guya Culture & Art House, 2021), 9–10.

146 Mokhtari Taleghani et al., *Khiaban-e Vali-e Asr Miras-e Memari va Shahrsazi-Ye Tehran [Vali E Asr Avenue Tehran's Architectural and Urban Heritage]*; Eskandar Mokhtari Taleghani, *Bonyan-Ha-Ye Khiaban-e Vali-e Asr (AJ) [Foundations of the Vali-e Asr (SA) Street]* (Tehran: Cultural Research Bureau-Tehran Municipality, 2020); Ghasemi, 'Molaghat Ba Khiaban (an-e) Dramatik-e Shahr [A Visit to the Street from a Dramatic Angel]'.

in the broader context of urban life over the last 90 years. As Mokhtari Taleghani, a senior heritage advisor to the municipality wrote: "Although the street was established on the basis of the authority of an individual [Reza Shah], it was the agency of the city and its inhabitants that gave it permanence, and the street became a container of memory".[147] The street was presented as an "exceptional example of the Iranian urban spaces of the Islamic period".[148] In short, by locating historical moments and sites of modern Iranian politics along the street, heritage planners of Tehran linked the Qajar period to the era of the Islamic Republic.

I first visited the Minaee House in October 2021. At the entrance of the permanent exhibition, I was pleasantly surprised to see pictures of unveiled poet Forough Farrokhzad, painter Iran Darroudi, and figures such as Reza Shah's first modernist minister, Mohammad Ali Foroughi. The exhibition blended traces of Tehran's pre-Revolutionary past with a thick Qajar accent, together with innocuous memories of ordinary people in confectioneries, cafes, cinemas, and photographer's studios over the previous nine decades. Without a doubt, the memories of residents and the participation of professionals had passed through the bureaucratic and discursive filter of the reformist city administration. But, for someone familiar with the official cultural context of the Islamic Republic, the technological, spatial, and discursive assemblage of the urban heritage of Vali-e Asr Street felt closer to the everyday experience of the ordinary public to an unprecedented degree.

In June 2022, I visited the house again to see if I could spot any traces of the then recent political changes in the museum. As expected, images of Forough Farrokhzad and Iran Darroudi wore headscarves and politically uncomfortable figures were smaller in size and nearly hidden by a set of recently added post-Revolutionary pictures. Also, the museum's Instagram activity had declined and was more conservative in

---

147   Mokhtari Taleghani, *Bonyan-Ha-Ye Khiaban-e Vali-e Asr (AJ) [Foundations of the Vali-e Asr (SA) Street]*, 118.
148   Mokhtari Taleghani et al., *Khiaban-e Vali-e Asr Miras-e Memari va Shahrsazi-Ye Tehran [Vali E Asr Avenue Tehran's Architectural and Urban Heritage]*, 118.

quality. A staff member of the municipality told me the museum's activities have been slowed down due to ideological opposition by the current government and Tehran's city administration on the museum's function. It was no surprise to see that after a political shift at the national level, urban heritage assemblage was being disassembled—from the macro level of administrative arrangements in the city council and municipality, to the micro layers of the composition of the pictures exhibited at Minaee House.

With the end of the reformist city administration in August 2021, the conservative factions took over the seats in the city council and the municipality. On Twitter, supporters and critics of Zakani, Tehran's new mayor depicted him on his way to Tehran in a war tank. Some said he had come to overturn the corrupt system of the reformists. Recalling the previous conservative government of the mid-2000s, others said he was coming to destroy gardens and historic neighbourhoods of Tehran.

Figure 60: 'The tank in the city', an illustration of Khabaronline News Agency showing Zakani with the logo of the municipality and a tank.

© Khabaronline, 2022

Figure 61: A cognitive map[149] *of Vali-e Asr Street created by a participant (Fatemeh Mahmoudi Panah) in the Minaee House workshops, exemplifying the discussed attempts to blend Tehran's official and popular heritage.*[150]

---

149 Following the conceptual framework introduced by Kevin Lynch: Kevin Lynch, *The Image of the City*, vol. 11 (Massachusetts: MIT press, 1960).
150 Vahid Ghasemi, *Khiaban-e Vali-e Asr Dar Khial-e Man [Vali-e Asr Street in My Mind]* (Tehran: Nashr-e Shahr (Municipality of Tehran), 2021), 116.

Conclusion

Urban heritage assemblage in Iran: A sequence of ephemeral territorialization endeavours foiled by de-territorializing forces

The national picture

The trajectory of socio-material formations around conservation and urban heritage planning tracked by this book shows a recurring pattern. Figure 62 maps the interplay of agents that have played significant territorializing and/or de-territorializing roles in the urban heritage sites studied. The map illustrates how the work of territorializers has been twisted, diverted, and dispersed in the maelstrom of frequent political changes. More specifically, processes that attempted to territorialize conservation have been repeatedly pulled back towards de-territorialization by anti-conservation ideologies, purge processes, corrupt administrations, wars, and revolutions. In this context, the formal structures of conservation and heritage planning have not been able to channel the social and economic forces into sufficiently solid and durable structures that can accommodate their function. Indeed, the network of formal structures in Iran—laws, governmental organizations, and academic concepts—has not succeeded in constraining the informal behaviours of actors at the governmental, parastatal, and private levels.

Any form of long-term planning, including heritage planning,[1] is consistently disrupted and interrupted by a short-term society.[2] As seen in the various cases studied, despite legally binding, long-term policies, processes tended to be stopped or put on hold following political changes. Moreover, as many have noted when studying urban administration systems in Tehran, a society characterized by the concentration of power and resources in the hands of the few often experiences profound corruption in its public organizations.[3] The cases discussed in this book show how public funds and urban spaces can be hijacked and diverted for the benefit of the elite.

The junior and senior public servants and private employees that I met during my field research were all well aware of the instability of the institutions they were working with. This awareness stymied their motivation to invest professionally and financially in long-term projects. In Tehran, for example, I witnessed a tendency towards short-term and small-scale projects. The popularity of short-term projects among experienced officials especially, often stemmed from a desire to claim credit for their accomplishments during their tenure, rather than allowing future political adversaries to benefit from their work. Nevertheless, it is important to acknowledge that limited financial resources also contributed to their preference for these projects.

In order to understand the functioning of the urban heritage bureaucracy in Iran, it is crucial to recognize the volatile political and economic conditions directly influencing its human resources. Rampant corruption and nepotism based on gender and ideology across

---

1   The term 'heritage planning' here is as used by Ashworth, see: Ashworth and Tunbridge, 'Old Cities, New Pasts: Heritage Planning in Selected Cities of Central Europe'.
2   Katouzian, 'The Short-Term Society: A Study in the Problems of Long-Term Political and Economic Development in Iran'.
3   Piran, *Az Shoma Harekat Az Khoda Barekat, Tose'e-Ye Mosharekat Mabna va Mosharekat Mehvar Dar Iran: Mored-e Tehran [God Helps Those Who Help Themselves: Participatory Local Development in Iran: The Case of Tehran]*; Abedi Jafari et al., *Sanjesh-e Fesad va Salamati Sazmani Shahrdari-e Tehran [Measuring Corruption and Organizational Health of the Municipality of Tehran]*.

academic and professional realms have resulted in widespread scepticism among conservation architects considering pursuing careers in Iran. Exacerbating this context is the ongoing political and economic instability in the country. Out of the 29 young professionals I interviewed between 2021 and 2022, 18 had either already emigrated from Iran or were making arrangements to do so.

The emergence of Iran's conservation bureaucracy in the early 1900s was the result of an intricate assemblage of the post-constitutional parliamentary administration, Western conservation doctrine, historic monuments, and official Iranian identity discourse. It involved collecting and distributing political and academic discourses, human resources, and funds, with Tehran playing a pivotal role in this process. The conservation workshops in Shiraz, Isfahan, and later Yazd played a significant material role as repositories of know-how for preserving stone and earthen architecture. Through generations, conservation architects learned the intricacies of working with local craftsmen and addressing the challenges posed by stone and mud brick structures in both archaeological and inhabited settings. Therefore, recognizing the material role within this discursive-material assemblage is crucial for a comprehensive understanding of the field of conservation in Iran.

Despite the disruptive effects of World War II and the Anglo-Soviet invasion of Iran, which resulted in a slowdown and even a halt in conservation activities during the 1940s and 1950s, the policy and practice of the 1960s remained connected to the pre-war conservation assemblage. In other words, although these political events had a de-territorializing impact on the conservation assemblage, the pause was temporary.

To provide a clearer understanding of Figure 62, let's briefly follow the trajectories of the conservation and heritage planning assemblage in Iranian cities discussed in this book.

Figure 62: Disrupted efforts to territorialize urban heritage planning in Iran from the Constitutional Revolution of 1905 to the unified rule of conservative factions in August 2021

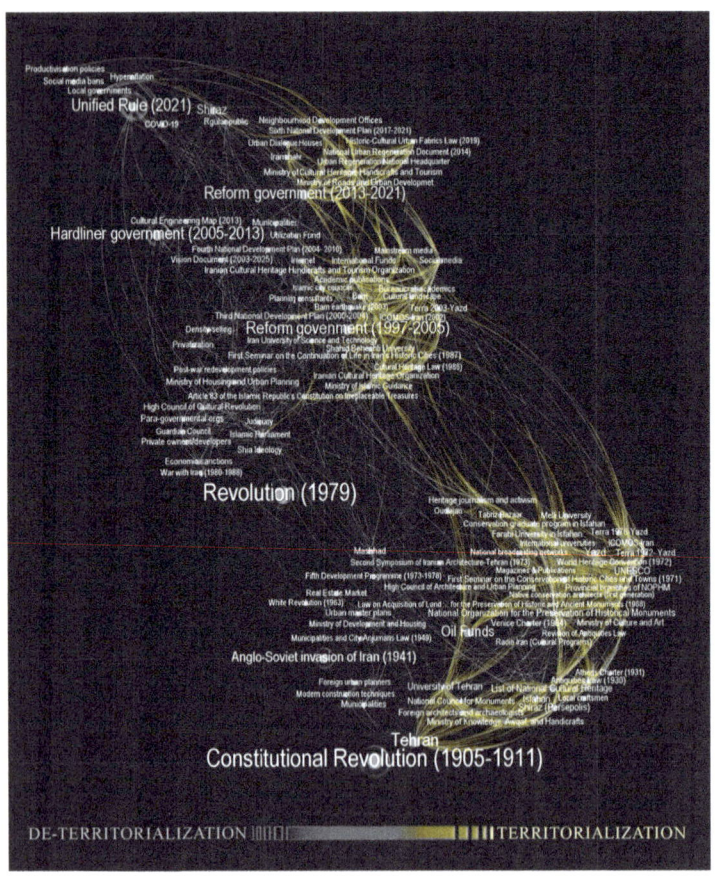

Author, 2023

In the broader historical context, conservation and urban heritage planning policy and practice in Iran have relied heavily on the institutional structures established during the 1960s and 1970s. These two decades witnessed an expansion and complexification in conservation and heritage planning assemblage across the country. During this period, the narrow scope of monument conservation gradually opened up into heritage planning, which included tourism economics and housing issues in cities.[4] Supported by oil funds, a centralized bureaucratic and legal infrastructure emerged, extending links to various provincial branches of NOPHM, universities, national broadcasting networks, and public educational institutions. It was within this network that generations of conservation architects and academics, who played an instrumental role in shaping heritage journalism and activism in the 1970s and beyond, emerged.

However, in the tense and uncertain atmosphere of the late 1970s, urban heritage assemblage, which was still in its formative stages, experienced a state of suspense. Progress in conservation and heritage planning again slowed down and was at times halted altogether. In contrast to the temporary pause that conservation assemblage experienced after World War II and the political shifts that followed, the suspension during the Revolution in the late 1970s led to a break with the previously established infrastructure.

Despite the achievements and expansion of conservation and heritage planning assemblage during this period, the established networks failed to build effective discursive and material-economic connections with a significant portion of the Iranian population, who maintained a traditional lifestyle in socially and physically decaying historic cities. The aftermath of the Revolution in the late 1970s, as depicted in newspapers and magazines of that time, highlighted the challenges faced by the conservation assemblage in relation with this particular population.

---

4   See: Ashworth, 'Conservation as Preservation or as Heritage: Two Paradigms and Two Answers'; Ashworth and Tunbridge, 'Old Cities, New Pasts: Heritage Planning in Selected Cities of Central Europe'.

Ideology-driven acts of vandalism and the surge of private property owners seeking the delisting of historic buildings following the Revolution and during subsequent conservative governments demonstrated the alienation between conservation doctrine and the traditional Islamic approach towards the built environment. In fact, the disconnection was already present in the preceding secular state; however, it became more prominently manifested with the advent of the post-Revolutionary Islamized state.

Following the 1979 Revolution, legal instruments concerned with conservation experienced fluctuating levels of effectiveness due to alternating conservative and reform-oriented regimes. Specifically, during conservative administrations, there was a noticeable decrease in attention given to heritage laws, which can be attributed to both economic and ideological factors.

Ideologically, the ontological contradictions between conservation as a concept developed in Western cultures and Islamic traditions have also played a significant role in the cases examined in this book.[5] An example of this is the prioritization of functional continuity over the authenticity of material and form in historic sites managed by Awqaf Organization and religious authorities. Another example is the prioritization of private property rights based on sharia law over modern heritage protection laws, leading to judicial approval to delist several historic buildings.

Given the transient nature of post-Revolutionary administrations, an independent and proactive academia and civil society could have ensured a certain degree of continuity. However, as reviewed throughout the previous chapters, both institutions across both of those sectors encountered systemic limitations. Even under the most favourable circumstances, in other words, during reformist governments, activism and academic engagement were only tolerated, and that was as long as they adhered to the discursive boundaries set by the reformist Islamic-Iranian identity narrative.

---

5   See: Yadollahi, 'Reflections on the Past and Future of Urban Conservation in Iran'.

Zooming in on Tehran

The examined cases in Tehran offer a close-up of the local socio-spatial assemblages in connection with the broader national heritage planning assemblage. When considered collectively, these cases illustrate the dynamics along the boundaries between the official realm of heritage planning and everyday urban life in a metropolis like Tehran. My ethnographic observations between 2019 to 2022 have allowed this study to further shift its focus to the micro-level of the informal socio-spatial dynamics of heritage planning in Iran's capital.

My fieldwork revealed that the reformist city administrations encountered a multifaceted political quandary when it came to heritage planning. The challenge was how to create a marketable concept of urban heritage, one that appealed to a wide range of social groups such as the middle class, women, and the educated. This intricate situation arose due to a distinctive political factor—unlike the conservative factions, the reformists had an interest in addressing the aspirations of these specific groups. The reformists encountered an immensely formidable task in attempting to appeal to Tehran's wider urban society, while simultaneously reconciling the presentation of an urban heritage that adhered to the official identity discourse and its associated economic-spatial structures.[6]

Drawing from my observations, particularly in Tehran, it becomes evident that heritage has functioned as a platform through which the general public expresses their political opinions, both through social media channels and at public gatherings. By closely examining the reformist city administration's strategy in Tehran, particularly their utilization of boundary objects to mitigate conflicts between official and non-official expressions of nostalgia, I have inferred that heritage

---

6   As defined, for example, in the Cultural Engineering Map, see: High Council of Cultural Revolution and Ahmadinejad, 'Mosavabe-Ye Naghshe-Ye Mohandesi-Ye Farhangi-Ye Keshvar [Decree on the Cultural Engineering Map of the Country]'.

planners acknowledged the political strife and taboo nostalgic sentiments prevalent among the general public. These sentiments frequently intertwined with recollections of the economic prosperity and social freedoms witnessed in Tehran during the 1970s. In light of this, the planners attempted to incorporate the less uncomfortable aspects of these nostalgic elements into spatial projects, while aligning them with official identity discourses.[7]

My online and offline field observations suggest that the reform-oriented urban government was indeed in the process of capturing Tehran's urban heritage assemblage by acting along the boundaries of the official and informal social spheres. Such boundary action helped them to overlap formal and informal, as well as public and private spaces, funds, and discourses. The objective behind this strategy, as I argue, was to facilitate a closer alignment between Tehran's official heritage planning policies one side, and the private sector and the target groups within the city's heritage market on the other. Additionally, the deployment of boundary objects such as reconstructed public spaces, museum-houses, and NDOs played a unifying role, bringing together various motivations and actors. As evidenced by the cases studied in Tehran, it is not uncommon for individuals involved in multiple areas of heritage planning to possess diverse and overlapping motives, combining interests in tourism, academia, and activism.[8]

As expected in a short-term society, the bureaucratic and legal infrastructures that underpinned this strategy proved to be short-lived. Despite the transitory nature of post-Revolutionary administrations, it

---

7   Uncomfortable or difficult heritage as discussed by: William Logan and Keir Reeves, *Places of Pain and Shame: Dealing with Difficult Heritage*' (Routledge, 2008); Sharon Macdonald, *Difficult Heritage: Negotiating the Nazi Past in Nuremberg and Beyond* (Routledge, 2010); Pendlebury, Wang, and Law, 'Re-Using "Uncomfortable Heritage": The Case of the 1933 Building, Shanghai'.

8   In this study, the exploration of subjectivity, desire, and the multifaceted nature of individual motivations draws from the writings of French psychoanalyst and philosopher, Felix Guattari's works, including his collaborations with Gilles Deleuze such as "Anti-Oedipus" and "A Thousand Plateaus," provide insights into the complexities of human motives.

is beneficial to consider the policy fluctuations of subsequent administrations within the broader framework of the Iranian state. Also, sociologists have contended, the reformist and conservative administrations should be viewed as two sides of the same coin, illustrating how the Iranian state possesses the capability to alternately relax and tighten its ideological constraints as it sees fit.[9] Or as noted by DeLanda, the collaboration between authoritarian states and the general public often exhibits an episodic nature.[10] Within this political context, the reformist administration examined in the case of Tehran witnessed the ephemeral nature of cultural reconciliation and participatory programmes that have been implemented through the strategy of boundary action. Following the conclusion of the reformist city administration, various discursive, technological, and spatial assemblages that encompassed place-making and storytelling gradually dispersed. This occurred for instance, with the new city council's declaration in 2021 that promoted a devotional lifestyle over the city nightlife that had been favoured by the reformists.[11] The new mayor further asserted a vision of Tehran as an exemplary metropolis of the Islamic world.[12] Additionally, the Revolutionary parliament imposed new constraints on internet access and social media, thereby introducing further restrictions on the public sphere.

The formal and informal connections between organizational, spatial, and social elements shaping the reform-oriented urban heritage assemblage gradually loosened by the end of the reformists' term and towards the beginning of the conservative government and city council

---

9   For instance see: Ali Gheissari and Vali Nasr, 'The Conservative Consolidation in Iran', *Survival* 47, no. 2 (2005): 175–90.
10 DeLanda, *A New Philosophy of Society: Assemblage Theory and Social Complexity*.
11 The topic was also widely discussed in the conservative newspapers. See for instance:'Montakhab-e Doeh-Ye Sheshom-e Shora-Ye Shahr Dar Bareh-Ye Zist-e Shabaneh Che Goft? [What Did the Elected Member of the Sixth Tehran City Council Said about Tehran's "Nightlife" Plan?]', *Tasnim News Agency*, 13 July 2021, https://tn.ai/2537595.
12 Alireza Zakani, 'Tehran Ra Kalanshahr-e Olgu-Ye Jahan-e Eslam Midanim [We Regard Tehran as a Role Model Metropolis of the Islamic World]', *Mehr News Agency*, 13 May 2022, mehrnews.com/xXG3n.

in 2021. It would be inaccurate to suggest that all the connections and friendships that were made, the spatial and infrastructural structures that were built, and the legal and administrative bases that were established to create the aforementioned assemblage have vanished. But it is fair to say that the change in political power has had a significantly detrimental effect on project-funding priorities and, more importantly, online and offline public life as an essential part of Tehran's urban heritage assemblage.

It is essential to exercise caution when dealing with heritage discourses that are rooted in nationalism, essentialism, ideology, or racism, as these discourses can have profound implications for heritage policy and practice.[13] However, after closely examining the evolution of urban heritage assemblages in Iranian cities, I have come to the conclusion that the most significant challenge facing urban heritage planning in Iran lies not in excessively rigid structures influenced by what Laurajane Smith calls 'Authorized Heritage Discourse' (AHD),[14] but rather in the absence of stable structures altogether. Smith's work is a comprehensive exploration of the ways in which heritage can be framed and controlled by institutions, experts, and dominant groups in society. However, I argue that in the context of ever-changing urban heritage policymaking in Iran, AHD has faced challenges in rooting itself in a stable and enduring discursive, spatial, and bureaucratic-legal framework.

In this context, the notion of sufficiently durable and solid structures refers to the establishment of robust scientific, professional, administrative, civil society, and legal frameworks that serve as binding points of reference for the various competing discursive-spatial forces

---

13 Grigor, 'Recultivating "Good Taste": The Early Pahlavi Modernists and Their Society for National Heritage'; Talinn Grigor, *Building Iran: Modernism, Architecture, and National Heritage under the Pahlavi Monarchs* (Periscope Publishing, distributed by Prestel, 2009); Gustav Wollentz et al., 'Toxic Heritage: Uncertain and Unsafe', *Heritage Futures. Comparative Approaches to Natural and Cultural Heritage Practices*, 2020, 294–312; Johanna M Blokker, 'Heritage and the "Heartland": Architectural and Urban Heritage in the Discourse and Practice of the Populist Far Right', *Journal of European Studies* 52, no. 3–4 (2022): 219–37.

14 Smith 2006

at play within cities. It is crucial to acknowledge, however, that the lack of durable structures in heritage planning in Iran is symptomatic of the proliferation of rigid ideological and political systems, along with their associated economic-spatial structures. In other words, the history of state-organized conservation in Iran consists of recurrent, short-lived episodes in which attempts at territorialization have been thwarted by de-territorializing forces.

Manuel DeLanda's concept of the 'knob' could provide a framework to understand the push-and-pull dynamics between actors engaged in territorializing and de-territorializing an assemblage.[15] In this book, I have borrowed the concept to explain the varying degrees of territorialization and de-territorialization witnessed within the investigated urban heritage assemblage (see Figure 62). To survive, each assemblage has to undergo experimentation to determine the optimal position of the knob, striking a balance to avoid the pitfalls of becoming excessively rigid at one extreme or descending into chaos at the other.

With that said, it is essential to underscore that this book does not propose practical suggestions. Nonetheless, it does provide a map of recurring patterns in Iran's urban heritage planning assemblage, offering glimpses into its potential future tendencies. Within the prevailing political and ideological landscape of Iran and the Middle East, the prospect of maintaining a stable legal, administrative, academic, and spatial backbone for urban heritage planning appears to be waning, and this poignant realization stands as a pivotal outcome of this research. Yet, through fostering connections that extend beyond our conventional boundaries, while bearing in mind the historical tendencies of the assemblage, academics and professionals have the potential to initiate a gradual transformation, bringing the assemblage closer to a state of equilibrium —balanced between chaos and rigidity. Persisting with this struggle and embracing the value of the human resources and the existing academic, spatial, and bureaucratic infrastructure (even if rooted in a troubled past) could inform our actions should we find ourselves in other instants of participating in a Body Without Organs.

---

15 DeLanda, *A New Philosophy of Society: Assemblage Theory and Social Complexity*.

References

Abedi Jafari, Hasan, Davoud Hosseini Hashemzadeh, Mohammad Fazeli, Hasan Mohadesi, and Leila Habibi. *Sanjesh-e Fesad va Salamati Sazmani Shahrdari-e Tehran [Measuring Corruption and Organizational Health of the Municipality of Tehran]*. Tehran: Research and Planning Centre of Municipality of Tehran, 2016.

Abid, SK. 'Imam Ali Shrine, Institution and Cultural Monument: The Implications of Cultural Significance and Its Impact on Local Conservation Management'. *Structural Studies, Repairs and Maintenance of Heritage Architecture XIV* 153 (2015): 87–98.

Afsar, Keramatollah. 'Arg-e ʿAlīšāh'. In *Encyclopedia Iranica*, 2:396–97, 1986. http://www.iranicaoranian Identity III. Medieval Islamic Periodnline.org/articles/arg-e-alisah-remains-of-a-colossal-mosque-built-in-tabriz-completed-1322.

Afsar, Keramatollah. 'Hefz-e Baft Ghadimi Shahrhay-e Tarikhi [Conservation of the Old Fabric of Historic Cities]'. *Agahinameh*, no. 34 (1978): 29–30.

Ahmadian, Hassan, and Payam Mohseni. 'Iran's Syria Strategy: The Evolution of Deterrence'. *International Affairs* 95, no. 2 (2019): 341–64.

Akbar E. Torbat. 'The Brain Drain from Iran to the United States'. *Middle East Journal* 56, no. 2 (2002): 272–95.

Akhundi, Abbas. 'An Interview with the Minister of MRUD'. *MRUD News Service*. 2018. http://news.mrud.ir/news/51902/.

Akhundi, Abbas. 'Barnamey-e Melli-e Baz-Afarini-e Shahri Be Ghalam-e Abbas Akhundi [The National Urban Regeneration Agenda, by Abbas Akhundi]'. *UN Habitat-Iran*. 2018. http://unhabitat.org.ir/?p=4708.

Akhundi, Abbas. 'Matn-e Kamel-e Estefa-Ye Abbas Akhundi [The Complete Text of Abbas Akhundi's Resignation]'. *Ensafnews*, 20 August 2018. https://cutt.ly/z2f92PN.

Akhundi, Abbas. 'Name-Ye Sarih-e Akhundi Be Rohani/ Dar Chenin Fazai Joz Naomidi, Forupashi Hambastegi-Ye Ejtemai va Nazar Shodan-e Iran Ayande-Ye Digari Nemitavan Entezar Dasht [Open Letter from Akhundi to Rouhani/ In Such an Atmosphere, Nothing Can Be Expected but Despair, the Collapse of Social Solidarity, and the Devolution of Iran.]'. *Khabaronline*, 13 June 2021. khabaronline.ir/xgY7W.

Akhundi, Abbas, Naser Barkpour, Meysam Basirat, and Habibollah Taherkhani. 'Asib Shenasi-e Model-e Edarey-e Omur-e Shahr Dar Iran [A Diagnosis of the Model of Urban Management in Iran]'. *Pajouheshhay-e Joghrafiai* 40, no. 63 (2007): 135–56.

Akhundi, Abbas, and Nasser Barkpour. 'Rahbord-Ha-Ye Esteghrar-e Nezam-e Hokmravai Dar Mantagheh-Ye Kalanshahr-e Tehran [Strategies For Establishing A Governance System In Greater Tehran]'. *Rahbord* 57, no. 19 (2010): 297–324.

Akhundi, Abbas, Nasser Barkpour, Iraj Asadi, Habibollah Taherkhani, Meysam Basirat, and Golzat Zandi. 'Hakemiyat-e Shar-Mantagheh-Ye Tehran: Chlesh-Ha va Ravand-Ha [The Governance Of The City-Region Of Tehran: Challenges And Processes]'. *Honar-Ha-Ye-Ziba* 29, no. 29 (2007).

Alamdari, Kazem. 'The Power Structure of the Islamic Republic of Iran: Transition from Populism to Clientelism, and Militarization of the Government'. *Third World Quarterly* 26, no. 8 (1 November 2005): 1285–1301. doi:10.1080/01436590500336690.

Aliasghar, Fatemeh. 'Hamid Baghaie Dar Miras-e Farhangi va Dolat-e Ahmadinejad Che Kard? [What Did Hamid Baghaie Do at ICHHTO and Ahmadinejad's Administration?]'. *Khabaronline*, 23 February 2017, sec. Jame'e. khabaronline.ir/x7sqm.

Ansari, Ali M. *Iran under Ahmadinejad: The Politics of Confrontation*. Routledge, 2017.

Ansari, Ali M. *The Politics of Nationalism in Modern Iran*. Vol. 40. New York: Cambridge University Press, 2012.

Ansari, Mojgan. 'Takhrib-e Cinema Iran-e Lalehzar, Shoru-e Takhrib-e Seriyali-e Cinema Ast [The Destruction Of Cinema Iran In Lalezar Signals The Beginning Of A Series Of Destructions Of Cinemas]'. *ISNA*. 29 December 2020. isna.ir/xdHnbz.

Arefi, Mahyar. 'Towards a Conceptual Framework for Urban Management: The Iranian Experience'. *City, Culture and Society* 4, no. 1 (2013): 37–48.

Art and Architecture. *Art and Architecture*. 15–16. Tehran, 1973.

Art and Architecture. 'News'. *Art and Architecture*, no. 15 (1974): 14–17.

Art and Architecture. 'News: The First Terra Conference in Yazd'. *Art and Architecture*, no. 14 (1972): 78.

Art and Architecture. 'The Declaration of the Second Symposium of Iranian Architecture-Tehran'. *Art and Architecture*, no. 15–16 (1973): 64–66.

Asgharian Jeddi, Ahmad, Farhad Fakhar Tehrani, and Ghadiri. 'Jozveh-ye Dars-e Tarh-e Maremmat-e Bana [Subject Transcript for Architectural Conservation]', 1990.

Ashraf, Ahmad. 'Bazaar-Mosque Alliance: The Social Basis of Revolts and Revolutions'. *International Journal of Politics, Culture, and Society*, 1988, 538–67.

Ashworth, Gregory J, and John E Tunbridge. 'Old Cities, New Pasts: Heritage Planning in Selected Cities of Central Europe'. *GeoJournal*, 1999, 105–16.

Ashworth, Gregory John. 'Conservation as Preservation or as Heritage: Two Paradigms and Two Answers'. *Built Environment (1978-)* 23, no. 2 (1997): 92–102.

Assadi, Ali, and Majid Tehranian. *Sedai Ke Shanide Nashod [The Voice That Was Not Heard]*. Tehran: Nashr-e Nei, 2016.

Assadi, Ali, and Marcello L. Vidale. 'SURVEY OF SOCIAL ATTITUDES IN IRAN'. *International Review of Modern Sociology* 10, no. 1 (1980): 65–84.

Athar. 'Fa'aliat-Ha-Ye Sazman: Kholase-Ye Gozaresh Sale 1358–1359 [Activities of the Organisation: Report of the March 1979-March 1980]'. *Athar* 2–4, no. 1 (1980): 185–89.

Athar. 'Seminar-e Bastanshenasi Dar Rasta-Ye Enghelab [Seminar on Archaeology in Line with the Revolution]'. *Athar* 2–4, no. 1 (1980): 246–48.

Atyabi, Maryam. 'Bazarcheh-Ye Oudlajan Dar Khatar Ast//Bonyad-e Tavon-e Naja Baft-e Tarikhi Ra Takhrib Mikonad [Oudlajan Bazaar Is in Danger // Bonyad-e Taavon-e Naja Is Destroying the Historical Fabric]'. *Honarnews*, 10 December 2011. https://honarnews.com/vdccosq1.2bq1i8laa2.html.

Ayatollah Zadeh Shirazi, Bagher, Saied Hejazi, Farangis Rahimiyeh, and Mohammad Mehryar. 'Behsazi-e Mahaley-e Oudlagan [The Improvement of the Oudlajan Neighbourhood]'. *Athar* 1, no. 2 (1980): 55–99.

Ayatollah Zadeh Shirazi, Bagher, Saied Hejazi, Farangis Rahimiyeh, Mostafa Robubi, and Naser Zad Rafie. 'Samandehi-e Bazaar-e Tehran [The Improvement of the Tehran Bazaar]'. *Athar* 1, no. 2 (1980): 9–48.

Political Studies and Research Institute. 'Ayatollah Taleghani Cheguneh Rah-E Behesht Ra Hamvar Mikard? [How Did Ayatollah Taleghani Pave The Way To Heaven?]'. 6 September 2014. https://psri.ir/?id=q5ol1zfj.

Azadi, Maryam, and Ghasem Hassanpour. 'Muzeh-Ye Miras-e Gheir-e Malmus [Museum of Intangible Heritage]'. *Keyhan-e Farhangi*, 2006.

Azadi, Pooya. 'The Structure of Corruption in Iran', 2020.

Azadi, Pooya, Matin Mirramezani, and Mohsen B Mesgaran. 'Migration and Brain Drain from Iran'. *Stanford Iran 2040* (2020): 1–30.

Azarkia, Solmaz. 'Tarh-e Samandehi-e Bazarcheh-Ye Oudlajan [Improvement Plan for the Oudlajan Cluster Bazaar]'. ICHHTO-Tehran, 2006.

Azarm, Mohsen. 'Shahr-e Farang-e Ali Hatami'. *Angah Magazine*, 2020.

Azhdari, Abolghasem, Mehdi Alidadi, and Dorina Pojani. 'What Drives Urban Densification? Free Market versus Government Planning in Iran'. *Journal of Planning Education and Research*, 2022, 0739456X221126625.

Azimi, Mohammadreza. 'Amalkard-e Shahrdari-e Esfahan Dar Tajrobeh-Ye Sakht-e Borg-e Jahan-Nama Dar Harim-e Meidan-e Naghsh-e Jahan [The Role of The Municipality of Isfahan in the Experience of Constructing the Jahan-Nama Tower in Naghsh-e Jahan Square's Buffer Zone]'. Tehran, 22 July 2015. https://chaharrah.tv/mohammadreza-azimi-a-1394-04-31/.

Azimi, Mohammadreza, and Yashar Soltani. 'Shahrdari Ba Miras-e Tarikhi Che Khahad Kard? [What Will Municipality Do with Historic Heritage?]'. Presented at the Bahamestan-Majma-e Hagh-e Bar Shahr, Tehran, 22 July 2015.

Bahrainy, H, and B Aminzadeh. 'Evaluation of Navab Regeneration Project in Central Tehran, Iran', 2007.

Baker, Tom, and Pauline McGuirk. 'Assemblage Thinking as Methodology: Commitments and Practices for Critical Policy Research'. *Territory, Politics, Governance* 5, no. 4 (2017): 425–42.

Bandarin, Francesco, and Ron van Oers. Reconnecting the City: The Historic Urban Landscape Approach and the Future of Urban Heritage. Wiley, 2014.

Barikani, Mohammad. 'Nekoodasht-e Sabt-e Jahani-e Kakh-e Golestan Be Onvan-e Nokhostin Banay-e Sabt-e Jahani-e Paytakht [Celebrating Golestan Palace as the Capital's First World Heritage Site]'. *Hamshahrionline*. 7 September 2013. hamshahrionline.ir/x3TFx.

Bavand Consulting Engineers. 'Sanad-e Hedayat-e Mahayeh-Ye Oudlajan [Guideline Document for the Oudlajan Neighbourhood]'. Municipality of Tehran, Renovation Organisation, 2010.

Bavand Consulting Engineers. 'The Detailed Plan of Tehran's 12th District'. Tehran: Tehran Urban Research and Planning Centre, 2006. Tehran Urban Research and Planning Centre.

Beheshti, S. Mohammad. 'Malekiyat Dar Eslam (2) [Ownership in Islam (2)]'. *Pasdar-e Eslam*, no. 2 (1982): 24–26.

Beheshti, S. Mohammad. 'Malekiyat Dar Eslam (3) [Ownership in Islam (3)]'. *Pasdar-e Eslam*, no. 3 (1982): 28–29.

Beheshti Shirazi, Seyyed Mohammad. *Dastan-e Tehran [The Story of Tehran]*. Tehran: Cultural Research Bureau, 2016.

Beheshti Shirazi, Seyyed Mohammad. Revitalisation of Tehran, Reflections on the Quality Improvement of Historic Fabric. Tehran Pajhouhi. Tehran: Cultural Research Bureau, 2017.

Beheshti Shirazi, Seyyed Mohammad. 'Tafakor, Hoviyat, Madaniyat [Thought , Identity, Civilisation]'. In *Atashgahi Dar Khab-e Atash-Ha [An Aperture To City Planning And Architecture In Iran, A Centennial Experience]*, edited by Ali A. Kiafar, 126–56. Mashhad: Kasra, 2018.

Beheshti Shirazi, Seyyed Mohammad, Elnaz Najjar Najafi, and Behnam Abutorabian. *Sheikh-e Bahai va Toop-e Morvarid [Sheikh Baha'i and the Pearl Cannon]*. Tehran: Rozaneh, n.d.

IRNA. 'Belataklifi Bala-Ye Jan-e Baft-e Tarikhi-Ye Shargh-e Meidan-e Naghsh-e Jahan-e Esfahan [Indecision, the Bane of the Historic District East of Naqsh Jahan Square in Isfahan]', 31 May 2022. https://irna.ir/xjJzhj.

Bernard, H Russell, Amber Wutich, and Gery W Ryan. *Analyzing Qualitative Data: Systematic Approaches*. Los Angeles: SAGE publications, 2016.

Bernhardt, Christoph, Martin Sabrow, and Achim Saupe, eds. *Gebaute Geschichte: Historische Authentizität Im Stadtraum*. Göttingen: Wallstein, 2017.

Bigio, Anthony, Rana Amirtahmasebi, and Guido Licciardi. *Culture Counts: Partnership Activities of the World Bank and Italian Development Cooperation on Cultural Heritage and Sustainable Development – Report (English)*. Washington, D.C: World Bank Group, 2013. https://documents.worldbank.org/en/publication/documents-reports/documentdetail/180971468163171229/culture-counts-partnership-activities-of-the-world-bank-and-italian-development-cooperation-on-cultural-heritage-and-sustainable-development-report.

Bilsaz, Amin. 'Tabriz Hal Nadarad [Tabriz Is Not Well]'. *Jam-e-Jam*, 4 March 2021. https://jamejamonline.ir/005UZg.

Birkerts, Sven. 'Walter Benjamin, Flâneur: A Flânerie'. *The Iowa Review*, 1982, 164–79.

Blokker, Johanna M. 'Heritage and the "Heartland": Architectural and Urban Heritage in the Discourse and Practice of the Populist Far Right'. *Journal of European Studies* 52, no. 3–4 (2022): 219–37.

Bod-e Puya Shahr Engineers. 'Project Report: Samandehi, Behsazi va Nosazi-e Khiaban-e Lalehzar (Had-e Fasel-e Khiaban-e Enghelab Ta

Kiaban-e Jomhuri) [Improvement, Reconstruction and Renovation of Lalehzar Street (between Enghelab Street and Jomhuri Street)]'. Municipality of Tehran, Deputy for Urban Planning and Architecture, 2019.

Bonyadi, Naser, Giti Etemad, and Farhad Golizadeh. 'Goftoguyi Dar Khosus-e Siyasat-Ha va Barnameh-Ha-Ye Behsazi va Nosazi-Ye Shahri Dar Iran [A Roundtable Discussion on Urban Improvement and Urban Renewal Policies in Iran]'. *HaftShahr*, no. 33–34 (2011): 129–34.

Borbor, Daryoush. 'Iran'. In *Encyclopedia of Urban Planning*, edited by Arnold Whittick, Vol. 29. Mcgraw-hill New York, 1974.

Bourbour, Daryoush. 'Nosazi-e Atraf-e Haram-e Motahar Hazrat-e-Rza, Mashhad [Projet de Renovation de Haram Hazrat-e-Reza Meched]'. *Art and Architecture*, no. 20 (1973): 30–41.

Buchta, Wilfried. *Who Rules Iran? The Structure of Power in the Islamic Republic*. Washington: The Washington Institute for Near East Policy and the Konrad Adenauer Stiftung, 2000.

Correia, M, P Jerome, M Blondet, and Maria Maddalena Achenza. 'Terra 2012. 12th SIACOT Proceedings. 11th International Conference on the Study and Conservation of Earthen Architectural Heritage', 2016.

Dagher, Sam. 'Devotion and Money Tie Iranians to Iraqi City'. *The New York Times*, 2009. https://www.nytimes.com/2009/05/31/world/middleeast/31karbala.html?smid=url-share.

Danati, Sogol, M. Karim Asayesh, and Zahra Nejadbahram. 'Dastandazi Be Piyadehro-Ha [Encroachment on Sidewalks]'. *Payam-e Ma Newspaper*. 14 December 2020, 1900 edition. Encroachment on Sidewalks.

Daneshdoost, Yaqoub. 'Tarhi Bara-Ye Tadavom-e Hayat va Hefz-e Baft-e Tarikhi-Ye Shahr-Ha [A Plan for the Survival and Conservation of Urban Historic Fabrics]'. In *Kholasehy-e Maghalat: Seminar-e Tadavom-e Hayat Dar Bafthay-e Ghadimi-e Shahrhay-e Iran [The Proceedings of the Seminar on the Continuation of Life in Iran's Historic Cities]*, 73–79. Tehran: Iran University of Science and Technology, 1987.

Daryaee, Touraj. Iranshar Tavahom va Eghragh Nist [Iranshahr is Neither an Illusion nor an Exaggeration], 27 October 2020. Etemad Newspaper.

Daryaee, Touraj, and Khodadad Rezakhani. *From Oxus to Euphrates: The World of Late Antique Iran*. Ancient Iran Series. H&S MEDIA, 2016.

Davari, Reza, Ahmad Jannati, Ahmad Ahmadi, Mahdi Golshani, and Iraj Fazel. 'Shoray-e Ali-e Enghelab-e Farhangi; Masuliat-Ha-Ye Ayandeh [High Council of Cultural Revolution Future Responsibilities]'. *Keyhan-e Farhangi*, 1997.

De Roo, Gert, and Jean Hillier. *Complexity and Planning: Systems, Assemblages and Simulations*. Routledge, 2016.

De Roo, Gert, Jean Hillier, and Van Wezemael. 'Complexity and Spatial Planning: Introducing Systems, Assemblages and Simulations'. In *Complexity and Planning: Systems, Assemblages and Simulations*, edited by Gert De Roo and Jean Hillier, 1–36. Oxon: Routledge, 2016.

DeLanda, Manuel. *A New Philosophy of Society: Assemblage Theory and Social Complexity*. London & New York: Bloomsbury Publishing, 2006.

DeLanda, Manuel. *Assemblage Theory*. Edinburgh: Edinburgh University Press, 2016.

Deldam, Eskandar. 'Khaterati az Shaykh Sadegh Khalkhali Givi, bakhsh Dovom [Memories from Shaykh Sadegh Khalkhali Givi, Part Two]', 14 August 2017. shorturl.at/kmxzG.

Deleuze, Gilles, and Felix Guattari. *A Thousand Plateaus*. Translated by Brian Massumi. Minneapolis: University of Minnesota Press, 1987.

Deputy of Cultural Studies -Parliament of Iran. 'Asibshenasi-e Jaigah-e Nafayes Melli va Monhaser-Befard Dar Nezam-e Ghanoon-Gozari [A Diagnosis of the Place of National and Irreplaceable Treasures in the Legislative System]'. Parliament of Iran-Research Centre, 2021.

Diba, Kamran, and Reza Daneshvar. *A Garden Between Two Streets*. Paris: Alborz, 2014.

Ecochard, Michel. 'Rénovation Du Centre de Mashad, Iran'. *L'Architecture d'Aujourd'hui* 169 (1973): 58–60.

Ehlers, Eckart, and Willem Floor. 'Urban Change in Iran, 1920–1941'. *Iranian Studies* 26, no. 3–4 (1 September 1993): 251–75. doi:10.1080/00210869308701802.

Ehlers, EHLERS, Eckart. 'Modern Urbanization and Modernization in Persia'. In *Encyclopedia Iranica*, V:623–29. Cities iv, 1991. http://www.iranicaonline.org/articles/cities-iv.

Emarat-e Khorshid Consulting Engineers. 'Tarh-e Maremmat va Samandehi-Ye Bazarcheh-Ye Tarikhi-Ye Oudlajan [Conservation and Rehabilitation Plan of The Historic Cluster Bazaar of Oudlajan]'. Emarat-e Khorshid Consulting Engineers, 2012.

Expediency Discernment Council. 'Sanad-e Cheshmandaz-e Jomhuri-e Eslami-e Iran Dar Ofoq-e 1404 [Twenty-Year Vision Document of the Islamic Republic of Iran for 2025]', 2003.

Fadaee Nejad, Somayeh. 'Behsazi, Nosazi va Bazsazi Dar Gozar-e Marvi [Rehabilitation, Renovation, and Reconstruction in Marvi Street]'. *Honar-Ha-Ye-Ziba* 32, no. 32 (2007): 61–71.

Falamaki, M. Mansour, ed. Avalin Seminar-e Maremat-e Banaha va Sharhay-e Tarikhi: Vojud va Ayandeye Marakez-e Maskuni-e Tarikhi [The First Seminar on the Conservation of Historic Cities and Towns: The Existence and Future of Historical Residential Centres]. Tehran: University of Tehran, 1971.

Falamaki, M. Mansour. 'Ayandeh-Ye Baft-Ha-Ye Shahri-Ye Tarikhi-Ye Iran: Padideh-Ha va Badil-Ha [The Future of Urban Historic Fabrics in Iran: Phenomena and Alternatives]'. In *Kholasehy-e Maghalat: Seminar-e Tadavom-e Hayat Dar Bafthay-e Ghadimi-e Shahrhay-e Iran [The Proceedings of the Seminar on the Continuation of Life in Iran's Historic Cities]*, 121–32. Tehran: Iran University of Science and Technology, 1987.

Falamaki, M. Mansour. Baz-zendeh sazi-ye banaha ya shahrhaye tarikhi [Revitalization of Historic Buildings and Cities]. Tehran: University of Tehran, 1977.

Falamaki, M. Mansour. 'Fardai Baray-e Yek Gharn Tajrobeh Maremat-e Shahri Dar Iran [A Future for a Quarter-Century of Urban Conservation Experience in Iran]'. In *Proceedings: Hamayesh-e Takhasosi-e Baft-Ha-Ye Shahri, 28–29 Khordad 1376-Mashhad-e Moghadas [Specialized Conference on Urban Fabrics, 18–19 June 1997, Mashhad]*, 713–34. Mashhad: Ministry of Housing and Urban Development, 1997.

Falamaki, M. Mansour. Harimgozari Bar Sarvat-Haye Farhangi-e Iran [Respect of the Cultural Goods of Iran]. Tehran: Faza Scientific and Cultural Institute, 2005.

Falamaki, M. Mansour. Nazariyehi Bar Manshur-e Maremmat-e Shahri [An Essay on Urban Restoration Charter]. Tehran: MRUD, 2008.

Falamaki, M. Mansour. Nosazi va behsazi-e shahri [Urban improvement and renewal]. Tehran: SAMT, 2013.

Falamaki, M. Mansour. Seiri Dar Tajarob-e Maremmat-e Shari, as Veniz Ta Shiraz [An Essay on Urban Conservation, From Venice to Shiraz]. Tehran: Faza Scientific and Cultural Institute, 2005.

Falamaki, M. Mansour. 'Taghir-e Shekl-e Vahed-Hay-e Memari Dar Baft Shahri [The Architectural Units' Change in Urban Fabrics]'. *Art and Architecture*, no. 15–16 (1973): 31–36.

Farahani, Ilia, and Shadi Yousefi. 'Public Housing, Intersectoral Competition, and Urban Ground Rent: Iran's First Public Housing Program That Never Was'. *Human Geography* 14, no. 1 (2021): 45–61.

Farasatkhah, Maghsoud. *The Adventure of University in Iran*. Tehran: Rasa, 2009.

Farmanfarmaian, Abdolaziz, and Victor Groen Institute. 'Master Plan of Tehran'. Sazman-e Barnameh va Budgeh, 1968.

Farouqi Qajar, Maryam. 'Qajar Yek Khanevadeh Nist [Qajar Is Not a Family]'. Translated by Human Zalpour. *Iran Newspaper*. 24 February 2020.

Fars. 'Az Tashil-e Sakht-o-Saz Dar Tehran Ta Raf-e Mozal-e Baft-e Farsoodeh [From Facilitating Construction in Tehran to Solving the Problem of Decayed Urban Built Environment]'. *Fars News Agency*. 13 September 2021. http://fna.ir/3p3q6.

Fars. 'Zakani: Tarh-e Tafsili Bayad Bazbini Shavad [Zakani: The Detailed Plan Should Be Revised]'. *Fars News Agency*. 2 January 2023. http://fna.ir/1u5oxj.

Fazeli, Mohammad. Iran Bar Labe-Ye Tigh, Goftar-Ha-Ye Jameshenasi-Ye Siyasi va Siyasat-e Omumi [Iran, on the Edge of the Blade Essays on Political Sociology and Public Policy]. Tehran: Rozaneh, 2021.

Flick, Uwe. An Introduction to Qualitative Research. Sage, 2009.

Fox-Rogers, Linda, and Enda Murphy. 'Informal Strategies of Power in the Local Planning System'. *Planning Theory* 13, no. 3 (2014): 244–68.

Fu, Shulan, and Jean Hillier. 'Disneyfication or Self-Referentiality: Recent Conservation Efforts and Modern Planning History in Datong'. In *China: A Historical Geography of the Urban*, 165–91. Springer, 2018.

Galdieri, Eugenio, and Kerāmat-Allāh Afsar. 'Conservation and Restoration of Persian Monuments'. In *Encyclopedia Iranica*, VI:134–38. New York, 1992.

Gasiorowski, Mark J. 'COUP D'ETAT OF 1332 Š./1953', VI, Fasc. 4,:354–56. Encyclopædia Iranica, 1993.

Gehl, Jan. *Cities for People*. Island press, 2013.

Gehl, Jan, and Birgitte Svarre. *How to Study Public Life*. Translated by Mohammad Saeid Izadi, Samaneh Mohammadi, and Samaneh Kheibari. Tehran: Elm-o-Sanat University Press, 2015.

Ghaderi, Zahed, Ehsan Aslani, Luc Beal, Mohammadhossein Dehghan Pour Farashah, and Moslem Ghasemi. 'Crisis-Resilience of Small-Scale Tourism Businesses in the Pandemic Era: The Case of Yazd World Heritage Site, Iran'. *Tourism Recreation Research*, 2022, 1–7.

Ghamami, Majid, ed. 'Goftegu Ba Doktor Abbas Akhundi [A Conversation with Dr. Abbas Akhundi]'. In Barresi-Ye Vaziyat-e Shahrsazi va Barnamehrizi Shahri va Mantaghei Da Iran-e Moaser [Observations on the State of Urban Planning and Urban and Regional Management in Contemporary Iran], 13–31. Tehran: Afrand Publishing House, 2013.

Ghanoun-e Budjeh Sal-e 1382 Koll-e Keshvar [Budget Law March 2003-March 2004]'. Parliament of Iran, 2003.

Ghari, Mohammad. 'A Conversation with Hooshang Seyhoin'. *Abadi*, no. 48 (2005): 130–34.

Ghasemi, Elham, and Mojtaba Rafieian. 'Analyzing Conflict of Interest in Large-Scale Participatory Projects with Emphasis on the "Public Private People Partnership" Model (4P) (Case Study: Isfahan Jahannema Citadel Project)'. *Motaleate Shahri* 9, no. 34 (2020): 90–104. doi:https://doi.org/10.34785/J011.2021.887.

Ghasemi, Vahid. *Khiaban-e Vali-e Asr Dar Khial-e Man [Vali-e Asr Street in My Mind]*. Tehran: Nashr-e Shahr (Municipality of Tehran), 2021.

Ghasemi, Vahid. 'Molaghat Ba Khiaban (an-e) Dramatik-e Shahr [A Visit to the Street from a Dramatic Angel]'. In *Khiaban-e Vali-e Asr (AJ); Tarrahaneh Andishidan [Vali-e Asr (AS) Street; Thinking Designerly]*, edited by Vahid Ghasemi, Aghil Bahra, and Syyedeh Pegah Hashemi Dogaheh, 9–10. Tehran: Guya Culture & Art House, 2021.

Ghazbanpour, Jasem. Zendegi-e Jadid-Kalbad Ghadim: Gozideh-i Az Bana-Ha-Ye Baarzesh-e Tarikhi [New Life – Old Structure: A Selection of Valuable Historic Buildings]. Tehran: Ministry of Housing and Urban Development, 1993.

Gheissari, Ali, and Vali Nasr. 'The Conservative Consolidation in Iran'. *Survival* 47, no. 2 (2005): 175–90.

Center for Human Rights in Iran. '"Girls of Revolution St" Protest Ignites Debate on Iran's Compulsory Hijab', 2018. https://iranhumanrights.org/2018/01/girls-of-revolution-st-protest-ignites-debate-on-irans-compulsory-hijab/.

'Gocaman Tabriz 6: Interview with Mr Akbar Taghizadeh', 2018. shorturl.at/los16.

'Gohar-hai Ke Khak Shodand: Masjed-e Mirza Jafar-Mashhad [Jems that turned into Soil: the destruction of Mirza Jafar Mosque-Mashhad]'. *Athar* 1, no. 1 (1980): 123–31.

Golkar, Saeid. 'Cultural Engineering Under Authoritarian Regimes: Islamization of Universities in Postrevolutionary Iran'. *Digest of Middle East Studies* 21, no. 1 (1 March 2012): 1–23. doi:10.1111/j.1949-3606.2012.00124.x.

Golkar, Saeid. 'Liberation or Suppression Technologies? The Internet, the Green Movement and the Regime in Iran.' *International Journal of Emerging Technologies & Society* 9, no. 1 (2011).

'Gozaresh-e Tarh-e Tajdid-e Nazar Dar Tarh-e Jame va Tafsili-e Esfahan [The Report on the Revision of Isfahan's Master and Detailed Plan]'. Housing and Urban Planning Organisation of Isfahan, 1988.

Gran-Aymerich, Ève, and Mina Marefat. 'GODARD, ANDRÉ'. *Encyclopaedia Iranica* XI (2001): 29–31.

Grigor, Talinn. Building Iran: Modernism, Architecture, and National Heritage under the Pahlavi Monarchs. Periscope Publishing, distributed by Prestel, 2009.

Grigor, Talinn. 'Recultivating "Good Taste": The Early Pahlavi Modernists and Their Society for National Heritage'. *Iranian Studies* 37, no. 1 (2004): 17–45. doi:10.1080/0021086042000232929.

Grigor, Talinn. 'The King's White Walls: Modernism and Bourgeois Architecture'. In *Culture and Cultural Politics under Reza Shah*, 109–32. Routledge, 2013.

Groat, Linda, and David Wang. *Architectural Research Methods*. 2nd ed. New Jersey: John Wiley & Sons, 2013.

Gurney, John, and Negin Nabavi. 'Dār Al-Fonūn'. *Encyclopædia Iranica* 6 (1993): 662–68.

Habibi, Behrouz. 'Ehya va Negahdari-e Shahr-e Ghadim [Revitalisation and Maintenance of the Old City]'. *Art and Architecture*, no. 15–16 (1973): 2–22.

Habibi, Mohsen. *Az Shar Ta Shahr [De La Cite a La Ville]*. Tehran: University of Tehran, 1996.

Habibi, Seyyed Mohsen. 'Shahr, Shahriyat, Shahrsazi Dar Iran [City, Urbanity, Urban Planning in Iran]'. In *Atashgahi Dar Khab-e Atash-Ha [An Aperture To City Planning And Architecture In Iran, A Centennial Experience]*, 279–316. Mashhad: Kasra, 2018.

Habibi, Seyyed Mohsen, Hamideh Farahmandiyan, Navid Pourmohammadreza, and Saleh Shokuhi Bidhendi. Khatereh-Ye Shahr, Bazkhani-Ye Sinematografik-e Shahr-e Irani: Dahe-Ha-Ye 1340–1350 [The Memory of the City, a Cinematographic Reencounter with the Iranian City: 1960s-1970s]. Tehran: Nahid, 2014.

Habibi, Seyyed Mohsen, and Mehran Foroughifa. 'Finding Some Strategies for Encouraging People to Cooperate in Urban Renovation Plans Based on the Game Theory'. *Honar-Ha-Ye-Ziba: Memary Va Shahrsazi* 18, no. 19 (2013): 5–14. doi:10.22059/jfaup.2013.51677.

Habibi, Seyyed Mohsen, and Malihe Maghsoodi. *Urban Restoration*. Tehran: University of Tehran, 2002.

Habibi, Seyyed Mohsen, Mehdi Taleb, Behrooz Hadi Zonuz, Esfandyar Borumand, Mehdi Mojabi, and Others, eds. Proceedings: Hamayesh-e Takhasosi-e Baft-Ha-Ye Shahri, 28–29 Khordad 1376- Mashhad-e Moghadas [Specialized Conference on Urban Fabrics,

18–19 June 1997, Mashhad]. Mashhad: Ministry of Housing and Urban Development, 1997.

Haftshahr. 'Gozaresh-e Avalin Hamayesh-e Behsazi va Nosazi-e Baft-Ha-Ye Farsoodeh, Mashhad, 1387 [Report of the First Conference on Regeneration and Revitalisation of Urban Distressed Areas, Mashhad, 2008]'. *HaftShahr* 4, no. 43–44 (2014): 145–61.

Hajaliakbari, Kaveh, and Amir Shafie. Tose-Ye Mahalli: Chaharchoobi Bara-Ye Mahalleh-Ha-Ye Nakaramad [Neighborhood Development: A Framework for Dysfunctional Neighborhoods]. Tehran: Research and Planning Centre of Municipality of Tehran, 2018.

Hamshahri. 'Hoshdar Be Van-Kafe-Ha-Ye Tehran Ke Mojavez Nadarand: Sabr-e Maraje-e Ghanuni Hadi Darad [Warning To Tehran Café-Vans That Don't Have A Licence; Judicial Authorities' Patience Has A Limit]'. *Hamshahrionline*. 2 June 2023. hamshahrionline.ir/x8jdG.

Hanachi, Pirooz. Maremat-e Shahri Dar Baft-Hay-Ye Tarikhi-e Iran [Urban Restoration in Historic Fabrics of Iran]. 1st ed. Tehran: University of Tehran Press, 2012.

Hanachi, Pirooz. 'Yaddasht-e Shrdar [Mayor's Note]'. In *Khiaban-e Vali-e Asr (AJ); Tarrahaneh Andishidan [Vali-e Asr (AS) Street; Thinking Designerly]*, edited by Vahid Ghasemi, Bahra Aqil, and Syyedeh Pegah Hashemi Dogaheh, 7. Tehran: Guya Culture & Art House, 2021.

Hanachi, Pirooz, Mozaffar Farhang, and Yaser Jafari. 'Hefazat Az Manzar-e Shahri Tarikhi Da Jedareh-Ha-Ye Tejari; Tabyin-e Chaharchoob-e Modakheleh Bar Mabnay-e Tajarob-e Behsazi Khiyaban-e Naser Khosrow Tehran [Protection of the Historic Townscape on Commercial Facades; Outlining the Intervention Framework Based on the Experience of the Redevelopment of Naser Khosrow Street in Tehran.]'. *Motaleate Shahr-e Irani-Eslami* 8, no. 32 (2018): 77–88.

Hanachi, Pirooz, M. Hassan Khademzadeh, Hamidreza Shayan, Hamed Kamelnia, and M. Javad Mahdavinejad. Barresi-e Tatbighi-e Tajarob Maremat-e Shahri Dar Jahan va Iran, Ba Negahi Vijeh Be Baft-e Yazd [A Comparative Study Of Urban Preservation Experiences In The World And In Iran, With A Special Focus On The City Of Yazd]. 1st ed. Yazd: Sobhan Noor, 2007.

Hanachi, Pirooz, Darab Diba, and M. Javad Mahdavinejad. 'Hefazat va Tose'e Dar Iran [Conservation and Development in Iran]' 32 (2007): 51–60.

Hanson, Brad. 'The "Westoxication" of Iran: Depictions and Reactions of Behrangi, Āl-e Ahmad, and Shariʿati'. *International Journal of Middle East Studies* 15, no. 1 (1983): 1–23.

Harris, Kevan. 'The Rise of the Subcontractor State: Politics of Pseudo-Privatization in the Islamic Republic of Iran'. *International Journal of Middle East Studies* 45, no. 1 (2013): 45–70. doi:10.1017/S0020743812001250.

Harrison, Rodney. 'Conclusion: On Heritage Ontologies: Rethinking the Material Worlds of Heritage'. *Anthropological Quarterly*, 2018, 1365–83.

Harrison, Rodney, Caitlin DeSilvey, Cornelius Holtorf, Sharon Macdonald, Nadia Bartolini, Esther Breithoff, Harald Fredheim, Antony Lyons, Sarah May, and Jennie Morgan. *Heritage Futures: Comparative Approaches to Natural and Cultural Heritage Practices*. UCL press, 2020.

Harvey, David C. 'The History of Heritage'. In *The Ashgate Research Companion to Heritage and Identity*, edited by Brian J. Graham and Peter Howard, 19–36. Ashgate Publishing, Ltd., 2008.

Hasanlu, Somayyeh. 'Pardebardari Az Yak Ettefagh Dar Baft-e Shiraz [Uncovering an Event in the Historic Shiraz]'. *ISNA*, 14 June 2022. isna.ir/xdLQ8W.

Hateftabar, Fahimeh, and Jean Michel Chapuis. 'The Influence of Theocratic Rule and Political Turmoil on Tourists' Length of Stay'. *Journal of Vacation Marketing* 26, no. 4 (2020): 427–41.

IRNA. 'Hayahoo-Ye Takhrib-e Asar-e Tarikhi Dar Mashhad Nooshdaru-Ye Bad Az Marg-e Sohrab [The Belated Outcry Over the Destruction of Historical Monuments in Mashhad]', 21 November 2018. https://irna.ir/xjrqFL.

Herzfeld, Michael. *Cultural Intimacy: Social Poetics and the Real Life of States, Societies, and Institutions*. Routledge, 2016.

Herzfeld, Michael. 'The European Crisis and Cultural Intimacy'. *Studies in Ethnicity and Nationalism* 13, no. 3 (2013): 491–97.

High Council of Cultural Revolution 'Ayin-Nameh-Ye Hefazat Az Miras-e Farhangi-e Keshvar [Iran's Cultural Heritage Conservation Guidline]', 2002.

High Council of Cultural Revolution, and Mahmud Ahmadinejad. 'Mosavabe-Ye Naghshe-Ye Mohandesi-Ye Farhangi-Ye Keshvar [Decree on the Cultural Engineering Map of the Country]'. Parliament of Iran-Research Centre, 2013. Parliament of Iran-Research Centre.

Hillier, Jean. 'More than Meat: Rediscovering the Cow beneath the Face in Urban Heritage Practice'. *Environment and Planning D: Society and Space* 31, no. 5 (2013): 863–78.

Hodjat, Mehdi. 'Arzesh-Ha-Ye Mojoud Dar Baft-e Tarikhi [Values of the Historic Fabric]'. In Kholasehy-e Maghalat: Seminar-e Tadavom-e Hayat Dar Bafthay-e Ghadimi-e Shahrhay-e Iran [The Proceedings of the Seminar on the Continuation of Life in Iran's Historic Cities], 58–65. Tehran: Iran University of Science and Technology, 1987.

Hodjat, Mehdi. 'Cultural Heritage in Iran: Policies for an Islamic Country.' Doctoral thesis, University of York, 1995. http://etheses.whiterose.ac.uk/2460/1/DX193597.pdf.

Hodjat, Mehdi. 'Goftari Dar Bab-e Miras-e Farhangi [A Speech about Cultural Heritage}'. Iran University of Science and Technology, Tehran, 5 July 2023. https://www.aparat.com/v/NjTgD.

Hodjat, Mehdi. Mirath-e Farhangi Dar Iran: Syasat Ha Baray-e Yek Keshvar-e Eslami [Cultural Heritage in Iran, Policies for an Islamic Country]. Tehran: ICHO, 2001.

Hodjat, Mehdi, Bagher Ayatollah Zadeh Shirazi, and Mehdi Chamran. 'Ostad Mohammad Karim Pirnia va Osul-e Memari-e Sonnati [Master Mohammad Karim Pirnia and the Principles of Traditional Architecture]'. *Kayhan Farhangi*. 1985.

Hokmravai-e Novin Shahri (ruykard-ha, mafahim, masael, va chalesh-ha) [New Urban Governance (approaches, concepts, Issues, and challenges)]. Vol. 1 and 2. Tehran: Tisa, 2017.

Holliday, Shabnam J. *Defining Iran: Politics of Resistance*. London: Routledge, 2016.

Honarfar, Lotfollah. 'Meidan-e Naghsh-e Jahan Isfahan'. *Honar va Mardom*, no. 104 (1971): 2–28.

Honarvar, Nilpar. 'Iranian Experiences Of Urban Restoration'. *HaftShahr* 1, no. 3 (2001): 14–31.

Hoseyni Dehkordi, Morteza, and Parvin Loloi. 'EY IRĀN'. In *Encyclopedia Iranica*, 2000.

Housing Development and Construction Company, and Housing Development and Construction Company-Fars. Dovomin Hamayesh-e Behsazi va Bazafarini-e Baftha-Ye Tarikhi, Farsoodeh-Ye Shahri va Sokunatgahha-Ye Gheir-e Rasmi, Shiraz, 1389 [Second Conference on the Improvement and Regeneration of Historic, Distressed Urban Fabrics and Informal Settlements, Shiraz, 2010]. Shiraz: Navid-e Shiraz, 2011.

ICHHTO. Asasnameh-ye Sandough-e Ehya va Bahrebardari az Banaha va Amaken-e Tarikhi-Farhangi [Statutes of the Rvitalisation and Utilisation Fund for Historical Places] (2005).

ICHHTO. 'Historic City of Yazd, World Heritage Nomination Dossier'. ICHHTO, 2017. https://whc.unesco.org/en/list/1544/documents/.

ICHHTO-East Azerbayjan. '2013 Winning Projects: Rehabilitation of Tabriz Bazaar-Tabriz, Iran'. Aga Khan Award for Architecture, 2013.

ICOMOS. 'Advisory Body Evaluation (ICOMOS)'. UNESCO, 1979. Paris. https://whc.unesco.org/en/list/115/documents/.

ICOMOS. *The Venice Charter*. Venice, 1964.

Institute for Research and Preparation of Urban Development Plans of Tehran. 'Tarh-e Rahbordi-Sakhtari-Ye Tose va Omran-e Shahr-e Tehran (Tarh-e Jame Tehran 1386) [Strategic-Structural Plan for the Development of the City of Tehran (Master Plan 2007)]'. MRUD, 2007.

International Monetary Fund, International Financial Statistics and data files. 'Inflation, Consumer Prices (Annual %) – Iran, Islamic Rep.' World Bank. Accessed 4 January 2023. https://cutt.ly/N2j1Wok.

Iran. 'Qajariyeh Be Ravayat-e Tajrobeh/Maryam Farooqi Qajar, Naveh-Ye Ahmad Shah Qajar [Qajar by Experience/ Maryam Farooqi Qajar, Descendant of Ahmad Shah Qajar]'. *Iran Newspaper*, 28 February 2019.

Iran Chamber Society. 'Persian Language & Literature Jalal Al Ahmad'. Iran Chamber Society, 2023 2001. https://www.iranchamber.com/literature/jalahmad/jalal_al_ahmad.php.

IRNA. 'Dar Marasem.e Jashn-e Sabt-e JahaniBazar-e Bozorg-e Tabriz [In the Celebration for Tabriz Grand Bazaar Inscription in the World Heritage List]', 31 July 2011. https://irna.ir/x3fzzW.

IRNA. 'Mohseni Ejeie: Hamid Baghaie Bazdasht Shod [Mohseni Ejeie: Hamid Baghaie Was Arrested]'. *IRNA*. 6 August 2015. https://irna.ir/xj9VRT.

IRNA. 'Negarini-Ye Yek Ozv-e Shora-Ye Shahr-e Tehran Az Enheraf Dar Bahrebardir-Ye "Khane Shahr" [A Member Of The Tehran City Council Is Concerned About The Inappropriate Exploitation Of The "City House"]'. *IRNA*. Accessed 14 October 2022. https://irna.ir/xjBKWb.

Islamic City Council of Tehran. 'Barnameh-Ye Dr. Hanachi [Dr. Hnachi's Program for Mayorship]'. Tehran, 29 April 2018. http://shora.tehran.ir/Portals/0/pdf/gozaresh dar sahn/برنامه دکتر حناچی.pdf.

Islamic City Council of Tehran. 'Barnameh-Ye Panjsaleh-Ye Sevom-e Tose-Ye Shar-e Tehran (1398–1402) [The Third Development Plan of Tehran (2019–2023)]'. Islamic City Council of Tehran, 2018.

Islamic City Council of Tehran. 'Ahmad Masjedjamei: Shahr Ra Ba Mosharekat-e Namayandegan-e Mahalat Edare Konim [Masjedjamei: Run the City with the Participation of Local Representatives]'. *Councilorship Coordination Headquarters of Tehran Islamic City Council*. 2019. Content code: 4138.

Islamic City Council of Tehran. Eslah-e Mavaredi az Mosavabeh-ye Tashkil-e Anjoman-ha-ye Shorayari-ye Shar-e Tehran [Amendment of Articles of the Decree on Establishment of Neighbourhood Councils in Tehran], Pub. L. No. 2560 (2019).

Islamic City Council of Tehran. 'Gozaresh-e Tafsili Dar Khosus-e Layehe-Ye 'Tarh-e Bahrebardari Az Piadehro-Ha [Detailed Report on the Bill on the Utilisation of Pedestrian Ways]'. Tehran Ciity Council-Archive, 2020.

ISNA. 'Amadand, Kharab Kardand, va Raftand ... [They Came, Destroyed and Left ...]'. *ISNA*, 25 June 2016. isna.ir/x9QrCW.

SNA. 'Ghabr-Ha-Ye Miliyardi Dar Shahecheragh! [Billion-Tuman Graves in Shahecheragh!]', 27 October 2014. isna.ir/x8sx4k.

SNA. 'Hokmi Ke Sabt-e Jahaniy-e Kakh-e Golestan Ra Tahdid Mikonad [A Decision That Threatens Golestan Palace's World Heritage Status]'. *ISNA*, 1 September 2022. isna.ir/xdKH9P.

Izadi, Mohammad Saeid. 'A Study on City Centre Regeneration: A Comparative Analysis of Two Different Approaches to the Revitalisation of Historic City Centres in Iran'. Doctoral thesis, Newcastle University, 2008. http://hdl.handle.net/10443/759.

Izadi, Mohammad Saeid. 'Rah Andazi-Ye Khane-Ha-Ye Gofteman-e Shahri Rahi Bara-Ye Maremat-e Baft-Ha-Ye Tarikhi [Establishment of Urban Dialogue Houses, an Approach to the Preservation of Historic Cities]'. *ISNA*, 19 November 2016. isna.ir/xcY47c.

Izadi, Mohammad Saeid. 'Sokhan-e Modir Masoul: Tahaghogh-e Gofteman-e Hagh-e Bar Shahr, Shart-e Lazem-e Bazafarini-Ye Paydar [Editorial: The Realisation of the Right to the City Discourse Is the Prerequisite for Sustainable Urban Regeneration]'. *HaftShahr* 4, no. 49–50 (2015): 2–3.

Jabari, Habib, ed. 'Modakhele Dar Baft-Ha-Ye Shahri va Masale-Ye Mosharekat [Interventions in Urban Fabric and the Participation Issue]'. *HaftShahr* 2, no. 4 (2001): 28–46.

Jacobs, Jane. The Death Andlife of Great American Cities. New York: Vintage, 1961.

Japan International Cooperation Agency, and Tehran Disaster Mitigation and Management Center. 'The Comprehensive Master Plan Study on Urban Seismic Disaster Prevention and Management for the Greater Tehran Area'. *JICA*, 2005.

Ja'fari Jazi, Mas'ud. 'SUVASHUN'. Encyclopædia Iranica, 2011. https://www.iranicaonline.org/articles/suvashun#prettyPhoto[content]/0/.

Jing, Feng, and Pedro A. Calderon. 'MISSION REPORT / Meidan Emam, Esfahan (Islamic Republic of Iran) (C 115)'. UNESCO World Heritage Centre, 2013. https://whc.unesco.org/en/list/115/documents/.

Jokilehto, Jukka. *Tarikh-e Hefazat-e Memari [History of Architectural Conservation]*. Translated by M. Hassan Talebian and Khashayar Bahari. Tehran: Rozaneh, 2008.

Jokilehto, Jukka, and Mehr-Azar Soheil. 'Development of ICCROM's Architectural Conservation Training in Reference to Council of Europe Initiatives'. *Monumenta* 3 (2015): 104–12. doi:https://doi.org/10.11588/monu.2015.0.42407.

ISNA. 'Joziyat-e Sabegheh-Ye Tarh-e Tafsili Dar Samaneh-Ye "Tehran-e Man" Montasher Mishavad [Extensive Background Information on the Detailed Plan Was Published in the "Tehran Man" Online System]', 27 June 2020. isna.ir/xdG7HY.

Judiciary Research Institute-Iran. Malekiyat-e Khosusi Ya Manfaat-e Omumi?: Naghd-e Raviye Shoabe Divane Edalat-e Edari Piramun-e Ebtal-e Tasmim-e Sazman-e Miras-e Farhangi va Tarikhi Dar Fehrest-e Athar-e Melli [Private Property or Public Interest? A Critique of the Administrative Court Branches' Procedure Regarding the Annulment of the Cultural Heritage Organization's Decision in the Listing of National Monuments]. Tehran: Judiciary of the Islamic Republic of Iran, 2014.

Kalantari, Hossein, and Ahmad Pourahmad. Fonun va Tajarob-e Barnamehrizi-e Maremat-e Baft-e Tarikhi-e Shahrha [Techniques and Experiences in Renovation Planning of Historical Area of Cities]. Tehran: Jahad-e Daneshgahi, 2005.

Kalantari, M. Mehdi. 'Domino-Ye Takhrib-e Baft-Ha-Ye Tarikhi [Domino Destruction of Historic Cities]'. *Shargh Newspaper*, 13 March 2022, 4242 edition. magiran.com/n4279124.

Kamrava, Mohammadali, Mehdi Azizi, Behnaz Aminzadeh, Hamidreza Parsi, Minoo Rafie, and Ferdows Shahrokhzadeh. Barresi-Ye Tarh-Ha-Ye Nosazi-Ye Baft-e Farsoodeh-Ye Tehran Da Panjah Sal-e Gozashteh [An Overview Of Renovation Projects In Tehran's Decaying Urban Fabric Over The Past Fifty Years]. Tehran: University of Tehran, Department of Applied Research, 2011.

Karbassian, Akbar. 'Islamic Revolution and the Management of the Iranian Economy'. *Social Research*, 2000, 621–40.

Karimi, Fatemeh. 'Tarak-Ha-Ye Jadid Tasir-e Shelik-e Toop Tahvil-e Sal Ru-Ye Borj-e Azadi? [New Cracks, the Impact of Cannon Fire on the Azadi Tower?]'. *Mehr News Agency*. 28 March 2021. mehrnews.com/xV27b.

Kasai, Reza. 'Hefazat va Ehyaye Bafthaye Kheshti [Conservation and Revitalisation of Adobe Urban Fabrics]'. *Agahinameh*, no. 5 (1976): 3–5.

Kasai, Reza. 'Khesht-e Kham [Mud Architecture}'. *Art and Architecture*, no. 14 (1973): 33–41.

Hamshahrionline. 'Kaseban-e Akherat [The Merchants of the Afterlife]', 10 March 2020. hamshahrionline.ir/x6JPW.

Katouzian, Homa. *Iranian History and Politics: The Dialectic of State and Society*. RoutledgeCurzon / BIPS Persian Studies Series. RoutledgeCurzon, 2003.

Katouzian, Homa. 'The Short-Term Society: A Study in the Problems of Long-Term Political and Economic Development in Iran'. *Middle Eastern Studies* 40, no. 1 (2004): 1–22.

Kearns, Ade, and Ronan Paddison. 'New Challenges for Urban Governance'. *Urban Studies* 37, no. 5–6 (2000): 845–50.

Keivani, Ramin, Michael Mattingly, and Hamid Majedi. 'Public Management of Urban Land, Enabling Markets and Low-Income Housing Provision: The Overlooked Experience of Iran'. *Urban Studies* 45, no. 9 (2008): 1825–53.

Keshavarzian, Arang. *Bazaar and State in Iran: The Politics of the Tehran Marketplace*. Vol. 26. Cambridge University Press, 2007.

Khanjani, Ramin S. Animating Eroded Landscapes: The Cinema of Ali Hatami. H&S Media, 2014.

Khosravani, Keyvan. 'Saving Oudlajan'. Accessed 23 May 2022. https://www.keyvankhosrovani.com/saving-oudlajan/.

Khosronejad, Pedram. Unburied Memories: The Politics of Bodies of Sacred Defense Martyrs in Iran. Routledge, 2013.

Kiani, Mostafa. *Memari-Ye Doreh-Ye Pahlavi-Ye Aval [Architecture During the 1st Pahalavi Dinesty]*. Tehran: Research Institute for Contemporary History of Iran, 2004.

Kuklan, Hooshang. 'The Administrative System in the Islamic Republic of Iran: New Trends and Directions'. *International Review of Administrative Sciences* 47, no. 3 (1981): 218–24.

Latour, Bruno. Reassembling the Social: An Introduction to Actor-Network-Theory. Oxford university press, 2005.

Le Corbusier, and CIAM. The Athens Charter for the Restoration of Historic Monuments. New York, 1931.
Lefebvre, Henri, and Donald Nicholson-Smith. *The Production of Space*. Wiley, 1991. https://books.google.de/books?id=SIXcnIoa4MwC.
Levers, LZ. 'Ideology and Change in Iranian Education'. *Education in the Muslim World: Different Perspectives*, 2006, 149–90.
Lewis, David. 'Civil Society and the Authoritarian State: Cooperation, Contestation and Discourse'. *Journal of Civil Society* 9, no. 3 (2013): 325–40.
Lewisohn, Jane. 'Flowers of Persian Song and Music: Davud Pirniā and the Genesis of the Golhā Programs'. *Journal of Persianate Studies* 1, no. 1 (2008): 79–101.
Lewisohn, Jane. 'The Rise and Fall of Lalehzar, Cultural Centre of Tehran in the Mid-Twentieth Century'. Music Department, SOAS, University of London, 2015.
Lochetto, Stephen M. 'Hybrid Ethnography: Online, Offline, and In Between', 2022.
Logan, William, and Keir Reeves. Places of Pain and Shame: Dealing with Difficult Heritage'. Routledge, 2008.
Lowenthal, David. 'Past Time, Present Place: Landscape and Memory'. *Geographical Review* 65, no. 1 (1975): 1–36. doi:10.2307/213831.
Lowenthal, David. 'The Heritage Crusade and Its Contradictions'. Giving Preservation a History: Histories of Historic Preservation in the United States, 2004, 19–43.
Lynch, Kevin. *The Image of the City*. Vol. 11. Massachusetts: MIT press, 1960.
Macdonald, Sharon. Difficult Heritage: Negotiating the Nazi Past in Nuremberg and Beyond. Routledge, 2010.
Macdonald, Sharon. 'Reassembling Nuremberg, Reassembling Heritage'. *Journal of Cultural Economy* 2, no. 1–2 (2009): 117–34.
Madanipour, Ali. 'City Profile: Tehran'. *Cities* 16, no. 1 (1999): 57–65.
Madanipour, Ali. 'Early Modernization and the Foundations of Urban Growth in Tehran'. *Fachzeitschrift Des VINI*, 2006.
Madanipour, Ali. *Tehran: The Making of a Metropolis*. World Cities Series. Chichester: John Wiley, 1998.

Madanipour, Ali. 'Urban Planning and Development in Tehran'. *Urbanization and the Iranian Revolution* 23, no. 6 (1 December 2006): 433–38. doi:10.1016/j.cities.2006.08.002.

Mahdizadeh, Sara, and Pirooz Hanachi. 'The Role of Western Orientalists in Restoration of Historical Buildings during the Pahlavi Era, Iran (1925–1979)'. *Honar-Ha-Ye-Ziba: Memary Va Shahrsazi* 21, no. 3 (2016): 5–14.

Malakouti, Moslem. *Masjed Masjed Shod [The Mosque Became a Mosque]*. First. Vol. 1–2. Tehran: Shafagh, 1985.

'Mamuriyat-e UNESCO Dar Iran, Kholaseh-Ye Gozaresh-e Bazdid Konandegan-e UNESCO Az Iran [UNESCO's Mission in Iran, a Summary of the UNESCO Visitors' Report)'. *Athar* 3, no. 7–9 (1983): 291–96.

Manavi, Saied. 'Taghirat-e Tarh-e Tafsili Che Bar Sar-e Tehran Avard? [What Damage Did the Changes to the Detailed Plan Do to Tehran?]'. *Payam-e Ma Newspaper*. 15 May 2021. https://payamema.ir/p/55395.

Manouchehrzaseh, Ramyar, and Negin Firoozi. 'Meidan-e Toopkhaneh'. Radio Nist. Accessed 10 April 2022. http://radionist.com/podcasts/ep28-meydantoopkhaneh/.

Mashregh. 'Ideology-Zodai Az Shahr, Barname-Ye Asli-Ye Eslahtalaban Bara-Ye Tehran/ Chera Hanachi Haman Akhundi Ast? [Ideological Cleansing, the Reformists' Main Program for Tehran / Why Hanachi Is the Very Same as Akhundi?]'. *Mashregh News*. 18 October 2018.

Masjedjamei, Ahmad. Jesm-o-Jan-e Shahr [The Body and Soul of the City]. Tehran: Rozaneh, 2016.

Masjedjamei, Ahmad. Negahi Be Darvazeh Ghar [A Glimpse of the Darvazeh Ghar]. Tehran: Sales, 2015.

Mason, Randall, and Erica Avrami. 'Heritage Values and Challenges of Conservation Planning'. In *Management Planning for Archaeological Sites*, edited by Gaetano Palumbo and Jeanne Marie Teutonico, 13–26. Corinth: Getty, 2002.

Masoumi, Gholamreza. 'Takhrib-e Athar-e Farhangi Tarfand-e Doshmanan-e Enghelab [Destruction of Cultural Properties, a Strategy of the Revolution's Enemies]'. *Jomhouri-e Eslami*. 16 January 1982, sec. Farhangi-Honari.

McFarlane, Colin. 'The City as Assemblage: Dwelling and Urban Space'. *Environment and Planning: Society and Space* 29, no. 4 (2011): 649–71.

Mehr News Agency. 'Darkhast-e E'ta Bara-Ye Sabt-e Meli-e Hamzaman-e 18 Cinema-Ye Lalehzar [E'ta's Request for Simultaneous National Registration of 18 Cinemas in Lalezar]'. Mehr News Agency, 1 May 2021. mehrnews.com/xTvqZ.

Mehr News Agency. 'Director of National Museum of Iran Dismissed'. *Mehr News Agency*. 7 December 2011. en.mehrnews.com/news/46922/.

Mehr News Agency. 'Sakht-o-Saz Ba Khesht Baray-e Avalin Bar Dar Keshvar Ghanooni Mishavad [Construction with Adobe Will Be Leagalised in Iran for the First Time'. *Mehr News Agency*, 2022. mehrnews.com/xY53N.

Meier, Hans-Rudolf. Denkmale in Der Stadt–Die Stadt Als Denkmal: Probleme Und Chancen Für Den Stadtumbau. Dresden: TUD press, 2006.

Memarian, Gholamhossein, Sorush Mokhtari, M. Mehdi Kalantari, and Saideh Asadian. 'Online Roundtable: Loder-Ha Be Ziafat-e Baft-e Tarikhi-e Shiraz Miravand? [Will the Loaders Head to the Historic City of Shiraz?]'. *Fars News Agency*, 20 January 2022. https://www.aparat.com/v/JL3rQ.

Merhavy, Menahem. 'Religious Appropriation of National Symbols in Iran: Searching for Cyrus the Great'. *Iranian Studies* 48, no. 6 (2015): 933–48.

Michaelsen, Marcus. 'The Politics of Online Journalism in Iran'. *Social Media in Iran: Politics and Society After*, 2009.

Ministry of Economic Affairs and Finance. 'Ayin-Nameh-Ye Ejrai-e Tabsareh-Ye (35) Ghanoon-e Budjeh 1368 [Executive Regulations Note (35) of the Budget Law of 1989]', 1989.

Ministry of Roads and Urban Development. 'Joziyat-e Mosavabeh-Ye Mashroot-e Tarh-e Jame-e Tabriz [In Hanachi's Letter to the Governor of Eastern Azerbaijan; Details of the Contingent Approval of the Tabriz Master Plan]'. *MRUD News Service*. 12 August 2016.

Ministry of Roads and Urban Development. 'Sanad-e Melli-e Rahbordi-e Ehya, Behsazi va Nosazi va Tavanmandsazi-e Bafthaye Farsudeh va

Nakaramad-e Shahri [The National Strategic Document for Revitalization, Rehabilitation, Renovation, and Reinforcement of Deteriorated and Dysfunctional Urban Fabrics]'. MRUD, 2014.

Ministry of Roads and Urban Development. 'Tey-e Nameh Az Suy-e Moaven-e Vazir-e Rah va Sharsazi Matrah Shod; Takid-e Mojadad Bar Roayat-e Mosavabat-e Shoray-e Ali-e Sharsazi Baray-e Hargooneh Sakht va Saz Dar Javar-e Bazar-e Sabt-e Jahaniy-e Tabriz [In a Letter from the Deputy Minister of Roads and Urban Development; Re-Emphasizing the Need to Comply with the Approvals of the High Council of Urban Planning for All Construction Projects in the Vicinity of the World Heritage Site of Tabriz Bazaar]'. *MRUD News Service*. 28 July 2018.

Miri, Seyyed-javad. 'Seyyed Javad Tabatabai Be Donbal-e Bastangerai Ast [Seyyed Javad Tabatabai Is Goal Is Seeking Archaism]'. *The Great Islamic Encyclopedia*, 2016. https://www.cgie.org.ir/fa/news/127659.

Moaveni, Azadeh. 'Iran and the US: When Friends Fall Out'. *Middle East Eye*, 2022. https://www.middleeasteye.net/big-story/iran-us-uk-oil-friends-fall-apart-cia-coup.

Moghtader-Andreef. 'Master Plan of Tabriz', 1970.

Mohammadmoradi, Asghar. 'Editor's Note: Zaroorat-e Maremat [The Essentiality of Conservation]'. *HaftShahr* 4, no. 12 (2003): 3.

Mohammadmoradi, Asghar, Atossa Amirkabirian, and Hojatollah Abdi Ardakani. *Revitalisation of Historic Urban Fabrics (a Review of Experiences)*. Tehran: University of Tehran, 2017.

Mohammadzadeh Mehr, Farokh, and MRUD. *Meidan-e Toopkhaneh-Ye Tehran [Toopkhaneh Square of Tehran]*. Tehran: Payam-e Sima, 2003.

Mohebali, Mohammad Hassan, and Maryam Jalilvand. 'Razha-Ye Magooy-e Chehrey-e Mandegar-e Miras-e Farhangi [The Untold Secrets of the Heritage Pioneer about the Cultural Heritage Organisation]'. *Seday-e Miras*, 2018. https://www.sedayemiras.ir/1397/05/29/.

Mohtaj, Aliasghar. 'An Interview with Keyvan Khosravani about the Sanitation of the Old Urban Fabric of Tehran'. *Tamasha*, 1978.

Moini, S. Mehdi. 'Afzayesh-e Ghabeliyat-e Piyadehmadari, Gami Be Suy-e Shahri Ensani-Tar [Enhancing Walkability, a Step Towards a More Humane City]'. *Honar-Ha-Ye-Ziba* 27, no. 27 (2006).

Moini, S. Mehdi. *Shahr-Ha-Ye Piyadehmadar* [Walkable Cities]. Tehran: Azarakhsh, 2011.

Mojab, Shahrzad. *The State and University: The"Islamic Cultural Revolution"in the Institutions of Higher Education of Iran, 1980–1987*. University of Illinois at Urbana-Champaign, 1991.

Mokhtari Taleghani, Eskandar. *Bonyan-Ha-Ye Khiaban-e Vali-e Asr (AJ) [Foundations of the Vali-e Asr (SA) Street]*. Tehran: Cultural Research Bureau-Tehran Municipality, 2020.

Mokhtari Taleghani, Eskandar, ed. *Gozaresh-Ha va Maghalat-e Salaneh-Ye Projeh-Ye Nejatbakhshi-e Miras-e Farhangi-e Bam-(Arg) [Anual Reports and Papers of the Bam Cultural Heritage Recovery Project-(Arg)]*. Vol. 1. 2. Tehran: Research Base of Arg-e Bam, 2005.

Mokhtari Taleghani, Eskandar, M. Hassan Talebian, Seyed Ahmad Mohit Tabatabaei, and Pirooz Hanachi. *Khiaban-e Vali-e Asr Miras-e Memari va Shahrsazi-Ye Tehran [Vali E Asr Avenue Tehran's Architectural and Urban Heritage]*. 2nd ed. Tehran: Tehran Beautification Organisation, 2019.

Molana, Seyyed Hamid, Mahmoud Lavasani, Mohammad Ali Taskhiri, and Mohammad Madadpour. 'Tamadon-Ha; Gof-o-Gu va Nazdiki Ya Ruyaruyi va Keshmakesh [Civilisations, Dialogue and Intercession or Confrontation and Conflict]'. *Keyhan-e Farhangi*, 1998.

Mollasalehi, Hekmatollah. 'Gereh-Ha-Ye Nagoshudeh-Ye Miras [The Unsolved Knots of Cultural Heritage]'. *Etelaat Newspaper*, 16 August 2017. https://www.ettelaat.com/archives/303389#gsc.tab=0.

Tasnim News Agency. 'Montakhab-e Doeh-Ye Sheshom-e Shora-Ye Shahr Dar Bareh-Ye Zist-e Shabaneh Che Goft? [What Did the Elected Member of the Sixth Tehran City Council Said about Tehran's "Nightlife" Plan?]'. 13 July 2021. https://tn.ai/2537595.

Mostaqasi, Shirin. 'Ravayati Az Takhrib-e Hammam-e Kosrow-Agha [A Narrative of the Demolition of the Khosrow Agha Bathhouse]'. *Iranian Students' News Agency*, 9 April 2022. isna.ir/xdMc64.

Mousavian, Seyyed Mojtaba. 'Gozaresh-e Neshast-Ha-Ye Takhasosi-Ye Sherkat-e Madar Takhasosi-Ye Omran va Behsazi-Ye Shahri-Ye Iran [Seminars in Iranian Urban Development and Revitalization Corporation (Session 3rd & 4th)]'. *HaftShahr* 4, no. 47–48 (2015): 138–45.

Mozaffari, Ali. 'Picturing Pasargadae: Visual Representation and the Ambiguities of Heritage in Iran'. *Iranian Studies* 50, no. 4 (2017): 601–34.

MRUD News Service. 'A Report of the Meeting Series on The Critique of Architecture and Urban Planning'. *MRUD News Service*. 2018. http://news.mrud.ir/news/50242/.

Müller, Martin. 'Assemblages and Actor-Networks: Rethinking Socio-Material Power, Politics and Space'. *Geography Compass* 9, no. 1 (2015): 27–41.

Municipality of Tehran, Paramadan Engineers. 'Bayaniyeh va sanad-e rahbordi-e modiriyat va hefazat-e baft va banahay-e tarikhi-farhangi-e Tehran [Declaration and strategic document of the management and conservation of the historic-cultural fabric of Tehran]'. Paramadan Engineers, 2014.

Municipality of Tehran, Public and International Relations. 'Baztab-e Mehvar-Ha-Ye Goftemani-Ye Modiriyat-e Shahri Da Eghdamat-e Shahrdari-Ye Tehran (1396–1399) [Discourse Lines of Urban Management in the Tehran Municipality's Actions between 2017 and 2021]'. Tehran Picture Agency, 2021.

n., n. *Agahinameh*. Vol. 1. 1. Tehran, 1975.

n., n. 'What Happened During the Second Terra Meeting?' *Agahinameh*, 1976.

n., n. 'The Second Terra Conference in Yazd'. *Agahinameh*, no. 3 (1976): 4–5.

n., n. 'Mosahebe Ba Rais Bakhsh-e Amoozesh Sazman [An Interview with the Director of the Department of Education]'. *Agahinameh*, no. 5 (1976).

n., n. 'Academic Cooperations between the Farabi University and the NOPHM [Hamkarihai Beine Daneshgah-e Farabi va Sazman-e Melli Hefazat-e Asar-e Bastani]'. *Agahinameh*, no. 17 (1977): 3.

n., n. 'Akhbar: Mosharekat-e Bazarian-e Tabriz Darmored-e Maremat-e Bazar-e Tarikhi-e Shar [News: The Participation of Merchants of Tabriz in the Restoration of the Historic Bazaar of the City]'. *Agahinameh*, no. 18 (1977): 19.

n., n. 'Announcement for Admission of Students for the Program, Conservation of Historic Monuments and Places (Second Phase) for the Academic Year 36–37'. *Agahinameh*, no. 18 (1977): 4.

n., n. 'Tashkilat-e Sazman [The Organisation]'. *Agahinameh*, no. 23 (1977): 8–9.

n., n. 'Asnad-e Fesad-e Hodud-e Nim-Triliard Tomani-e Hamid Baghaie Montasher Shod [Hamid Baghai's Corruption Documents of About Half a Trillion Tomans Were Published]'. *Young Journalists Club*. 20 March 2018. https://www.yjc.news/ooRBRd.

n., n. 'International Conference on Reconstruction of the War-Damaged Areas, University of Tehran, Iran (6–16 March 1986)'. *Athar* 7, no. 12–14 (1987): 97–101.

n., n. 'Masjed-e Jame-e Esfahan, Dayeratol-Ma'aref-e Eyni-e Honar-Ha-Ye Eslami [The Jame Mosque of Isfahan, an Encyclopedia of Islamic Architecture]'. *Kayhan Farhangi*. 1985.

n., n. 'The Magazin of Radio Tehran [Inja Tehran Ast]', 65 1947. Tehran. National Library of Iran.

Najmi, Mohammad. 'Moraghebe Ezhar-e Nazar-Hayetan Bashid [Watch Your Mouth]'. *Etemad Newspaper*. 26 January 2023. https://www.etemadonline.com/tiny/news-593602.

Nashriyeh-Ye Daneshkadeh-Ye Honarha-Ye Ziba (1341–1343) [Magazine of the College of Fine Arts 1962–64]. Vol. 2. Tehran: University of Tehran, 1964.

Nazar Research Center for Art, Architecture & Urbanism. 'Ruykard-e Ejtemai Lazemeh-Ye Ehya-Ye Khiaban-e Lalehzar [Social Approach as a Prerequisite for the Revitalisation of Lalehzar Street]'. *Nazar-Online*. 22 October 2019.

NOPHM. *Agahinameh*. Vol. 36. Tehran, 1978.

Oevermann, Heike, Eszter Gantner, and Sybille Frank. *Städtisches Erbe – Urban Heritage*. Informationen Zur Modernen Stadtgeschichte. Berlin, 2016.

Organic Engineering Consultancy. 'Detailed Plan of Isfahan'. Ministry of Housing and Urban Development, 1975.

Oruji, Ardeshir. 'Darshayi Ke Az Zelzeleh-Ye Bam Mitavan Amookht [Lessons to Be Learnt From the Bam Earthquake]'. *HaftShahr* 5, no. 17 (2005): 86–89.

Page, Max, and Randall Mason. Giving Preservation a History: Histories of Historic Preservation in the United States. Routledge, 2004.

Paknia, Bahman. 'Masael-e Shahri [Urban Issues]'. *Art and Architecture*, no. 15–16 (1973): 23–26.

Parliament of Iran. 'Ghanoon-e Mohasebat-e Omumi-e Keshvar [The Public Audit Act]'. The Official Magazine: Rooznameh-e Rasmi-e Keshvar, 1987.

Parliament of Iran. 'Ghanoon-e Mojazat-e Eslami [Islamic Penal Law 5th Vol.]'. The Official Magazine: Rooznameh-e Rasmi-e Keshvar, 1996.

Parliament of Iran. 'Ghanoon-e Sabt-e Athar-e Melli, Aban 1352 [National Heritage Listing Law,1973]', 1973.

Parliament of Iran. 'Ghanoun-e Tashkilat va Ekhtiarat-e Sazman-e Awqafva Omour-e Kheiriyeh [Law of the Establishment of Awqaf Organization]'. The Official Magazine: Rooznameh-e Rasmi-e Keshvar, 1984.

Parliament of Iran. 'Ghanun-e Akhz-e Mablagh-e Bist Rial Avarez Az Har Ton Siman Be Naf-e Anjoman-e Asar-e Melli [The Law on the Taxation of an Amount of Twenty Rials per Ton of Cement for the Benefit of the Anjoman-e Asar-e Melli]'. The Official Magazine: Rooznameh-e Rasmi-e Keshvar, 1968.

Parliament of Iran. 'Ghanun-e Asasname-Ye Sazman-e Miras-e Farhangi-e Keshvar [Law of the Statute of the ICHO]'. The Official Magazine: Rooznameh-e Rasmi-e Keshvar, 1986. Tehran.

Parliament of Iran. 'Ghanun-e Barnamey-e Chaharom-e Tose-Ey-e Eghtesadi, Ejtemai va Farhangi-e Jomhuriy-e Eslami-e Iran [The Law of the Fourth Plan of Economic, Social and Cultural Development of Islamic Republic of Iran]'. *The Official Magazine: Rooznameh-e Rasmi-e Keshvar*, 2004.

Parliament of Iran. 'Ghanun-e Barnamey-e Panjom-e Tose-Ey-e Eghtesadi, Ejtemai va Farhangi-e Jomhuriy-e Eslami-e Iran [The Law of the Fifth Plan of Economic, Social and Cultural Development of Islamic

Republic of Iran]'. *The Official Magazine: Rooznameh-e Rasmi-e Keshvar*, 2011.

Parliament of Iran. 'Ghanun-e Barnamey-e Sevom-e Tose-Ey-e Eghtesadi, Ejtemai va Farhangi-e Jomhuriy-e Eslami-e Iran [The Law of the Third Plan of the Economic, Social and Cultural Development of Islamic Republic of Iran]'. *The Official Magazine: Rooznameh-e Rasmi-e Keshvar*, 2000.

Parliament of Iran. 'Ghanun-e Barnamey-e Sheshom-e Tose-Ey-e Eghtesadi, Ejtemai va Farhangi-e Jomhuriy-e Eslami-e Iran [The Law of the Sixth Plan of Economic, Social and Cultural Development of Islamic Republic of Iran]'. *The Official Magazine: Rooznameh-e Rasmi-e Keshvar*, 2017.

Parliament of Iran. 'Ghanun-e Divan-e Edalat-e Edari [Law of the Administrative Court of Justice}'. *The Official Magazine: Rooznameh-e Rasmi-e Keshvar*, 2006.

Parliament of Iran. 'Ghanun-e Hemayat Az Ehya, Behsazi va Nosai-e Bafthaye Farsudeh va Nakaramad-e Shahri [The Law of Safeguarding the Revitalization, Rehabilitation and Renovation of Decayed and Dysfunctional Urban Fabrics]', 2011.

Parliament of Iran. 'Ghanun-e Hemayat Az Maremmat va Ehyay-e Bafthay-e Tarikhi-Farhangi [The Law on Promotion of Restoration and Revitalisation of Historic-Cultural Urban Fabrics]', 2019.

Parliament of Iran. 'Ghanun-e Kharid-e Arazi Abniyeh va Tasisat Baray-e Hefazat Asar Tarikhi va Bastani [Law on Acquisition of Land and Real Estate for the Preservation of Historic and Ancient Monuments]'. *The Official Magazine: Rooznameh-e Rasmi-e Keshvar*, 1968.

Parliament of Iran. 'Ghanun-e Tashkilat va Ain-e Dadresi Divan-e Edalat-e Edari [Law on the Organization and Procedure of the Administrative Court of Justice]'. *The Official Magazine: Rooznameh-e Rasmi-e Keshvar*, 2013.

Parliament of Iran. 'Ghanun-e Tashkil-e Sazman-e Miras-e Farhangi-e Keshvar [Law for the Establishment of the Iranian Cultural Heritage Organisation]'. *The Official Magazine: Rooznameh-e Rasmi-e Keshvar*, 1986.

Parliament of Iran. 'Municipalities and City Anjomans Law [Ghanoon-e Tashkil-e Shahrdari-Ha ve Anjoman-e Sahrha va Ghasabat]', 1949.

Parliament of Iran. 'The Constitution of Islamic Republic of Iran'. The Official Magazine: Rooznameh-e Rasmi-e Keshvar, 1979.

Parliament of Iran. 'The Constitution of Islamic Republic of Iran, Article 83'. The Official Magazine: Rooznameh-e Rasmi-e Keshvar, 1979.

Parliament of Iran. 'The Law on Antiquities', 1930.

Pazouki, Nasser. 'Mabani-e Miras-e Farhangi [Principles of Cultural Heritage]'. *Mirath-e Farhangi*, no. 17 (1997): 82–84.

Pendlebury, John. *Conservation in the Age of Consensus*. London: Routledge, 2008.

Pendlebury, John. 'Conservation Values, the Authorised Heritage Discourse and the Conservation-Planning Assemblage'. *International Journal of Heritage Studies* 19, no. 7 (2013): 709–27. doi:10.1080/13527258.2012.700282.

Pendlebury, John, Yi-Wen Wang, and Andrew Law. 'Re-Using "Uncomfortable Heritage": The Case of the 1933 Building, Shanghai'. *International Journal of Heritage Studies* 24, no. 3 (2018): 211–29.

Piran, Parviz. Az Shoma Harekat Az Khoda Barekat, Tose'e-Ye Mosharekat Mabna va Mosharekat Mehvar Dar Iran: Mored-e Tehran [God Helps Those Who Help Themselves: Participatory Local Development in Iran: The Case of Tehran]. Tehran: Sazman-e Nosazi-e Tehran, 2010.

Pirnia, Mohammad Karim. 'The Boulevard Disease'. *Honar va Mardom* 2, no. 69 (1968): 39–43.

Pourhassan, Ghasem, Seyyed-javad Miri, and Mohammad-Ali Moradi. 'Naghd va Barresi-e Andishey-e Iranshahri [Reflecting on the Iranshahri Thought]'. Institute for Humanities and Cultural Studies, Tehran, 31 October 2017. https://www.aparat.com/v/oJa3t.

Premiership of Iran. Layehe-ye Ghanooni Tajdid-e Gharadad va Ejareh-ye Amlak va Amvale Mowqufeh va Tajdid-e Entekhab-e Motevalian va Omana ava Nozar-e Amaken-e Motebarekeh Mazhabi va Masajed [The bill on the renewal of the leasing contract for endowment properties and the re-appointment of administrators of mosques and religious places] (1979).

Purcell, Mark. 'Excavating Lefebvre: The Right to the City and Its Urban Politics of the Inhabitant'. *GeoJournal* 58, no. 2 (2002): 99–108.

Rahemi, Mohammad Mohsen. 'Iranshahri Mordeh Ast [Iranshahri Is Dead]'. *Farhikhtegan*, Islamic Azad University, 20 October 2018. http://fdn.ir/23522.

Rahimi, Amin. 'Shabneshini Be Sarf-e Aramesh, Food Street-e Khiaban-e Si-e Tir Patogh-e Shabaneh Baray-Ye Khanevadeh-Ha [Night Stop For Recreation, The Food Street In Si Tir Street Is A Nightly Meeting Place For Families]'. *Hamshahri*. 26 May 2018.

Rahnamaei, M. Taghi, and Parvaneh Shah Hosseini. *Process of Urban Planning in Iran*. 2nd ed. Tehran: SAMT, 2012.

Rahvan Shahr Consultant Engineers. 'Sanad-e Jame' Modiriyat va Hefazat-e Baft-Ha va Bana-Ha-Ye Tarikhiy-e Tehran [The Comprehensive Document for the Management and Conservation of the Historic Buildings and Urban Fabric of Tehran]'. Tehran: Municipality of Tehran, 2012. Research and Planning Centre of Municipality of Tehran.

Rakel, Eva. Power, Islam, and Political Elite in Iran: A Study on the Iranian Political Elite from Khomeini to Ahmadinejad. Brill, 2008.

Rastegar, Raymond, Zohreh Zarezadeh, and Ulrike Gretzel. 'World Heritage and Social Justice: Insights from the Inscription of Yazd, Iran'. *Journal of Sustainable Tourism* 29, no. 2–3 (2021): 521–40.

Revue Du Touring Club de l'Iran [Majale-Ye Jahangardi]', September 1936. Tehran. National Library of Iran.

Revue Du Touring Club de l'Iran [Majale-Ye Jahangardi]', August 1937. Tehran. National Library of Iran.

Rezaei, Naimeh, and Pirooz Hanachi. 'Mahaleh-Ye Oudlajan, Miras-e Shahri Dar Taghabol Bein-e Sonnat va Modernite [The Oudlajan Neighbourhood, Urban Heritage at the Crossroads of Tradition and Modernity]'. *Journal of Iranian Architecture Studies* 4, no. 7 (2015): 19–34.

RFE/RL's Radio Farda. 'Iconic Iranian Antihijab Protester Jailed For One Year; Human Rights Lawyer's 13-Year Sentence Upheld'. *Radio Farda*, 2017. https://www.rferl.org/a/iconic-iranian-antihijab-protester-jailed-for-year/29879887.html.

Rizvi, Kishwar. 'Art History and the Nation: Arthur Upham Pope and the Discourse on" Persian Art" in the Early Twentieth Century'. In *Muqarnas, Volume 24*, 45–66. Brill, 2007.

Roberts, Peter, and Hugh Sykes. *Urban Regeneration: A Handbook*. Translated by Mohammad Saeid Izadi and Pirooz Hanachi. University of Tehran Press, 2014.

Roundtable: Be Bahaneh-Ye Tose'e-Ye Haram City Center Misazand/ Az Tamallok-e 8 Milliun Tomani Ta Forush-e Maghaber-e 1 Miliard Tomani [Construction of a City Center Under the Pretext of Shrine Development/Land Acquisition for 8 Million Tomans per Square Meter and Its Sale for 1 Billion Tomans as Graves.]. Tehran: Ensafnews, 2022. http://www.ensafnews.com/366407/.

Rvitalisation and Utilisation Fund. Sanad-e Ehya va Bahrebardari Az Amaken Tarikhi va Farhangi [Guidelines for the Revitalisation and Utilisation of Historic and Cultural Places]. Second. Tehran: Gang-e Shayegan, 2009.

Ryberg-Webster, Stephanie, and Kelly L. Kinahan. 'Historic Preservation and Urban Revitalization in the Twenty-First Century'. *CPL Bibliography* 29, no. 2 (2014): 119–39.

Sadiq, I. 'Anjoman-e Athar-e Melli'. In *Encyclopedia Iranica*, II:83, 1985.

Saeidi, Ali A. 'The Accountability of Para-Governmental Organizations (Bonyads): The Case of Iranian Foundations'. *Iranian Studies* 37, no. 3 (1 September 2004): 479–98. doi:10.1080/0021086042000287541.

Safamanesh & Co. Engineers. 'Tarh-e Behsazi va Bazsazi-Ye Khiaban-e Lalehzar [Improvement and Reconstruction Plan for Lalehzar Street]'. Tehran Beautification Organization, 1994.

Sakurai, Keiko. 'University Entrance Examination and the Making of an Islamic Society in Iran: A Study of the Post-Revolutionary Iranian Approach to "Konkur"'. *Iranian Studies* 37, no. 3 (2004): 385–406.

Salimi, Keyvan. 'A Stitch to the Earth, Meeting Keyvan Khosravani'. *Memar*, no. 113 (2019): 4–9.

Samadi, Younes. Cultural heritage in domestic and international Law in Iran [Miras-e Farhangi dar Hoghugh-e Dakheli va Benalmelali]. Tehran: ICHO, 2003.

Samadi, Younes. The collection of Laws, Regulations, Guidelines, Circular Notes, and Conventions of the Cultural Heritage Organization [Majmue' Ghavanin, Ayinnameh-ha, Bakhshnameh-ha va Moahedat-e Sazman-e Mirath-e Frhangi-e Keshvar]. Tehran: ICHO, 2004.

Sareminia, Mostafa. 'Takhrib-e Baft-e Tarikh-Ye Mashhad Taaroz Bar Hoviyat-e Eslami va Farhang Irani Ast [The Destruction of the Historic Fabric of Mashhad Is an Attack on Islamic Identity and Iranian Culture]', 25 June 2022. isna.ir/xdLTmh.

Shahidi, Hossein. Journalism in Iran: From Mission to Profession. London: Routledge, 2007.

Shahryar. 'Booy-e Eidi [The Scent of Eidi]'. *Irangardi Shahriyar Dar Shanbeh*, 3 June 2010. 25.5.2020.

Shargh Newspaper. *Vijhenameh-Ye Shahr va Shora-3 [Special Issue: City and Shura-3]*. Edited by Mehdi Rahmanian. Tehran: Entekhab Resaneh, n.d.

Shirazi, Faegheh. 'The Veiling Issue in 20th Century Iran in Fashion and Society, Religion, and Government'. *Religions* 10, no. 8 (2019): 461.

Shirazian, Reza. Tehran Negari; Bank-e Naghsheh-Ha va Anavin-e Makani-e Tehran-e Ghadim [Documentation of Tehran; Database of Maps and Place Names of the Old Tehran]. Tehran: Dastan, 2017.

Asrshahrvand. 'Shirini-Ye Faranse Polomp Shod [The French Pastry Was Sealed]'. Accessed 3 September 2022. https://asrshahrvand.com/?p=283818.

Shirvani, Shahrzad. 'Making Histories of "Sacred" Mausoleums'. *Traditional Dwellings and Settlements Review* 29, no. 2 (2018): 55–71.

Silverman, Helaine. 'Heritage and Authenticity'. In *The Palgrave Handbook of Contemporary Heritage Research*, 69–88. London: Springer, 2015.

Siroos, Bood-o-Nabood-e Yek Mahalleh [Siroos, The Existence and Inexistence of a Neighbourhood]. Documentary, 2014.

Smith, Laurajane. *Uses of Heritage*. London: Routledge, 2006.

Star, Susan Leigh, and James R Griesemer. 'Institutional Ecology,Translations' and Boundary Objects: Amateurs and Professionals in Berkeley's Museum of Vertebrate Zoology, 1907–39'. *Social Studies of Science* 19, no. 3 (1989): 387–420.

Storper, Michael, and Allen J. Scott. 'Current Debates in Urban Theory: A Critical Assessment'. *Urban Studies* 53, no. 6 (2016): 1114–36.

Submitted by: and Iranian Cultural Heritage, Handicrafts and Tourism Organization. 'Vali-e Asr Street'. UNESCO World Heritage Centre, 2019. https://whc.unesco.org/en/tentativelists/6387/.

Supreme Council of Chiefs of State and Government for Economic Coordination. 'Mosavabeh-Ye Movaledsazi-Ye Darayi-Ha-Ye Dolat [The Act on the Productivization of State Assets]'. Ministry of Economic Affairs and Finance, 24 November 2020.

Tabatabai, Javad. 'Iran be onvan-e Iranshahr [Iran as Iranshahr]'. Presented at the Twenty-fourth Meeting of the Iransharian Thought and Civilization, Tehran, 10 March 2017.

Tabatabai, Javad. *Khajeh Nezam-al-Molk*. Tehran: Tarh-e Now, 1996.

Alef Analytical News Association. 'Taghirat-e Ahmadinejadi Tarh-e Tafsili-Ye Tehran Hazf Mishavad [Ahmadinejadian Changes in the Tehran Detailed Plan Will Be Removed]'. 5 May 2014.

Tajbakhsh, Kian. 'The Political Economy of Fiscal Decentralization under the Islamic Republic of Iran'. *The Muslim World* 111, no. 1 (2021): 113–37.

Takmil Homayoun, Naser. Ruydad-Ha va Yadmanha-Ye Tarikhi-Ye Tehran, Az Darolkhelafeh-Ye Naseri Ta Piroozi-Ye Mashrooteh [Historical Events and Monuments in Tehran, from the Naseri Caliphate to the Victory of the Constitutional Revolution]. Tehran: Cultural Research Bureau, 2015.

Talebian, M. Hassan. 'The Role of Authenticity in Conservation of World Heritage Sites the Experiences from Dur-Untash for Authenticity-Based Conservation'. University of Tehran, 2005.

Tamadonfar, Mehran. 'Islam, Law, and Political Control in Contemporary Iran'. *Journal for the Scientific Study of Religion* 40, no. 2 (2001): 205–20.

Tasnim. 'Ezharat-e Kechuyan Darbareh-Ye Monazereh-Ash Ba Seyyed Javad Tabatabai+Film[Kechuyan's Statements on His Debate with Seyed Javad Tabatabai + Video]'. *Tasnim News Agency*, 6 January 2014. 29.10.2020. https://tn.ai/387906.

Tavassoli, Mahmoud. 'Baft-e Ghadim, Moghadameh-i Bar Masaleh [The Historic City, an Introduction to the Issue]'. In Kholasehy-e

Maghalat: Seminar-e Tadavom-e Hayat Dar Bafthay-e Ghadimi-e Shahrhay-e Iran [The Proceedings of the Seminar on the Continuation of Life in Iran's Historic Cities], 5–15. Tehran: Iran University of Science and Technology, 1987.

Tavassoli, Mahmoud. 'Baft-e Ghadim, Moghadameh-i Bar Masaleh [The Historic City, an Introduction to the Issue]'. In Kholasehy-e Maghalat: Seminar-e Tadavom-e Hayat Dar Bafthay-e Ghadimi-e Shahrhay-e Iran [The Proceedings of the Seminar on the Continuation of Life in Iran's Historic Cities], 5–15. Tehran: Iran University of Science and Technology, 1993.

Official Website of the President of the Islamic Republic of Iran. 'Tazahom-Ha-Ye Miras-e Farhangi Ra Hal Konid Ta Mardom Nafas Bekeshand [Address Heritage-Related Disturbances so That People Can Breathe a Sigh of Relief]', 14 July 2022. https://www.president.ir/fa/138393.

Tehranian, Majid. 'Communication and Revolution in Iran: The Passing of a Paradigm'. *Iranian Studies* 13, no. 1–4 (1980): 5–30.

Tester, Keith. *The Flâneur*. London: Psychology Press, 1994.

The Council of Ministers. 'Ayin-Nameh-Ye Amval-e Farhangi Honari va Tarikhi-Ye Nahad-Ha-Ye Omumi va Dolati [Code for Cultural, Artistic and Historical Properties of Public and State Institutions]'. Parliament of Iran, 2003.

The Council of the Islamic Revolution. 'Layehey-e Ghanouni-e Raj'e Be Kakhhay-e Niavaran va Saadabad va Nahvey-e Arzyabi va Negahdari-e Amval-e Marboot[The Legal Bill on Niavaran and Saadabad Palaces and The Evaluation and Maintenance of These Properties]', 1980.

The World Heritage Committee. 'Operational Guidelines for the Implementation of the World Heritage Convention'. UNESCO World Heritage Centre, Paris, 2021.

UDRC. 'Iranian Urban Development And Revitalization Corporation Operation Report (2013–2017)'. MRUD, 2017.

UNESCO. 'Convention for the Protection of Cultural Property in the Event of Armed Conflict with Regulations for the Execution of the Convention'. Hague, 1954. https://en.unesco.org/protecting-heritage/convention-and-protocols/1954-convention.

UNESCO, WHC. 'Recommendation on the Historic Urban Landscape', 2011.

UNESCO-Tehran, and ICHO. 'The BAM Declaration and Recommendations'. UNESCO, 2004. https://unesdoc.unesco.org/ark:/48223/pf0000190150.

Vadie, Kazem. 'Bazaar Dar Baft-e Novin-e Shahri [Bazaar in the Modern Urban Fabric]'. In Avalin Seminar-e Maremat-e Banaha va Sharhay-e Tarikhi: Vojud va Ayandeye Marakez-e Maskuni-e Tarikhi[The First Seminar on the Conservation of Historic Cities and Towns: The Existence and Future of Historical Residential Centres], edited by M. Mansour Falamaki, 89–93. Tehran: University of Tehran, 1971.

Varjavand, Parviz. 'Acknowledge Yazd Before It Is Too Late [Ta Be Afsoos Nanshesteim, Baft-e Yazd, Takhtgah-e Kavir Ra Daryabim]'. *Honar va Mardom*, no. 192–191 (1978): 2–17.

Wells, Jeremy C. 'The Affect of Old Places: Exploring the Dimensions of Place Attachment and Senescent Environments'. In *Place Meaning and Attachment*, 1–15. Routledge, 2020.

Wells, Jeremy C, and Barry L Stiefel. Human-Centered Built Environment Heritage Preservation: Theory and Evidence-Based Practice. New York: Routledge, 2019.

Wilber, Donald Newton. Regime Change in Iran: Overthrow of Premier Mossadeq of Iran, November 1952-August 1953. Nottingham: Spokesman Books, 2006.

Wollentz, Gustav, Sarah May, Cornelius Holtorf, and Anders Högberg. 'Toxic Heritage: Uncertain and Unsafe'. *Heritage Futures. Comparative Approaches to Natural and Cultural Heritage Practices*, 2020, 294–312.

World Heritage Committee. *Decision 38 COM 8B.45*. Doha: UNESCO World Heritage Convention, 2014.

Yadollahi, Solmaz. 'Prospects of Applying Assemblage Thinking for Further Methodological Developments in Urban Conservation Planning'. *The Historic Environment: Policy & Practice* 8, no. 4 (2 October 2017): 355–71.

Yadollahi, Solmaz. 'Reflections on the Past and Future of Urban Conservation in Iran'. *Built Heritage* 4, no. 1 (2020): 1–13.

Yadollahi, Solmaz. 'The Iranian Bazaar as a Public Place: A Reintegrative Approach and a Method Applied towards the Case Study of the Tabriz Bazaar'. Doctoral thesis, Brandenburg University of Technology, 2017. https://opus4.kobv.de/opus4-btu/frontdoor/index/index/docId/4294.

Yadollahi, Solmaz. 'Tracing the Identity-Driven Ambitions of the Iranian Urban Conservation Apparatus'. *The Historic Environment: Policy & Practice*, 30 June 2019, 1–20. doi:10.1080/17567505.2019.1637081.

Yadollahi, Solmaz. 'When Values-Based Conservation Theory Meets Planning Practice in Tehran'. In *Conservation Theory and the Urban Realpolitik*, edited by Solmaz Yadollahi, Vol. 10. Kulturelle Und Technische Werte Historischer Bauten. Berlin: Birkhäuser, 2024.

Yarshater, Ehsan. 'IRAN Ii. IRANIAN HISTORY (2) Islamic Period (Page 6)'. *Encyclopaedia Iranica* XIII, no. 3 (2012): 243–46.

Yaworski, Jeff. 'The Downing of Ukraine International Airlines Flight 752: Factual Analysis'. Global Affairs Canada, 24 January 2021. https://www.international.gc.ca/gac-amc/publications/flight-vol-ps752/factual_analysis-analyse_faits.aspx?lang=eng.

Yin, Robert K. *Case Study Research: Design and Methods*. Thousand Oaks: SAGE Publications, 2009.

Zakani, Alireza. 'Tehran Ra Kalanshahr-e Olgu-Ye Jahan-e Eslam Midanim [We Regard Tehran as a Role Model Metropolis of the Islamic World]'. *Mehr News Agency*, 13 May 2022. mehrnews.com/xXG3n.

Zweiri, Mahjoob, and Aljohara AlObaidan. 'The Second Succession in the Islamic Republic of Iran: Change or Continuity?' *Journal of Balkan and Near Eastern Studies* 23, no. 3 (2021): 473–89.

Index

1979 Revolution, 39, 53, 64, 65, 68, 72, 92, 117, 143, 172, 194, 198, 208, 209, 220

A
academia, 28, 67, 78, 110, 114, 129, 220, 222
activism, 69, 112, 155, 219, 220, 222
assemblage, 26, 27, 31–35, 39, 40, 64, 65, 88, 98, 111, 115, 117, 125, 127, 128, 138, 172, 173, 179, 181, 183, 185, 189, 200, 207, 211, 212, 215, 217, 219, 221–223, 225
    network, 27, 28, 51, 65–67, 87, 110, 163, 183, 184, 186, 207, 215, 219
Awqaf, 8, 9, 41, 66, 70, 71, 83, 89, 91, 127, 130, 133, 150, 204, 220
Azadi Tower, 141, 142, 173

B
Bam, 27, 63, 96, 97, 101
bazaar, 47, 56–58, 147, 149–151, 153, 167, 168, 171, 172, 184, 203
beautification, 10, 66, 164, 165, 192, 198, 202, 209, 210
Body Without Organs, 30, 32, 40, 62, 64, 65, 225
bonyad, 9, 87, 104, 127, 156, 178
boundary objects
    boundary action, 28, 163, 188, 190, 209, 221–223
brain drain
    migration, 75, 164, 217

C
Constitutional Revolution, 40, 43, 45, 85, 90, 147, 181, 189, 192, 199, 218
COVID-19, 20, 127, 151, 174, 184, 203

Cultural Engineering, 74, 121, 189, 221
Cultural Revolution, 74–76, 78, 88, 89, 121–123, 189, 221

D
discourse, 23, 45, 51, 52, 55, 82, 88, 118, 135, 159, 162, 180, 188, 217, 221

E
Enghelab, 9, 68, 72, 88, 172, 173, 175, 202
ethnography, 33–35, 121, 200, 221

F
film, 159, 170, 171, 192, 200

I
identity, 35, 79, 87, 88, 91, 99, 101, 109, 110, 119, 121, 123, 179, 188, 189, 204, 217, 220–222
Iran-Iraq War, 75, 90, 209
Iranshahr, 10, 118–123, 128
Isfahan, 27, 41, 44, 47, 49, 51–53, 63, 74, 75, 77, 80, 82, 83, 90, 98, 112, 119, 129, 138, 139, 155, 217

J
journalism, 69, 98, 110, 114, 219

L
Lalehzar, 184, 188, 196, 198–205, 207

M
Mashhad, 47, 58, 60, 68, 72, 84, 92, 93, 95, 99, 100, 129, 130, 191
museum-house, 90, 123, 124, 208, 222
music, 170, 182, 188, 200

N
nafayes, 108, 134

O
Oudlajan, 62, 77, 131, 147, 151, 153, 155–158, 166, 168–170, 172, 207

P
Pahlavi, 40, 41, 63, 89, 104, 141, 142, 174, 189, 191, 193, 195, 197, 208–210, 224
para-governmental, 65, 68, 70, 87, 102, 104, 127, 150, 156
parastatal, 67, 78, 83, 87, 91, 117, 129, 130, 132, 133, 160, 204, 215
place-making, 154, 178–182, 185, 193, 202, 223
public sphere, 33, 48, 110, 114, 116, 133, 135, 137, 140, 174, 195, 199, 200, 208, 221, 223

Q
Qajar, 43, 90, 141, 142, 147, 148, 155, 171, 172, 179, 187–189,

R

reform, 44, 66, 67, 87, 88, 96, 110, 115–117, 125, 138, 142, 149, 159, 178, 204, 205, 220, 222, 223

S

Shah, 41, 44, 51, 58, 60, 63, 83, 141, 171, 172, 191, 194, 208, 210, 211
sharia, 69, 72, 79, 80, 88, 92, 103, 198, 220
Shiraz, 27, 41, 47, 63, 82, 84, 92–95, 100, 112, 113, 130–132, 134, 138, 143, 174, 178, 217
social media, 28, 29, 33, 110, 120, 130, 136–138, 140–143, 155, 161–163, 172, 174, 182–184, 187, 188, 190, 191–194, 198, 199, 208, 209, 211

T

Tabriz, 47, 48, 56, 57, 59, 72, 74, 75, 82–86, 92, 98, 100, 108, 109, 120, 140, 150
territorialization
 de-territorialization, 31, 64, 66, 128, 215, 225
Toopkaneh, 194
tourism, 44, 47, 54, 67, 79, 84, 87, 105, 106, 111, 113, 128, 139, 163, 165, 170, 184, 185, 187, 188, 192, 193, 219, 222

U

UNESCO, 24, 25, 51, 69, 81, 94, 96–98, 180, 209, 210
Urban Dialogue House, 121, 122, 138, 195
urban regeneration, 11, 101, 117, 119, 125, 127, 128, 133, 159, 180

W

World Heritage, 24, 51, 56, 67, 92, 96–98, 104, 108, 109, 112, 127, 128, 140, 141, 209, 210

Y

Yazd, 27, 44, 47, 55, 56, 58, 63, 77, 96, 98, 99, 114, 119, 126–128, 217

[transcript]

PUBLISHING. KNOWLEDGE. TOGETHER.

transcript publishing stands for a multilingual transdisciplinary programme in the social sciences and humanities. Showcasing the latest academic research in various fields and providing cutting-edge diagnoses on current affairs and future perspectives, we pride ourselves in the promotion of modern educational media beyond traditional print and e-publishing. We facilitate digital and open publication formats that can be tailored to the specific needs of our publication partners.

OUR SERVICES INCLUDE

- partnership-based publishing models
- Open Access publishing
- innovative digital formats: HTML, Living Handbooks, and more
- sustainable digital publishing with XML
- digital educational media
- diverse social media linking of all our publications

Visit us online: www.transcript-publishing.com

Find our latest catalogue at www.transcript-publishing.com/newbookspdf